THE PATH TO DISCIPLESHIP

A YEAR IN JOHN 1 - 11

RONNIE COLLIER STEVENS

RAMPART
PUBLICATIONS

Rampart Publications
PO Box 13455
Bakersfield, California 93389
www.rampartpublications.com

ISBN: 978-1-7328778-0-1

Cover art:
The Four Apostles by Albrecht Dürer, 1526
Oil on wood, left panel
Alte Pinakothek, Munich

Cover Design:
The Marcom Group, Bakersfield, California

To the Memory of My Mother
Rachael Swindle Stevens
(1926-2014)
Who first showed me the Path

Special thanks to Tom Hinkle, who first challenged
me to follow Jesus.

And to Johnny Lawler, Phil Prince, and Michael Blackburn
who taught me early and teach me still.

Most of all, thanks to Jane, best loved Companion on
the Path to Discipleship.

January 1

In the beginning ...
John 1:1

The echo is obvious.
The first words of the Bible become the first words
of this Gospel.
Is the time frame identical because the words are identical?
We think not.
Moses tells us what the original Creation was like.
John tells what the eternal Creator is like.
Genesis addresses terrestrial realities.
Here we have celestial realities.
"Beginning" here is something we call "Eternity Past."
This is the beginning without beginning.
God is a being without limits in space or time.
God is a noun impossible of modification by the
word "before."
What we know about God must be revealed by the God who is
before all things.
He abides outside our capacity for unassisted discovery.

Heavenly Father, thank You for revealing what we
could not discover.
Thank You for writing Your own autobiography.
Thank You for telling of realities which precede
human existence.
As we learn may we profit.
May we show that profit in prayer and thanksgiving.
In Jesus' own Name we ask it.
Amen

In the beginning was the Word...
John 1:1

The WORD.
The "word" John wrote was LOGOS.
A Greek word bigger than the English word.
A word pregnant with implication.
Theology = Theos plus Logos.
Theology is the study of God.
This writer writes like a philosopher.
He writes of something bigger than philosophy.
He writes of God.
That surprised his contemporaries since he had no
formal training.
They called him ignorant and unlearned (Acts 4:13).
He worked outside.
He worked all night.
You could guess the nature of his work by the smell
of his hands.
He was qualified because He spent time with God.
He learned of God from God's own Son.
He invites us by these words to learn from the God who
makes Himself known.

Heavenly Father, thank You that by Your gracious providence
these words have come down to us.
Thank You for bending low to teach.
May we reach high to learn.
May it happen through the gracious work of Your Spirit for we
ask it in the blessed Name of Your Son.
Amen

In the beginning was the Word...
John 1:1

Before the picture came the caption.
Before there was a world there was the Word.
Before there was a sound there was the Word.
What is the difference between a sound and a word?
A sound must be interpreted.
A word is the interpretation of a sound.
A word brings meaning.
The presence of the Word at the beginning signals the
presence of Intelligence before the beginning.
Those who do not know God insist that the beginning
was meaningless.
After eons meaning bubbled up randomly from below.
This writer says no.
Meaning was handed down from above.
In the beginning was the Word.

*Dear gracious Father, thank You for revealing
meaning to us.
Meaning which was before all time.
Meaning which will outlast time.
Thank You in the name of the living Word.
Jesus Christ Your only Son.
Amen*

...and the Word was with God...
John 1:1

God has always been, and God has always been One.
But God has never been alone.
The Word has always been with God.
The Word too is Eternal.
If co-eternal, then also co-equal.
At this early stage God's Companion is called the LOGOS.
John in the space of one verse moves from declaring God's
existence to describing God's essence.
And His essence is relational.
From this opening God's primary relationship begins to
be disclosed.
Here at first we are told of God and the LOGOS.
Because we have learned more of the story we know that we
are being introduced to the Father and the Son.
Soon the whole point of the story will emerge.
And the point is that we grow in knowledge and relationship
with God through the LOGOS.

Father, we thank You that we know of Your existence and
relationship through this gracious disclosure.
We know You because of the LOGOS.
Thank You that Your Holy Spirit moved John to write.
Thank You for the opportunity to read.
May that same Spirit who moved the writer to write, help
us understand as we read.
Amen

...and the Word was God...
John 1:1

There is only one God.
And the God who is there is One.
And God who is there is tri-Personal.
It means that the one God exists in three Persons.
Here we learn of the Second Person.
In due course we will learn of the Spirit, the Third Person of the God-head.
It's a mystery of course.
But the mystery need not shock us.
It would be more surprising if what we know about God fit neatly into all our human constructs.
As we ask how God can be one and three at the same time we may also ask why we should expect an infinite reality to be fully explicable in terms of human mathematics.
We must take into account that the three Persons are infinite realities.
When we ask how many infinities there can be it becomes easier to recognize that there is one infinite God in three infinite Persons.
And an infinity can only be one.

Heavenly Father, thank You for making us persons.
Thank You for designing us in a way that makes it possible for us to know You, the personal God, person to Person.
May we be attentive.
May we take it all in.
May we learn faithfully what You teach perfectly.
In Jesus' own Name.
Amen

January 6

He was in the beginning with God.
John 1:2

So the LOGOS is a He, not an it.
We know in advance that the LOGOS is a son.
In human generation the father always exists before the son.
Not so in divine generation.
The Son proceeds from the Father.
But the Father does not precede the Son.
In human generation the son never looks precisely like the
father for the simple reason that father and son can never be
the same age.
Not so in divine generation.
Remember the Father and Son are co-eternal.
The Word who is the Son is the express image of His Person.
The Father has never been without the Son.
The Father has never been older.
The Son has never been younger.
The Father and the Son are from the beginning.
Because the Father and Son are eternal.

*Heavenly Father, thank You for what it cost You to
send Your Son.
He was with You from the beginning.
But You sent Him to be with us.
Forever.
Thank You for making it possible for sinners who believe
to become part of a relationship which has always existed.
Thank You in the Name of Your Son who is the
eternal LOGOS.
Amen*

All things were made through him...
John 1:3

The universe is not the accidental collision of
primeval forces.
The human is not the incidental result of an
inexplicable beginning.
We are not a result.
We are a Rendering.
"If there were ever only nothing there would still be
only nothing."
So wrote a Professor named CS Lewis.
The Cosmos is the expression of the Divine Intelligence.
We are not the relics of an explosion lately cooled.
We are the objects of a love intensely warm.
We were intended.
The universe is not the explosion of the worlds.
The universe is the Exposition of the Word.
Because the LOGOS made the world nothing is left
to chance. Nothing is happenstance.
Everything was purposefully wrought.
The LOGOS saw to that.

*Heavenly Father, thank You for the assurance that we
were intended.*
*Because we know that we can live our lives with the
intentionality of stewards.*
Aim our lives toward the targets You design for us Lord.
For Jesus' sake who lived and died with purpose.
Amen

...without him was not anything made that was made.
John 1:3

It would be difficult to enhance the claim.
It marks a kind of upper limit.
The claim is comprehensive.
The claim is universal.
And the claim is exclusive.
All things were made by the LOGOS.
No thing was made without the LOGOS.
The Word is without border or boundary.
There lives nothing outside His creative reach.
Everything proceeds from Him and is preserved by Him.
To Him alone we attribute the "every" and the "all."

Heavenly Father, thank You for the gift of creation.
Thank You for including us in the "all things" made by Your
Son, the LOGOS.
We were made, and we were made to praise You.
So we praise You now in Jesus' Name.
Amen

In Him was life...
John 1:4

He was not only the maker of things but the giver of life.
He made life, yes, but not that only.
Life proceeded from Him.
Life proceeded from Him because life was in Him.
Life, we learn in other places is not only from Him
but for Him.
Breath and movement, consciousness and feeling, all flow
from Him.
Because He originates He also owns.
He is the Sole Proprietor of life.
All rival claimants are impostors.
Quite simply He is our Life.
Life is not the accidental progression of a force.
Life is the intentional conferring of personhood by a Person.

Lord, may we ever avow that our life is not our own.
We proceed from You.
We are preserved by You.
We proceed toward You.
Lord we thank You for life.
And we thank You for Yourself.
For You are our life.
Amen

In him was life, and the life was the light of men.
John 1:4

He gave us Life; He gives us light.
By His life we exist.
By His light we see.
By the light of His own life we understand all life.
The puzzle of our lives is solved by the light of His life.
"LOGOS" may be translated "explanation."
It is folly to seek meaning apart from God's own explanation.
The LOGOS made the world and the LOGOS explains
the world.
Apart from the LOGOS the COSMOS is a riddle without
an answer.
Apart from the Logos man himself is a riddle.
The LOGOS appeared to show God to us.
But He also appeared to show us ourselves.
By His light we know what we are.
By His light we know what we were.
By His light we know what we shall yet be.

Father, thank You for shining the light of the LOGOS.
Without Him we could never know the wonderful truth
about You.
Without Him we could never know the difficult truth
about ourselves.
May we see by this light now.
May we abide in this light forever.
For Christ's own sake.
Amen

In him was life, and the life was the light of men.
John 1:4

The LOGOS shines a light on who we are.
The LOGOS shines a light on what we are.
It is no easy thing to define the human.
The Darwinist says we are the chance product of evolution.
The key they offer is biological.
Are we really no more than a higher animal?
The Fascist says the key is racial.
The Marxist insists the key is economic.
But the Gospel tells a different story.
And we find in the Gospel an explanatory power.
Scripture teaches that to be human is to be a fallen
image-bearer.
How to account for the nobility of the lost?
They are all made in the image of God.
How to account for the iniquity of the saved?
We are all of us fallen.
To be human is to be a fallen image-bearer who can only be
rescued by a Wounded Healer.
The LOGOS is the Wounded Healer.
In this Gospel we will learn His Name.

Father, without this light we would guess and grope.
By this light we see and know.
Thank You for fashioning our lives.
Thank You for shining the light of the LOGOS onto our lives.
In the Name of Jesus, our light and our life.
Amen

January 12

The light shines in the darkness…
John 1:5

The great distinctive of light is contrast.
We notice light when it contrasts the surrounding darkness.
Light was the first of created things in the material universe.
But there was a light uncreated.
God is light.
And the Creator created light by speaking.
In John's Gospel we see the uncreated realities which find
correspondence in the created realm:
LOGOS, Life and Light.
Speculation apart from the LOGOS is not merely lesser light.
Guessing without God does not yield comparative brilliance.
All speculation inevitably distorts the reality that is God.
Speculation apart from revelation is dangerous.
The Bible calls it darkness.

Heavenly Father, we see light and we see by the light.
Thank You for the light which protects against error.
Thank You for the light which scatters darkness.
Make us to see, live and abide.
In Christ's Name who is our light we ask it.
Amen

January 13

**The light shines in the darkness, and the darkness
has not overcome it.
John 1:5**

Some translate, "The darkness does not comprehend
the light."
Both are true.
The darkness cannot understand the Light and the darkness
cannot overcome the Light, who is the LOGOS, who is Jesus.
There is neither comprehension nor victory in opposition
to the Light.
The darkness cannot overcome because its power is temporary
and its influence is temporary.
This Light shone before the world was.
This Light will shine after the world is no more.
The Hebrew Scriptures say that the wicked walk in darkness
and know not over what they stumble.
The Apostle tells us the man of flesh cannot know things
which are spiritually discerned.
The darkness cannot comprehend the Light.

Heavenly Father, may we grow as we walk in Light.
May we grow in our love for the Light.
This we ask in our Saviour's Name.
Who is the Light of the world.
Even Jesus our Lord.
Amen

There was a man sent from God, whose name was John.
John 1:6

The perspective shifts suddenly.
The subject is now historical.
The scene becomes local.
A Sovereign never arrives first.
He is preceded.
A Sovereign never arrives alone.
He is accompanied.
So it was with Jesus.
Outriders, servants, courtiers and guards precede the arrival
of earthly Kings.
This heavenly King was preceded by an entourage of one.
The forerunner was named John.
He was not the Disciple who became an Apostle, who wrote
the book we read.
He was the prophet who baptized.
He drew the attention of men by living apart from men.
He came before the LOGOS as a herald.

Heavenly Father, thank You for sending the many who told
us of Jesus.
The herald who went before.
The Evangelists who came after.
Thank You for their faithfulness in their generation.
Grant us like faithfulness in our own.
In Jesus' Name.
Amen

He came... to bear witness about the light...
John 1:7

It is not necessary to call attention to the sun at its rising.
Not necessary unless we are asleep.
The Logos arrived while the world slept.
John was sent to rouse.
He was sent to prepare the way.
He was sent as a witness.
His role is vital but secondary.
His own light shone fragmentary and inferior.
Like the moon he reflects the greater.
His calling was to point a way.
And to that calling he was faithful.

*Heavenly Father, make us remember that we are
not the center.
Our Lord Jesus is original and primary.
We are something secondary.
We ourselves are derived.
May we understand as John understood.
May we shine our own light in His direction.
For we ask it in His Name who is Christ the Lord.
Amen*

**The true light, which gives light to everyone,
was coming into the world.
John 1:9**

If we see at all we see by the Light John proclaims.
THIS Light is true.
Every man who sees, sees by this Light.
Every woman who understands, understands because
of this Light.
Contradictory lights are false and mask a hidden darkness.
That darkness is poisonous.
It is in fact a darkness which slays.
But blessedly the LOGOS who made the world has
entered the world.
He arrives to shine His own Light.
The Light He shines is uncreated.
His Light outshines all the false lights which are displayed.

*Heavenly Father, thank You for shining the Light of Jesus
into our lives.
Thank You for inclining us to the Light, causing us to believe
the Light and teaching us to love the Light.
Left to ourselves we would have remained in darkness.
Thank You in the Name of Jesus.
Amen*

January 17

He was in the world, and the world was
made through him...
John 1:10

The Maker made manifest!
The Invisible seen walking abroad in the world.
He walked as Creator among creatures.
No theme could be more dramatic.
The Word, having made the world, enters the world.
The Author writes Himself into the script.
His story will shape our own story decisively.
Indeed, His Story means our own story need never end.
His role could be nothing less than central.
For the eternal has entered time.

Heavenly Father, thank You that You made the world
through Your Son.
Thank You that You sent Your Son into the world that
He might redeem us from the world.
It was a mercy for which we could never have dared to ask.
Thank You that the mercy unasked became the
mercy bestowed.
We are eternally grateful.
And we offer thanks in Jesus' Name.
Amen

**He came to his own, and his own people
did not receive him.
John 1:11**

The maker arrives unrecognized.
Later he will depart unrewarded.
The repudiation was personal.
As Man He came for His people.
It was no mere force they resisted.
It was no simple thesis they disbelieved.
The rightful owner was defrauded.
The true King was uncrowned.
Christ appeared like a Suitor offering the sincerest of loves.
He made the greatest offer ever tendered.
But they received Him not.
For those who refused, it became the greatest error ever made.

*Heavenly Father, thank You for sending Your Son on the
saving errand.
Apart from grace we too would have rejected.
So we praise You for grace.
And we thank You for the gift the Son sent down in love.
Amen*

But to all who did receive him...
John 1:12

Blessedly the rejection was not unanimous.
God reserved for Himself a remnant.
There was an election of grace.
Some among His people did receive Him.
And took the message to all peoples.
It received a joyful reception among many.
Those who receive and those who reject mark a
final division.
A division not according to race or gender, rich or poor,
slave or free.
But according to something final and profound.
Some received Him.
Some did not.

Heavenly Father, thank You for preserving the faithful core.
Thank You for the inspired witness published abroad.
Thank You that the news spread even to us.
So that we could receive Him too.
In Christ's Name we thank You.
Amen

But to all who did receive him… he gave the right...
John 1:12

It is the common conviction of democracies that rights
are intrinsic.
But in one celebrated formula we hear that even
unalienable rights are endowed.
They are endowed by the Creator.
Privileges may be conferred by men.
Rights are the gift of God.
We may seek democracy as something ideal.
We seldom encounter it as something real.
It may sound undemocratic to suggest that not all
have a claim on the Fatherhood of God.
But as God offered His Son to all, He offers His
adoption to all.
All do not receive the franchise.
All do not receive it, because all do not desire it.

Heavenly Father, thank You that when we receive Him we
receive everything.
Including the right to call You Father.
Amen.

But to all who did receive him, who believed in his name, he gave the right to become children of God...
John 1:12

If an heir would qualify he must first believe.
Those are the terms of Covenant and Testament.
Faith is little valued by human measure.
By the divine standard it is a thing monumental.
The thing which fills the distance between hell and heaven.
Unbelief locks the door of heaven.
Unbelief doubts whether there is a heaven.
Faith sees Heaven's Gate from afar in the present.
Faith delivers the believer inside the door in the future.
That is a part of what "receiving" means.
We receive the promise when we believe the promise.

*Heavenly Father, thank You for promises exceedingly great
and precious.*
*Thank You for the promised gift of admission into
Your family.*
Thank You for the gift to believe so that we may receive.
Thank You in the name of Your Son Jesus.
Amen

**...who were born, not of blood nor of the will of the flesh
nor of the will of man, but of God.
John 1:13**

Three cardinal events are now linked in this section of
John's Gospel:
Receiving.
Believing.
Being born.
We may argue about which comes first.
But there should be no argument about the Source which
ignites the entire process.
The analogy is to biological birth.
Men have desires and from those desires, children are born.
But even in the case of biology none of us is born because
of our own desire, but rather the desire of our parents.
In every sense our new birth, our spiritual birth, cannot
be self-originated.
It cannot be precipitated by our desire alone.
The whole thing is wrought in God.
He is the sole Source and Giver of this New Life.

Father, thank You for moving toward us in Creative Love.
Thank You for moving a second time in Redemptive Love.
When You moved You moved our hearts to love You.
You made us to be.
And You made us to be born again.
Thank You in Jesus' Name.
Amen

January 23

And the Word became flesh and dwelt among us...
John 1:14

This is the solitary verse on the Nativity in John's Gospel.
It constitutes his one reference to Christmas.
You will notice in this instance that John is concerned
to summarize theology, not to narrate history.
This is that part of theology we call Incarnation.
The Word Who has always been Spirit from all Eternity
becomes flesh in time.
He becomes flesh while never ceasing to be Spirit.
He is the unique God-Man incomparable without
precedent or peer.
The LOGOS who is God becomes Man.
Who made Him thus?
It is a thing accomplished by the Father's decree.
It is a thing accomplished by the Holy Spirit
overshadowing the virgin.
It is a thing volunteered for freely by the Son.
Which means it is a Trinitarian transaction.
Which means it is a thing beyond the range of
human comprehension.

Heavenly Father, we are accustomed to seeking the
highest place.
We thank You that Your Son sought the lowest place.
That we might move to a higher place.
Incarnation – it is a thing no angel would have dared suggest.
Thank You for Your plan.
Your plan for us which leads to REDEMPTION.
In Jesus' Name.
Amen

...and we have seen his glory...
John 1:14

His was not a history rumored second hand.
His was not a hidden work unwitnessed.
The neighbors in Nazareth watched Him from childhood.
He healed the sick in Galilee.
He preached to crowds in Judaea.
The Twelve shared His life day by day.
The glory was displayed.
To those who were there, it was a prodigy unforgettable.
It was a thing to make fishermen write books.

*Heavenly Father, thank You that You sent Your Son in a
visible Body to speak with an audible voice, to touch with a
transformative hand.*
Thank You that He came to us and that He came for us.
Thank You in the Name of Christ our Saviour.
Amen

And the Word became flesh and dwelt among us, and we have seen his glory, glory as of the only Son from the Father, full of grace and truth.
John 1:14

Any man or woman may possess part of the truth.
All made in God's image will display a piece of grace.
But only One is full of grace.
Only One is full of truth.
Grace brings us news of God's son.
Grace helps us to believe.
It is grace which distributes benefits made possible by the Incarnation.
The Gospel is the truth which dispenses grace.
Grace flows from the Person who is truth.
He could be no other than truth.
For He is THE Incarnate Word.

Father we know only Jesus could dispense grace without depletion.
We worship Him as the Lord of infinite source.
Thank You that we have seen His fullness.
Thank You that we have partaken of the same.
For grace and truth, we thank You.
Amen

January 26

John bore witness about him, and cried out...
"...he was before me."
John 1:15

But how could Jesus be BEFORE?
John was, after all, born first.
But John KNEW.
It was his vocation to reveal the Christ.
And He knew that Jesus possessed an identity before and
beyond the human.
Jesus of Nazareth took on human flesh in Bethlehem
of Judea.
He became flesh, yes.
But from all eternity He had been someone higher and
someone other.
He became the Son of Mary.
But His existence did not originate in either Bethlehem
or Nazareth.
His existence did not originate on our planet.
In fact, His existence did not originate at all.
He had always been.
He had always been the only begotten of the Father.
John understood that.
The Spirit taught it to him.
And so, he declared the same.

Heavenly Father, thank You for sending Jesus to take on
something lower and weaker, so we could take on something
higher and stronger.
Thank You for the heavenly intersection with earth
called Incarnation.
Thank You for accomplishing such a thing in the history
of the world which transformed our personal history and
our eternal future.
Thank You in Jesus' Name.
Amen

For from his fullness we have all received...
John 1:16

The Son of God became Man for a transcendent purpose.
The life of God became the life of a Man so that the life of
God could belong to all who believe.
This is the end and purpose of salvation.
God fashioned the original man out of dust in His
own image.
God conforms those who believe to the likeness of His Son
by the Spirit.
Such is the fullness of Jesus that all may receive while his
store yet overflows.
We may always be replenished.
He can never be diminished.
His treasury never wanes, is never meager.
Such is our bank of endless supply.
Such is His bounty of infinite love.

Heavenly Father, thank You for making us rich with a
wealth unalienable.
Thank You that He bent low and became a despised thing.
That we might reach high to become as those exalted.
Thank You in His own Name who is our Jesus.
Amen

...fullness...grace upon grace.
John 1:16

What is this fullness which enriches the believer's estate?
To be sure, it is grace.
Grace added to grace.
Grace succeeding grace.
Grace multiplied by grace.
There are wonders in nature to be sure.
But the wonders of grace are better by far.
The wonders of nature show what God makes.
But the wonders of grace show who God is.
There are wonders of nature which abide unseen.
They hide under seas.
The repose beyond stars.
Just so we have only the foretaste of marvels which grace
will unfold.
The glory of promise is wondrous and divine.
The glory of fulfillment will surpass by far.
And it will all be of grace.

Heavenly Father, for grace we thank You.
Because of grace we are able to thank You.
And by that same grace we will always be thanking
You forevermore.
In Jesus' Name who is the proof of Your grace.
Amen

January 29

**For the Law was given through Moses; grace and truth
came through Jesus Christ.
John 1:17**

The Law could only point to the Promised Land.
It never took anyone over Jordan.
Moses himself could only gaze.
He himself never entered in.
Only grace could bear us through the swelling current.
And land us safe on Canaan's side.
The Law is true and pure, but partial.
It shows us what to do.
It never delivers the power of performing.
The Law set the standard.
In the fullness of time One came who would
meet the standard.
Moses was the Law-giver.
The One who came later was the Law-keeper.
He was the Gospel-giver.
He would keep the Law.
Then He would make us free.

Heavenly Father, thank You so much for the Law.
Without it we would never know the scope of Your holiness.
Without it we could never grasp the depth of our sin.
Thank You for sending Jesus to keep the Law.
And rescue those who cannot.
In Christ's own Name.
Amen

No one has ever seen God; the only God, who is at the Father's side, he has made him known.
John 1:18

The words surprise us.
This same Bible informs us that Adam and Eve saw God.
Abraham and Moses saw God.
Isaiah saw God high and lifted up.
If the earlier reports are true what does this report mean?
We may be permitted to understand the words this way:
"No one has ever seen God, except of course when they see
Jesus, the only begotten of the Father."
We know that the visible God of the New Testament is God
the Second Person Incarnate.
These words suggest that the visible God of the Old Testament
is God the Second Person pre-Incarnate.
We infer then that these God-sightings in the older Testament,
what the scholars call "theophanies" are manifestations of
God the Second Person.
When God makes Himself visible on earth it is Christ
who is seen.
One reason He is called LOGOS is because He is what
we hear of God.
One reason He is called Light is because He is what we
see of God.
Personally, we call Him Jesus of Nazareth, and He is
God in human form.
The accolades lavished upon the Lord Jesus are piled
High in this chapter.
Though if the one true God became the one perfect Man the
praise accorded here is no more than we should expect.

Heavenly Father, thank You for all You have made known to
us about Yourself.
Thank You for the final and decisive disclosure in
Your only Son.
Thank You for Jesus, His Incarnation and birth.
His wondrous words and works.
In His holy Name we thank You.
Amen

**(John)… saw Jesus coming toward him, and said,
"Behold, the Lamb …"
John 1:29**

We've been listening to the Gospel writer called John the
Evangelist, one of the Twelve.
In verse 18 he revealed that no one had ever seen God,
except...except of course when Jesus showed God to us.
Now this other John, Jesus' older cousin called the Baptist,
bids us see something else.
Jesus is LOGOS, Jesus is Light.
We learned that at the first.
Now we hear that Jesus is also the Lamb.
Isaac asked his father Abraham one of the great Old
Testament questions.
"Father, where is the lamb...?" (Genesis 22:7)
The father answers, "My son, God will provide for
Himself a lamb."
The answer is beautiful.
The answer is accurate.
The answer is incomplete.
The full answer waits for 2000 years.
"There He is Isaac," answers that Prophet baptizing
down at the Jordan.
Look at Him.
There is the Lamb.
He walks toward us at the River.

*Heavenly Father, thank You that You not only sent Jesus to us,
but You sent Jesus for us.
Thank You that the sacrifice was provided to take the place
of Isaac.
Thank You that the sacrifice was sent in our place as well.
Thank You for this Saviour Jesus.
In His own Name.
Amen*

February 1

**"Behold the Lamb of God, who takes away
the sin of the world!"
John 1:29**

The Law which commanded could not take sin away.
The Prophet who warned could not take sin away.
The Priest who made sacrifice could not take sin away.
But the Law, the Prophets, and the Priests could
bear witness.
All of these anticipated something else.
Something greater and other.
Something approaching from the outside.
It would be the perfection required but unknown.
It would be the righteousness to purge the deepest guilt.
It would be the purity to cleanse the blackest stain.
It would be a Man.
The Man who walked toward John at the River.
The Man he called a Lamb.

*Heavenly Father, thank You that You did not leave us to the
consequences of our choices.
Thank You that You did not require that we repair
what we ruined.
Thank You that You sent Jesus to do all that.
Amen*

February 2

(John) looked at Jesus...and said,
"Behold the Lamb of God!"
The two disciples heard him say this,
and they followed Jesus.
John 1:36-37

John directs attention away from himself.
He points to Jesus.
He tells the truth about Jesus.
And others follow.
He thus fulfills his mission.
This is the supreme ministry achievement.
For him it meant a leave taking, with the resultant subtraction
from among his own number.
The true Prophet longs for this.
The godly Pastor aims at this.
It defines the crown of Gospel labor.
It meant goodbye to those he loved.
He was human so he likely sighed.
They had been his own disciples.
But now they followed another.
But what an other!
Herein is authentic joy.
Herein is true vocation.
To speak of Him and others follow.

Heavenly Father, thank You that we are not only told
but we are shown.
Thank You for the model called John the Baptist.
May we go and do likewise.
In the power of the Holy Spirit.
In the Name of Jesus.
Amen

February 3

**Jesus turned …and said to them,
"What are you seeking?"
John 1:38**

The demand is for clarification.
It is a question which warrants an answer.
Einstein complained that his own age combined a
refinement of means with a confusion of goals.
Our own generation has advanced no further.
What are we really looking for anyway?
Jesus asked questions to teach, not to learn.
His question works as an effective diagnostic.
He demands candor.
He asks for motive.
His question forces us to think about the subject we
care about most.
We mean the subject of ourselves.

*Father, invest us with the sobriety required to answer the
important questions.
And help us understand which questions are important
and which are not.
Lord, make us to look for the most important thing.
We mean the knowledge of the One who is Himself
Eternal Life.
For in His Name we do ask it.
Amen*

February 4

…they said to Him… "Where are you staying?"
John 1: 38

A simple question fetched a simple answer.
Well, not quite an answer, because they responded
with a question.
But we know what they meant.
They were following because they wanted to know
where He lived.
This is one of the chief reasons we become Christians.
We just want to see where He lives.
And the only way to see is to believe and follow.
Let us follow then.
Follow with resolve.
Follow with faith.
Follow fully.
When we see the Cross looming let us not shrink back.
Let us then quicken our pace.
It means we are almost home.

Heavenly Father, we thank You that these two disciples
wanted to follow Jesus.
We know it was so because the Lord Jesus drew them along.
May He draw us to Himself as well.
That we too may follow.
For His own sake we ask it.
Amen

February 5

He said to them, "Come and you will see."
John 1:39

Jesus' response is more than an answer.
It is an invitation.
But it is also more than an invitation.
It is a methodology.
Jesus' answer constitutes the methodology at the heart of
Christian apologetics.
Christianity invites all creatures to believe in Jesus Christ.
But before believing any seeker is permitted to draw close, to
study, to test, to prove.
It is a considered and informed faith which is in view, not a
faith thoughtless and blind.
Any sinner unready to look to Christ is invited to
look at Christ.
The claims are to be tested both rationally and experientially.
This is the invitation issued to John's disciples on the road at
the beginning.
This is the invitation by the angel at the tomb to the women
at the end.
Come and see.

Heavenly Father, thank You for the offer of your Son.
We have come, and we have seen.
We know Him to be more than enough, far beyond all desert
and even beyond all imagining.
How we thank You for Him.
In whose Name we pray.
Amen

**...they came and saw where he was staying, and they
stayed with him that day,
for it was about the tenth hour.
John 1:39**

They saw something which made them want to stay.
Something compelled them beyond the lateness of the hour.
It was not just that they saw WHERE He lived.
They saw HOW He lived.
And they saw that He was Life.
They never returned home for they stayed with Him
three years.
After He returned to the house of His Father they could never
return to the house of their fathers.
They went to the world to invite others to come and see.
To declare to them that the hour was late.
To plead that it was a good thing for others to stay
with Him too.

*Heavenly Father, we thank You that as it was in the beginning
it is now and ever shall be.
We thank You that even now Jesus is preparing a place for
us to stay.
So that where He is, there we may be also.
For that we bless You and praise You.
In Jesus' own Name.
Amen*

February 7

**One of the two ...Andrew...found his own
brother Simon and said to him,
"We have found the Messiah"
(which means Christ).
John 1:40-41**

Jesus is a change agent.
After those men spent time with Jesus they were changed.
The change was immediate.
And it was profound.
Spending time with Jesus made them want to tell others.
Telling others became their chief preoccupation.
Quiet men became vocal.
Fishermen became authors.
What choice had they?
They were compelled.
The news was too good to keep hidden.
That's why they called it Gospel.

*Heavenly Father, thank You that through Your Word
and Your Spirit You have made it possible for us to
spend time with Jesus.
Thank You for sending Jesus to save our lives and to
change our lives.
Don't let us miss opportunities to tell others.
That may be the main reason You left us on this planet.
In Jesus' Name.
Amen*

"We have found the Messiah" (which means Christ).
John 1:41

This One was expected.
The Law foreshadowed Him.
The Prophets foretold Him.
God had, after all, promised Him.
But He was different from what they had imagined.
Far different.
And far greater.
They would be overwhelmed.
How could they not be?
God is always greater than our capacity to imagine.
And this Man was very God of very God.

Heavenly Father, thank You for fulfilling what You promised.
Now make us to do as we are commanded.
Make us to yield to Him His rightful place.
May we always tell others.
May He always be preeminent.
This glorious Jesus, in whose Name we pray.
Amen

Jesus looked at him and said, "You are Simon the son of John. You shall be called Cephas" (which means Peter).
John 1:42

After his brother's invitation Peter expected to be introduced to Jesus.
But Peter never expected Jesus to introduce him to himself.
Jesus called Peter's name and the name of his father before they were introduced.
Shortly thereafter Jesus informed Peter that he would have a new name.
What kind of Man was this?
What kind of Man indeed!
A Man who knew Peter's past for the same reason He knew Peter's future.
A Man who named Peter as a mark of ownership.
A Man who owns Peter because He made Peter.
The Man called Christ.

Heavenly Father, we are secure because Christ has taken ownership of our lives.
We are hopeful because He gives us our names and controls our future.
May we always bear the marks of those who belong to Him.
In Jesus' own Name we ask it.
Amen

He found Philip and said to him, "Follow me."
John 1:43

Though it was declared only of Philip, they were all four
found by Jesus.
Just as He found them so also did He find us.
Though we may persuade ourselves that we initiated, it is God
who always makes the first move.
We seek Him out because He bids us come and follow.
We may hear no audible sound, but He bids us all the same.
Following is essential in the life of a Christian.
When we choose one end of the road we choose the
other also.
The way leads by a Cross, but it doesn't end there.
Better a Cross with Jesus than a smooth path without Him.
The great thing is to be with Jesus.
Our great Companion on the way.
The Way has a name.
The name is discipleship.

Heavenly Father, thank You for the privilege of following
Your Son.
Thank You that we learned His name and heard His voice.
Thank You that we, even we, can be counted among
His disciples.
For such a mercy we praise You.
Amen

"We have found him of whom Moses...wrote..."
John 1:45

John wrote that Jesus found Philip.
Philip declared that he had found Jesus.
John's version is definitive and the more
theologically accurate.
But we know what Philip means.
In a way he had found Jesus long before in the
writings of Moses.
Moses gave the Law, but Moses couldn't keep the Law.
Moses could lead the people to the Promised Land,
but he couldn't take them in.
So, he wrote about another Prophet.
A Prophet who could do both.
The Prophet whom Philip called Joseph's son.
The Prophet from Nazareth named Jesus.

Heavenly Father, we thank You for the witness of Moses.
We thank You for the witness of John's Gospel.
Thank You that Jesus came and that He called disciples to
Himself on the road.
We have joined that once small band now swollen to millions.
Keep us close on the road.
For Jesus' sake we ask it.
Amen

**Nathanael said to him, "Can anything good
come out of Nazareth?"
John 1:46**

It was an understandable prejudice.
The Messiah was to come from Bethlehem,
David's own city.
The circumstances of Jesus' birth were not well
known at the beginning.
In the First Century Nazareth was a muddy little
village of 50 or so houses.
It was a place justifiably obscure.
Such was the humility of the God-Man.
Such are the ways of God.
He passes by the self-regarding.
He takes the lowly and lifts them up.
Nazareth would not be long unknown.
Her exaltation was drawing nigh.

Father, You make the humble to hope.
Your choices surprise us and build us up.
Thank You for seeing what the world misses.
Thank You that nothing escapes Your notice.
Thank You for making a place of contempt the
dwelling place of Your only Son.
Many of us have felt the sting of discrimination.
Many have had their Nazareth moments.
Thank You for blessing Nazareth and reforming Nathanael.
Thank You in the Name of Jesus the Nazarene.
Amen

February 13

Philip said to him, "Come and see."
John 1:46

Philip echoes Jesus' first words to the first disciples.
Hear the perpetual invitation of Christianity.
"Come and see."
Biblical faith is not abetted by a vacuum.
Christianity requires faith to be sure, but that faith is supported
by evidence and strengthened by experience.
The complementary sides of our nature find resonance
in the salvation Jesus offers.
Observation and emotion, feeling and experience are
mutually confirmatory.
It is Nathanael the unbeliever, not some religious zealot,
who proves himself the bigot in this exchange.
As a remedy he is offered opportunities of
first-hand investigation.
Only the hardest cases resist a personal encounter
with this Jesus.
And Nathanael would not be a hard case.

Heavenly Father, thank You for sending someone or
something to point us to Jesus.
Thank You for all the influences which brought us
face to Face.
We find Him to be more than what was publicized.
More than what was promised.
And for that we offer everlasting praise.
Amen

**Jesus saw Nathanael coming toward him and said of him,
"Behold an Israelite indeed, in whom there is no deceit!"
John 1:47**

What was Jacob's chief character trait?
Was it not deceit?
One scholar paraphrased Jesus' salutation this way:
"Behold an Israel in whom there is no Jacob."
The introduction of apparent strangers is noteworthy
for its contrast.
Nathanael hears of Jesus and discounts Him by a prejudice.
Jesus greets Nathanael and exalts him by a compliment.
Nathanael degraded Jesus by an assumption
born of ignorance.
Jesus lauds Nathanael BECAUSE HE KNOWS
EVERY HEART.
From Him nothing could be hidden.
He passed over a great error to publicize a great virtue.
No virtue can compensate for a low opinion of Jesus.
But Jesus answers the insult with good will.
This marks the first sighting of a great mercy.
The massive extent of that mercy is a primary New
Testament theme.

Heavenly Father, we are ever slighting your Royal Son.
He is ever blessing and encouraging us.
He lifts us up.
Teach us by Your Spirit to value Him supremely and
worship Him sincerely.
For His own dear sake we ask it.
Amen.

February 15

Nathanael said to him, "How do you know me?"
John 1:48

Jesus' claims are staggering.
And Jesus' claims are verifiable.
They are verifiable by evidence.
They are verifiable by experience.
Our faith subsists upon something, not nothing.
Faith will not long survive in a vacuum of confirmation.
It must have sustenance.
Discovering that what Jesus says about ourselves is true
strengthens our conviction that what He says about Himself
is also true.
We advance in our knowledge of God as we discover His
knowledge of us.
Early in our Christian lives it begins to dawn upon us that we
are thoroughly known.
Adam and Eve had not the option of hiding in the trees.
So it is with ourselves.
Jesus knows who we are.
And He loves us anyway.
Nathanael made this discovery at the outset.
Jesus knew him because He made him.
He made him because He is the Son of God.
The sooner we learn the lesson for ourselves, the better off
we will be.

Heavenly Father, we believe You know us because You
made us.
Thank You for the power that caused us to be.
Heavenly Father, we believe You love us because You
redeemed us.
Because You know us, You know that we need redeeming.
Thank You for the love that caused us to be redeemed.
Thank You for the Creator/Redeemer love shown to us by
the Lord Jesus.
Thank You in His Name.
Amen

Nathanael said to him, "How do you know me?" Jesus answered him, "Before Philip called you, when you were under the fig tree, I saw you."
John 1:48

Nathanael could have discredited Jesus' claim.
But he did not.
On the contrary, he was converted by it.
First, Jesus declared what Nathanael was like on the inside.
Then Jesus described the place where Nathanael thought he was unobserved.
The aptitude demonstrated was something akin
to omniscience.
The reason for this would soon become obvious.
Nathanael had asked Jesus how He knew what He knew.
Only God is omniscient.
The clues were falling into place.
And they all pointed in the same direction.

Heavenly Father, thank You for sending Jesus to answer the questions of skeptics.
Thank You that Jesus offers satisfactory answers to reasonable questions.
Thank You that He came not only to show us who He is, but He came to show us who we really are.
Since He made us He is the only one who can know for sure.
Thank You, Father, for disclosing truth we could never attain by unaided effort.
Thank You in Jesus' Name.
Amen

February 17

Nathanael answered him, "Rabbi, you are the Son of God!
You are the King of Israel!"
John 1:49

It took but a few words to bear Nathanael over the
threshold of conversion.
He had heard enough.
The skeptic came around.
What he heard brought him across that line.
We mean the dividing line between Life and Death.
Very likely something transpired between Nathanael
and Jesus which will remain opaque to outsiders.
All will have experiences incommunicable to others.
Some experiences will pass solely between God
and ourselves.
Nathanael may recently have been accused of deception.
Jesus could have unburdened him by what sounded like
an acquittal.
Or Nathanael could have prayed, "Lord if You are real,
if You can see me, confirm it by convincing means."
Jesus appears, recalls the recent scene, then declares,
"I saw you."
It would have been sufficient.
But we are guessing.
Whatever it was, Nathanael was electrified to a point of
irrevocable commitment.

Heavenly Father, thank You for our own exposure to
converting truth.
Thank You for introducing us to this same Jesus.
He has convinced us as well.
And we know it was not our perception but Your grace which
brought us to this Kingdom.
Amen

Nathanael answered him, "Rabbi, you are the Son of God!
You are the King of Israel!"
John 1:49

Here are three endorsements in one confession.
Nathanael comprehended much in a short space.
By his declaration he shows himself a thoroughly
converted believer.
He assigns Jesus the title, "Rabbi" which sets Him forth a
teacher both accredited and worthy.
This is a plaudit few would begrudge Him.
But to call Him Son of God!
Could Nathanael have known all that meant?
Decidedly not.
Nor do we.
God is boundless with respect to time, for He is eternal.
God is borderless with respect to space, for He is infinite.
His center is everywhere; His circumference is nowhere.
So declared the ancients, and the faithful shout, "Amen."
We believe these truths about God readily enough.
We comprehend them but dimly.
They are beyond our intellectual range.
Nathanael had not comprehended everything, but he had
believed enough.
He had seen enough to know that Jesus of the formerly
despised Nazareth was the Son of God.
Jesus called Nathanael an Israelite.
Nathanael called Jesus the King of Israel.
It was a certification of the Messianic identity to be sure.
But it was more than that.
Nathanael was saying, "You are my King."

Father, we say with Nathanael, that Jesus is our King.
You have sent Him, let us crown Him.
Crown Him with worship, crown Him by obedience and love.
By His own Name we pray.
Amen

February 19

**Jesus answered him, "Because I said to you 'I saw you
under the fig tree' do you believe?"
John 1:50**

In a brief instant Nathanael traversed the substantial distance
between skepticism and faith.
He did this of course, by the gracious aid of God the
Holy Spirit.
Jesus does not let the great change go by unremarked.
Jesus had exhibited the qualities of God's own Son.
Having noted the same, Nathanael enrolled as Christ's
own subject.
Philip's original claim would have sounded extravagant
to most in Israel.
Nathanael's estimate was more lavish still.
Philip asked Nathanael to come and see.
What Nathanael saw was more than Philip forecast.
Messiah, yes, but also divine and Israel's true King.
Nathanael met in the Nazarene far more than He expected.
It is ever thus with this Jesus.

*Heavenly Father, we have had the same experience with
Your only Son.
He has far outshone His publicity.
No promise could exceed the reality of who He is and
what He offers.
We see in Him all that is good.
We find in Him everything needful.
We praise You for such a Saviour and King.
We praise You in His wonderful Name.
Amen*

**Jesus answered him, "Because I said to you,
'I saw you under the fig tree' do you believe?
You will see greater things than these."
John 1:50**

Apparently this disciple, after his first skeptical bluff, required minimum demonstration to advance toward maximum faith.
Note the verbs in the Lord's commendation: "I said...You believe ...You will see."
The progression models a worthy pattern for any disciple to follow.
It is in fact a kind of Disciple's Credo.
"Jesus says it. I believe it. I will see it."
How different from the worldling's motto!
The man of flesh must always say, "If I see what you say, then I will believe."
But by then it may be too late.
The words of Jesus are our better eyes.
They provide a higher vision.
Our own eyes may deceive us.
His Word is the only infallible sense we possess.

*Heavenly Father, may we believe the words of
Your Son invariably and implicitly.
What grace You show by bringing His words
into our hearing.
May we answer grace with faith.
In Christ's own Name we ask it.
Amen*

February 21

"...You will see greater things than these."
John 1:50

Even a small faith opens a wide vista.
But initial faith yields but a foretaste.
At the first Nathanael saw enough to persuade.
But it was only a beginning.
Portentous confirmations lay ahead.
Nathanael's trust in Jesus' ability to deliver what He
promised would be rewarded.
There would be miracles more numerous.
There would be miracles more dramatic.
Faith shines like a star.
But the dawn outshines the stars.
Our faith awaits a vindication.
One glad morning faith will be eclipsed by sight
at His appearing.
We have no surer expectation.
Nor do we need one.

Father, we have seen much, and we are satisfied.
But we have the further prospect of the greater promise.
Grow our faith to the proportion of Your promises.
We await eagerly Lord.
We await with expectation.
In Jesus' Name.
Amen

February 22

"...you will see heaven opened, and the angels of God ascending and descending on the Son of Man."
John 1:51

The chapter begins with words found in the first of Genesis.
The chapter ends with words from another famous
Genesis episode.
Jacob saw a vision of something like a ladder stretching
between heaven and earth.
The ladder was not built-up from below.
It was let down from above.
Upon that ladder angels went up and angels came down.
Nathanael, Jesus promised, would see what Jacob saw.
Jacob's vision was one proof of God's own presence.
Nathanael would know a greater proof.
Nathanael already enjoyed a greater presence.
Where Jacob saw the shadows in a dream Nathanael
would enjoy the substance in the light.
There can be but one way to reach heaven from earth.
That way is a Man.
The Man who stood before Nathanael at the close of
John's first chapter.

Heavenly Father, thank You that by Your Spirit we can stand
in Your Presence.
All because of Your Son.
Thank You for showing us the way to heaven in Him.
Thank You that Nathanael's promise is our promise.
Thank You for the sure and certain prospect of
faith's vindication.
In Christ's own Name we thank You.
Amen

"...you will see...the angels of God ascending and descending on the Son of Man."
John 1:51

This astonishing prophecy is not random.
There is context and that context goes all the way back to the first book of the Bible.
"Behold an Israel in whom there is no Jacob" was one interpretation of the Lord's greeting to Nathanael we noted earlier.
The Jacob connection abides to the end of the chapter.
In his famous vision Jacob saw angels ascending and descending upon a ladder.
Jesus came to fulfill promises made long earlier.
He also came to reveal the substance of which Old Testament types and patterns are but shadows.
Jesus is here telling Nathanael that one day he would see what Jacob saw.
Except Nathanael would see more.
The ladder was but the shadow.
Jesus of Nazareth is the substance.

Heavenly Father, we thank You that You deliver more than You promise.
Thank You for giving us Your Son who is far greater than anything we could imagine.
Thank You that Nathanael's prospect was greater than Jacob's past.
Thank You that we too will see Faith's vindication.
We will see the attendance of angels upon the Son of Man.
For that we thank You and praise Your Name.
Amen

**On the third day there was a wedding at Cana in
Galilee, and the mother of Jesus was there.
Jesus also was invited to the wedding with his disciples.
John 2:1-2**

Jesus retraces the steps of our first parents.
Unlike Eve Jesus is not deceived.
Unlike Adam Jesus does not give in.
Jesus retraces the path of Israel.
Unlike Israel Jesus does not murmur or fall short.
When we survey the Gospels together we see that Jesus is
tempted in the wilderness after His baptism.
He then proceeds to the wedding.
Adam fell low in the Garden.
Jesus, our second Adam, stands firm in the desert.
One of the many things sin ruined was marriage.
Shame followed sin and blame followed shame.
Jesus approaches marriage as a physician approaches
a patient.
He comes to deliver and to heal.
No one can predict at the outset what pressing need will
emerge first.
Marriage is God's own idea.
It can only be mended by God's own remedy.

*Heavenly Father, we thank You for Jesus' presence
in Cana.
We thank You that He goes where He is invited.
At this moment we invite Him afresh into our own families
and into our own wedded lives.
May He be the third partner in every Christian marriage.
We thank You that He is as available to us as He was to them.
And even more so.
In His own Name we pray.
Amen*

February 25

When the wine ran out, the mother of Jesus said to him,
"They have no wine." And Jesus said to her,
"Woman what does this have to do with me?
My hour has not yet come."
John 2:3-4

We hear only an observation. Jesus hears a request.
Francis Bacon insisted that Jesus would not answer
mere words.
Especially words masking the true concern of the heart.
He responds rather to thoughts.
She said, "They have no wine."
The remark is benign enough for us.
But there was something deeper.
It was that deeper thing her Son addressed.
She wanted the time-table advanced
She wanted Him to launch.
She wanted His true identity to come forward.
"We have waited quite enough," she seemed to say.
His answer was, "No."
He would choose the time.
He would choose the place.
Had she fully understood, patience would have come easier.
Once known, He would be opposed.
And once opposed, He would be killed.

Dear Father, we know You created time.
And we know one day You will bring time to an end.
We are certain that You are never too early.
We know that You are never too late.
We rest in knowing that our times are in Your hands.
We thank You for Jesus' timing in this enterprise.
We thank You He did the right thing at the right time.
We thank You that He took the time to rescue our souls.
Amen

His mother said to the servants,
"Do whatever he tells you."
John 2:5

In the Lord's response to His mother, we hear only a "no."
His response sounds curt.
It takes us off guard.
There is no evidence it took her off guard.
She apparently heard a "yes."
No one knew Him better than she.
She fielded the apparent rebuff with a noble faith.
There is probably no harder time to do the Lord's
bidding than at that moment we believe He has denied
us something dear.
Indeed, such moments may invite defiance.
Hurt may make us sluggish at the next opportunity
for obedience.
That's what makes Mary's response so exemplary.
Immediately she runs to the servants.
"Do everything He tells you," she says.
Listen well to that.
Is it not the best strategy?
Could there be a better?
She gave the wisest counsel.
Definitely the wisest possible counsel.
In the long history of our world.

Father, may we listen with an attentive heart.
May we obey with prompt feet.
May we wait with a strong confidence.
May we know the joy of servants who are used.
In Christ's own Name we ask it.
Amen

**Jesus said to the servants, "Fill the jars with water."
John 2:7**

He did not give her everything her heart desired at
that moment.
But He was not unresponsive.
He acted.
He moved immediately, dramatically and efficiently.
He gave her something no other could have given.
But before He gives, He commands.
The command was somewhat mysterious, actually
wearisome, and apparently futile.
The volume in those water-pots would have exceeded
seventy gallons.
To fill the pots by hand would have been tedious in
the extreme.
No Servant balked. No Servant complained.
They were servants indeed.
And the miracle of transformation, what John will call the first
sign, was worked through the servants' hands.

*Heavenly Father, we do thank You that You have brought us
into vital contact with the Life-giver called Jesus.
We thank You for the fact of salvation.
We thank You for the way of salvation.
We thank You that we have life.
We know that we have life because You gave life to Him and
He gave life to us.
Thank You, Heavenly Father, for giving us this wonderful gift
through your Son Jesus.
Amen*

When the master of the feast tasted the water now become wine, and did not know where it came from (though the servants who had drawn the water knew)...
John 2:9

The "when" of the miracle is debatable.
We are not told the precise moment the commonplace water became the exceptional wine.
Perhaps when the water was poured into the pots.
Perhaps when the contents were poured into the cups.
Perhaps when the cups were raised to the lips.
Dynamically the miracle happened somewhere between the command and the obedience.
It was the connection between the two which brought the marvelous result.
The steward in charge knew nothing of the source.
The ones who knew were those who obeyed.
The obedience came first.
The benefits came next.
The understanding came after.
The sequence is instructive.
We expect that sequence to be repeated throughout our Christian lives.

Heavenly Father, we thank You that Your Son's fatiguing commands lead on to refreshment.
We thank You for the surprising benefits which follow obedience.
We thank You for the understanding which comes to us when we look back on the faith of others.
We thank You in Jesus' Name.
Amen

February 29

"Everyone serves the good wine first, and when people have drunk freely, then the poor wine. But you have kept the good wine until now."
John 2:10

The best was saved until last.
It is ever thus with the Lord.
The evil one recruits by exaggerating the pleasures of sin.
He obscures the fact that those pleasures diminish
over time.
He denies that sin chases sinners toward a bad end.
Jesus hides no hard thing from those who follow Him.
He forecasts stern battles.
He promises a Cross.
The time will come when enemies will regard killing disciples
as a service to God.
Those who hate Jesus will hate His followers.
But after the Cross, the Crown.
And, better still, the divine accolade, the "Well done, good
and faithful servant."
That is the highest reward.
But rewards don't come at the outset.
Great victories follow hard fighting.

Heavenly Father, we thank You for the privilege
of participation.
Thank You that we don't merely watch the Christian
life go by, we get to live it every day.
Thank You for the prospect of future rewards.
Thank You in Jesus' wonderful Name.
Amen

**This…Jesus did at Cana in Galilee, and
manifested his glory.
John 2:11**

How did Jesus manifest His glory by this miracle?
He manifested the glory of His love by rescuing the hosts
from embarrassment.
He manifested the glory of His power by doing what no one
else could do.
He manifested the glory of His generosity by providing the
wine for others.
He manifested the glory of His humility by refusing to
publicize the miracle.
He manifested the glory of His providence by extending
the celebration.
Christians may have the reputation of dampening the
fervor of the celebration.
They did not get the reputation from their King.
The presence of Jesus sends a different signal.
One lesson of the miracle is this:
The celebration need not be cut short.
The Lord Jesus is still here.

Heavenly Father, thank You for weddings.
Thank You for the joy they bring to the participants but
thank You even more for the lesson they teach to us all.
Thank You for the way weddings foreshadow that final
wedding feast in heaven after the Last Day.
Thank You for the way Jesus' presence at the wedding in
Cana foreshadows the final wedding in heaven.
Because He will always be in heaven, joy will always
be in heaven.
The joy will never run out.
Thank You in Jesus' own Name.
Amen

**...and Jesus went up to Jerusalem. In the temple he found
those who were selling oxen and sheep and pigeons, and
the money-changers sitting there. And
making a whip of cords, he drove them all out of the
temple... and overturned their tables. And he told those
who sold the pigeons, "Take these things away; do not
make my Father's house a house of trade."
John 2:13-16**

The sacrifice of animals was required by Law.
Animals were sold close-by to ease the burden of pilgrims.
Without those Jerusalem sellers, worshippers would have to
herd live animals over long distances.
Why then did the Lord drive those animals away?
He acted because a legitimate need for convenience had
spawned an illegitimate traffic in greed.
The faithful worshiper approached the Temple with a
resolve to sacrifice.
These merchants approached with an appetite for gain.
The spectacle of these profiteers filled the landscape.
Their commerce subverted God's design.
Rightly did Jesus accuse them of making His Father's house
of worship into a house for their own profit.
This ministry of eviction (occurring twice in the Gospels) is
the only time the Son resorted to physical coercion.
Here for once the Lord is provoked.
Here is the action of Deity offended and aroused.

*Heavenly Father, thank You for a Saviour who is not supine.
We know He was provoked for our sakes.
We thank You that the violence He visits is a holy violence.
We thank You that the war He wages brings a just peace.
We pray that the emotions of our own natures would be
controlled by the Holy Spirit and directed toward
righteous ends. For Jesus' sake we ask it.
Amen*

...Take these things away...
John 2:16

A common notion persists that Jesus was overcome by anger and out of control.
There is no denying that He was angry.
Anger itself is not necessarily unrighteous.
Anger at unrighteousness is rather the proof of righteousness.
And Jesus' own anger is proof of that very truth.
It is instructive that the scourge of cords is the only thing we know that this Carpenter ever made.
Stopping to fashion that scourge took patient deliberation.
Jesus drove the merchants and their slow-footed stock away from the holy place.
It would have been easy for the owners to recover those large animals.
But he did not drive the birds away as their recovery would have been impossible.
He rather asked the owners to remove them.
This proves His mastery over His emotion.
He would not rob those sellers of their property.
He would not have His Father robbed of His honor.

Heavenly Father, thank You for all we learn from what Jesus said.
Thank You for all we learn from what Jesus did.
Thank You that His action was an expression of love and an instrument for correction.
Conform our own actions to His perfect pattern.
Amen

**So the Jews said to him, "What sign do you show us
for doing these things?"
Jesus answered them, "Destroy this temple, and in
three days I will raise it up."
John 2:18-19**

For the second time in the same chapter Jesus appears to be
answering a question which has not been asked.
It may be difficult for us to relate His response to the context.
But it will be simple if we remember what was before noted:
Words we can hear are often used to hide motives we
cannot see.
We may be sure this is the case here.
But nothing can be hidden from this Jesus.
Those profiting from the Temple commerce were enraged.
They demanded a proof of authority.
But Jesus knew they had already judged Him and had already
pronounced sentence in their hearts.
No matter what proof would be forthcoming (and it would be
massive) their wrath would not be turned aside.
They had decided He must die.
His answer, though mysterious and indirect, speaks to that
murderous intent.
"One day I will permit you to do what you want," He is
saying. "You may kill Me," He says.
"But death can hold Me no more than three days."

*Heavenly Father, we know that the Lord Jesus saw everything
hidden in human hearts.
We know that even now He sees our own hearts.
We know that He is the great discerner of motives.
We praise You because He is able to explain us to ourselves.
We thank You that He is able to rescue us from ourselves and
make us to be different.
May we see what He shows us about ourselves.
May we believe in His power to change us. To change us and
make us like Himself. For His own dear sake, we ask it.
Amen*

...for he himself knew what was in man. Now there was a man ...named Nicodemus...
John 2:25-3:1

The New Testament was originally written in capital letters
without punctuation or spaces between words.
Punctuation and word division became the task of scholars in
later years.
Chapter and verse numbers were assigned centuries after the
original composition.
These innovations dramatically aid memory and citation.
But the advantage is not unmixed.
Sometimes the flow is disturbed.
This is the case between chapters two and three in
John's Gospel.
Jesus "knew what was in man," we are told at the end of
chapter two.
"Now, there was a man," follows close on as chapter
three commences.
The implication is obvious.
Nicodemus approached Jesus to learn what He could.
He was startled to discover that the Lord Jesus already knew
everything there was to know about Nicodemus.

*Heavenly Father, we praise You that we are perfectly
known by You.*
*We praise You that though You know us perfectly You
also love us perfectly.*
*Thank You for teaching us about ourselves by teaching us
about Nicodemus.*
*Most of all thank You for teaching us about the Lord Jesus
by what He says to Nicodemus.*
Thank you in Jesus' own name.
Amen

Now there was a man...named Nicodemus ...(who) came to Jesus... and said to him, "Rabbi, we know that you are a teacher come from God"...Jesus answered... "unless one is born again he cannot see the kingdom of God."
John 3:1-3

Once again Jesus speaks to a subject remote from context.
Once again we offer the same explanation: Jesus is addressing unspoken thoughts.
Nicodemus is an eminent ruler of the Jews.
He approaches the young rabbi as an examiner.
He will validate or invalidate the claims of this new sensation in Israel.
His errand could have been private and self-originated.
It is more likely he took the assignment from his colleagues on the Council.
According to Jewish expectations Jesus is from the wrong place.
According to Jewish qualifications Jesus had no training.
According to Jewish standards Jesus spent time with the wrong people.
But Jesus does not subject Himself to Nicodemus' judgment.
Jesus transforms the agenda into an examination of Nicodemus' own credentials.
And Jesus declares that those credentials are lacking.
Unless Nicodemus becomes someone else, he will never see God's Kingdom.
God did not send His Son to be judged by Nicodemus and the other rulers.
God sent His Son to judge Israel and offer a new, better way.

Heavenly Father, all we truly are is laid bare in the presence of Christ Jesus our Lord.
We know that our first birth has made us sinners.
Thank You that because of Jesus' death we have second birth.
May we always walk by faith in the fullness of this born-again life until we see our Jesus Face to face.
In His own high Name we pray.
Amen

**Jesus answered, "Truly, truly, I say to you, unless one is
born of water and the Spirit,
he cannot enter the kingdom of God...."
Nicodemus said to Him, "How can these things be?"
Jesus answered him, "Are you the teacher of Israel and yet
you do not understand these things?"
John 3:5, 9-10**

The key to understanding what Jesus meant lies in the
question posed to Nicodemus.
How could he be a teacher and not know these things?
The inference is that Jesus was not introducing a novelty but
rather referencing something revealed before in the
Hebrew Scriptures.
The reference is to the prophecy of Ezekiel 36 which tells of
clean water, a new spirit, and a new heart.
In Ephesians 5 Paul wrote of the cleansing power of the
water of God's word in marriage.
Jesus tells of the power of the Spirit and the water of the
Word in bringing about the New Birth.
That which is born of the flesh is flesh, said Jesus, and the
implication is that no advantage or achievement of our human
nature apart from God's grace can help us qualify for Heaven.
Nicodemus evidently enjoyed every advantage of birth.
He was SOMEBODY in Israel.
The only problem was that he needed a new birth.
He needed to become somebody else!

*Heavenly Father, we thank You that the new birth is a great
promotion high above our original birth.*
*We thank You that we have the promise of a life acceptable to
You through a death that was acceptable to You as payment
for our sins.*
For all of this we praise You in Jesus' name.
Amen

March 8

"...And as Moses lifted up the serpent in the wilderness, so must the Son of Man be lifted up..."
John 3:14

The reference is to events recorded in Numbers 21.
The episode there was as unexpected as it was instructive.
His hearers must have been shocked that Jesus would link His own ministry to the case of the brazen serpent.
Israel had sinned against God in an unusually offensive way.
A rampage of fiery serpents unleashed was the consequence.
After they cried out for relief God told Moses to lift the image of a bronze serpent high upon a pole.
Those who looked to that serpent were healed of that plague.
The event is strange because God chose the very vessel of wrath - the serpent who brought suffering in the current emergency - as the medium of deliverance.
The choice is all the more unexpected since it was the serpent who tempted our first parents to bring sin into the world.
That mode of deliverance foreshadowed the great deliverance at Calvary. The Son of God was treated as a cursed thing and nailed to a cross. But those who look to that curse for deliverance are safe from God's wrath and the consequences of their own sinfulness.
Here Jesus interprets the past as a Teacher unsurpassed.
Here Jesus forecasts the future as a Prophet infallible.
The Jews had considered only the exalted and glorious aspects of Messiah's appearing.
Jesus cited passages which signal indignity and suffering in Messiah's future career.
Nicodemus would have been stunned by the recovery of truth he had long overlooked.

Father, thank You that Jesus opens our eyes like no other.
We thank You for the light He shines for the formerly blind.
We see nothing without Him.
We understand nothing without Him.
We are no less dazzled than Nicodemus of old.
Thank You for the truth unfolded for us in Christ Jesus.
Amen

"... the Son of Man..."
John 3:13, 14

Here the Lord Jesus employs His favorite self-designation.
He called Himself "Son of Man" more than any other title.
So great were His mighty acts, so undeniable were the proofs
of Deity, that those who looked on would need assurance that
He was fully human.
But the title was more than a reference to His humanity.
"Son of Man" pointed back to the heavenly events of Daniel 7.
In that chapter the Son of Man received all the authorization of
heaven for all dominion on earth.
All biblically literate Jews would have recognized the citation.
By calling Himself Son of Man, Jesus was identifying Himself
with that majestic heavenly being.
Here, then, is the paradoxical connection between that cursed
thing high on a pole and the exalted Personage high in heaven.
No contrast could be more extreme.
No other candidate could conform to such radically
contrasting elements more perfectly than this Jesus.
The two realities are foretold by the whole of Scripture.
His honor in the courts of Heaven is asserted.
But His humility on the Cross of Calvary is not obscured.
Both are combined in a Personality unimaginable
and uncreated.
Jesus Christ our Lord.

*Father, we praise You for sending Your Son to show us true
God and perfect Man at the same time, in the same Person.
By Your wisdom You have conceived such a thing.
By Your great power You have accomplished it.
By the humility of His condescension Christ has shown it.
How we bless You for Him.
How we want to see everything He shows.
How we want to do everything He commands.
In Christ's own Name we ask it.
Amen*

"For God so loved..."
John 3:16

This verse is justly celebrated and often misunderstood.
Our default reflex is to interpret God in human terms.
That is to be expected.
What could be more natural for us humans?
But the Bible was given to school us in something higher than human understanding.
God loves of course.
We are even told that God is love.
But it is not human love.
It is rather a love inexpressibly divine.
Inexpressible yes but paradoxically demonstrated in the most concrete of ways.
His love is something higher, something to make us wonder, worship and sing.
God not only declares His love for us in the Bible; He proves His love for us in the Life and Death of His only Son.
It is this proof that John will now explore.

Father, Your love for us can only be denied by the worst form of blindness.
Father, Your love for us can only be explained by the purest form of grace.
Thank You for telling us You love us.
Thank You for sending Your Son to prove Your love.
Amen

March 11

"For God so loved the world, that he gave his only Son..."
John 3:16

Because we have long known the Bible's story line we do not
adequately measure the colossal shock His words brought to
the original hearers.
Familiarity has dulled our capacity to appreciate how
unexpected the Gospel was in the First Century.
God's ways are not our ways.
His thoughts are far above our thoughts.
And the most counterintuitive thing God discloses about
Himself is the way He determined to rescue the guilty
and undeserving.
God did not give in some abstract and indeterminate way.
God's love was not hypothetical.
He loved concretely.
He loved by handing over an infinitely loved Son to
the torturers.
Can there be a more shocking concept than that?
In the long history of human thought has anything more
counterintuitive been encountered?

Father, Your love for us was proved by something
fierce and daring.
Something unimaginable.
Let us never be casual in our response to Your shocking
and sacrificial love.
Teach us to return Your love fiercely and with abandon.
We ask it in the name of the Son whom You sent.
Even Jesus our Lord.
Amen

"For God so loved the world, that he gave...
that whoever believes..."
John 3:16

The initiation had to be on God's side.
No angel would have dared suggest the transaction.
The very idea that God should sacrifice His Son would not
have originated in a created mind.
From provenance to consummation the whole thing had to
be of God.
But the truth of this does not rule out human participation.
The sinner is given a role and the role is important to the
point of being critical.
The plan involved rescue and ransom.
But the plan assigns to faith a catalytic force.
That is, we must believe in God's plan.
We must believe in the goodness of God's motives.
We must believe in the justice of God's actions.
So corrupt are we that such faith does not come easily.
Our very belief is also something only God can give.
Faith is a gift which God alone can confer.
But faith is a responsibility which the sinner must express.

*Heavenly Father, thank You for the unutterable price You
paid to ransom us from sin and death.
Thank You for the grace to believe.
Thank You for giving us faith to agree that we are sinners
and we need rescuing.
Thank You for giving us faith to believe that Jesus is
competent to rescue by His atoning blood.
Thank You in Jesus' own Name.
Amen*

**"For God so loved the world, that he gave his only Son,
that whoever believes in him
should not perish but have eternal life."
John 3:16**

The choices are stark and they are mutually exclusive.
God has not offered us the option of retreating to a
neutral corner.
Neutrality was never among the options.
We may dismiss from our minds any alternative not
disclosed here.
There are no third destinies.
Either we receive everlasting life, or we perish.
Our perishing is not a death without continuing
consciousness just as Christ's sacrifice was not a death
without ultimate resurrection.
If the choices are not to our liking that is one symptom
of our sin.
If we rise up in protest, that, too, is a symptom of sin.
When we want our plan to displace God's plan we are
coveting divine prerogatives.
Like the fallen angel originally called Lucifer we may want
to take the place of God.
That is one of the terrible things we need to be saved from.

*Heavenly Father, the amazing thing is that You gave us any
choice at all.*
*We could have perished immediately and everlastingly the
first moment we defied You.*
*But instead You sent Your Son to die so that we might receive
everlasting life.*
Make us everlastingly grateful.
For Jesus' own sake we ask it.
Amen

**"For God so loved the world, that he gave his only Son,
that whoever believes in him
should not perish but have eternal life."
John 3:16**

The Life we receive through the gift of God's Son
is everlasting.
But the gift includes much more than mere longevity.
It would be a mistake to understand the term "everlasting"
here as a mere perpetuation of our current earthly existence.
The life we receive at our first birth is physical.
This offer is of a new, spiritual birth.
It is that Birth which the Lord Jesus is helping Nicodemus
to understand.
We are tempted to regard the spiritual as something less real
than the physical.
Because spiritual life is not visible to our senses we may
suspect that spiritual life is something insubstantial.
That is a great mistake.
We associate "life" with the physical life of the senses.
It's easy to forget that this everlasting life confers a power to
see, hear and touch in ways inaccessible to the life which is
perishing. It is a thing supremely FELT.
Indeed, this new life is the only sphere which may properly be
called Life.
All else is darkness and death.

*Father, there is much that is good in this disappearing
physical life we received at our first birth.
So much so that we are reluctant to let go of the physical.
Let us assess the relative value of the temporary life we
received at birth and the everlasting life we receive by faith.
We KNOW that this second-birth life is far better.
Make us to FEEL it we pray.
And may our choices conform to what we know.
For Christ's sake we ask it.
Amen*

"And this is the judgment: the light has come into the world, and people loved the darkness rather than the light because their works were evil."
John 3:19

The connection between a man's theology and a man's morality is profound.
God's character in God's revealed Law is the only objective basis for morality.
But the connection reaches still deeper.
Our moral inclinations affect our response to God's righteousness at the deepest level.
Our sinful nature bids us hide from the presence of God's righteousness.
Our first parents hid from that presence and we are born with their nature.
We are attracted to the darkness of moral confusion, denial of God's Word or even the denial of God Himself, because we seek a cloak for our unrighteousness.
But there is only one covering for sin.
God Himself has provided it.
Bible students call it Atonement.
The covering is found in the perfect life and sacrificial death of God's own Son.

Gracious Father, reorder our loves we pray.
Let us hate the darkness from which we came.
Let us love the light You have brought us to.
We ask it in the name of this lovely Jesus.
He who Himself is light.
Amen

March 16

"But whoever does what is true comes to the light, so that it may be clearly seen that his works have been carried out in God."
John 3:21

This is the first of four remarkable verses in John's Gospel which address the question, "What about those who have never heard?"
Or, "What about really good people who have never heard the Gospel?" (The other three are John 6:45; 7:17 and 18:37).
Sooner or later most of us are bothered at the thought that there must be creatures noble and deserving, who do good things while living outside the pale of Gospel witness.
That notion tempts us to question God's fairness.
Rather than doubting God's fairness we would be far better employed in intercessory prayer and sacrificial investment in missionary labors.
We may be sure that these noble creatures who are the object of our concern are mythological.
But if they do exist this verse offers comfort.
We are told that all who have a personal affiliation with the truth find their way to God's light.
Indeed, the verse reveals more than that.
We learn that praiseworthy things done by noble people find their origin in God.
All goodness issues from Him.
All reward for goodness flows from Him.

Heavenly Father, grant us the capacity to assess what is good and what is not.
May we trust that Your own competence to do what is just is far greater than our own.
Make us always to exhibit confidence that the judge of the whole earth will do right.
And may we dedicate our lives to bringing those in darkness to the light. For Christ's sake we ask it.
Amen

March 17

"The one who has the bride is the bridegroom."
John 3:29

God the Second Person accommodates a myriad of titles.
That is not surprising since He is an infinite Personality.
He must occupy more than one office.
He alone can perfectly combine the work of Prophet, Priest and King.
He benefits His people in numberless ways.
When Christians sing "He's everything to me...," it is no mere sentiment.
It is literal fact.
He is LOGOS, Son, and Redeemer.
Here John calls Him Bridegroom.
The Gospel is a Romance.
The Church is in the place of a Bride.
Her suitor woos by His wounds.
It is a truth which shocks and overwhelms.

Heavenly Father, thank You that John the Baptist discharged his role faithfully.
Thank You that our heavenly Bridegroom has pursued us at maximum cost to Himself.
Thank You that the Holy Spirit has been faithful in His role.
He has made Jesus lovely to us.
Lovely and necessary.
Thank You that like a Bridegroom the Lord Jesus has offered to take us to His home to live with Him forever.
For that we praise You in His Name.
Amen

"He must increase, but I must decrease."
John 3:30

At the beginning John the Evangelist told us how this thing
called the Christian life begins.
It was a matter of believing and receiving, he wrote.
Now John the Baptist relates at least one way that
life proceeds.
As faith matures the old life is gradually supplanted.
But it is common for the life we receive when we are
born again, to be held back by weakness.
We are, after all, addicted to the old ways.
As long as we live in these fallen bodies the original
fleshly life will always seek to reassert itself.
In other places we are told that there is a war raging inside us.
We are to fight.
And we must be sure we fight on the right side with the
right weapons.
We will not fight well without firm resolve.
Indeed, without resolve we may not fight at all.
We are to hold the old life - the life we lived independently
from God - in the place of death.
These words record the firm resolve of that stalwart John
the Baptist.
As we learn to manage this new life we have been given,
indeed the new Creation we have become, we will see the
transformation which John here makes his resolve.
Less of self; more of Jesus.
This is one sign that the new birth has really taken hold.
This is the true joy-giver.
It is a joy far above all that went before.

Heavenly Father, our fondest wish is to see our earthly
weakness replaced by the heavenly character of our
Saviour Jesus.
Grant it dear Father, through your Holy Spirit.
For we ask it in the Name of your Holy Son.
Amen

The Father loves the Son and has given all
things into his hand.
John 3:35

The Baptist's resolve to decrease is followed by this blaze of
divine disclosure.
Here is heavenly truth so large it does not fit into an
earthly mind.
By the Spirit's aid we aim at comprehension.
We lose nothing when we decrease because we have Christ.
On the contrary, in Christ we gain everything.
In Chapter 1 we were told that Christ the LOGOS made
all things.
Now we learn that Christ the Son was given all things
by the Father.
Why?
Because of love.
The Father's love for the Son is the original love, love
at the fount.
That love prevailed from eternity past and that love will
extend through the everlasting future.
The Father's love for the Son is the key to everything.
We don't mean it is merely the key to theology, or the Bible,
or to our spiritual lives.
We mean it is the key to everything.
It is the grand theme we have been given to master.

*Heavenly Father, we thank You for disclosing to us the
truth about Your great love for Your Son.
We praise You, that by a terrible expense, that love has
spilled over Trinitarian bounds to include creatures so
low as ourselves.
We have gained everything by gaining Your Son Jesus.
May we steward the love carefully.
May we share the love faithfully.
All our days.
For Jesus' sake we ask it.
Amen*

March 20

And he had to pass through Samaria.
John 4:4

It is almost impossible for anyone in the 21st Century to
measure the impact of Jesus of Nazareth in the First Century.
We don't mean worldwide impact.
During the short span of Jesus' biological life few outside
Israel would have heard of Him.
But His impact on those who heard Him speak and saw Him
act would have been unforgettable.
Because the Gospel accounts are familiar, their original shock
value is often lost upon us moderns.
Entering Samaria was a thing not done by pious Jews of the
First Century.
Lingering deliberately would be a thing unheard of.
But the world had never seen a Man like this Jesus.
He had to go through Samaria.
He stationed Himself there on purpose.
It was because He knew this woman would be there.
The woman He determined to save.
It was something He settled on in the long ago.
Before there was enmity between Samaritans and Jews.
Before there were wells.
Even before the foundation of the world.

*Heavenly Father, we thank You for the determination of the
Lord Jesus Christ.
We thank You that all His actions were according to purpose.
Thank You that He cast aside prejudice for the love of sinners.
Thank You that He went as a Shepherd to search out the
lost sheep.
Amen*

**So he came to a town of Samaria....Jacob's well was there;
so Jesus, wearied as he was from his journey, was sitting
beside the well. It was about the sixth hour.**
John 4:5-6

Behold the spectacle of Incarnate Deity.
What a picture!
The Lord of glory exhausted at the well head.
He was susceptible.
He subjected Himself to the same weariness which overtakes
all the children of men.
He had come to the place where the Patriarch Jacob made it
possible for Rachel to drink.
And now great Jacob's greater Son sits at the same well
wanting water Himself.
The narrative is known by two names.
Either the story of the Woman at the Well or the story of the
Samaritan Woman.
We could just as well call it the story of the Man at the Well.
What she did was totally predictable for a woman of her time
and caste.
What He did was unprecedented and wholly unanticipated.
It was noon and He waited.
Almost never in that time and place did a woman visit a well
alone at noon.
But He knows she will come.
He waits for the woman more than He waits for water.
Something momentous is about to happen.
It will shock everyone but Himself.

*Heavenly Father, thank You for sending this Jesus to suffer
thirst like ourselves.*
*Thank You that He humbled Himself to the point that He asked
water from sinners like ourselves.*
We praise You that He offered Water as He asked for water.
Thank You that the water He offers takes away thirst forever.
In His own righteous Name we pray.
Amen

March 22

**A woman from Samaria came to draw water.
Jesus said to her, "Give Me a drink."
John 4:7**

Here more than in most texts we try to understand the
conventions of time and place.
His request was an affront to manners.
For a Jewish man to speak to a Samaritan woman while
alone was a thing not done.
It was bound to cause offense and arouse suspicion.
Pious Jews would not tread on Samaritan soil.
Samaria was a place of defilement.
The great thing was to avoid contact.
But this rabbi asks for refreshment from Samaritan hands.
He asks water from a woman avoided by the
Samaritans themselves.
Likely it would be a drink from her own cup.
"Let me put my mouth where your mouth has been," He asks.
It was a request to stagger the Jewish universe.
It was an appeal which did not originate in our world.

*Heavenly Father, thank You that Jesus showed us the
Heavenly culture.
Thank You that He showed us what You think of racism.
Thank You that He became thirsty, so we could receive
His water.
Thank You that He asked for drink to effect reconciliation
between us and You.
Between ourselves and those we thought were enemies.
Amen*

The Samaritan woman said to him, "How is it that you, a Jew, ask for a drink from me, a woman of Samaria?" (For Jews have no dealings with Samaritans).
John 4:9

The woman was not unacquainted with men.
That acquaintance would have proceeded along predictable lines in many cases.
She stereotyped Him as male.
She stereotyped Him as a Jew.
Her question was rhetorical.
Her experience of men made her confident she knew the answer to her question.
In her thought world there could be only one motive for an overture so personal in a place so deserted.
But He was not subject to the limitations of her thought world.
Indeed, He did not originate in her world at all.
He came into her world to invite her to His own.
This was no average Jewish man.
This was the Jewish Saviour.
He came to sit at the Samaritan well.
He now knocked upon the Samaritan door.

Heavenly Father, we know that because Jesus sought her out, He is seeking us out.
As He speaks to her we hear Him speaking to us.
Let us pay attention.
Let us learn.
We know the story was not contrived.
We know there is true history here.
We know there is real salvation here.
If we are not saved let us believe.
If we have believed let us adore.
Let us love more deeply the Saviour of Jews, Samaritans and sinners like ourselves.
For Christ's own sake we ask it.
Amen

**Jesus answered her, "If you knew the gift of God, and who
it is that is saying to you, 'Give me a drink,' you
would have asked him, and he would have
given you living water."**
John 4:10

At this early stage Jesus' words would have startled.
The Lord Jesus at every juncture comes forth with
the unanticipated.
But the Lord is just beginning.
He is master at bringing those afar off into immediate
contact with God.
From the outset He introduces key essentials of
Gospel witness.
He relates the necessity of foundational knowledge.
That God offers a gift - not a "merit granted due to works
rendered" plan - is made plain.
There is also the matter of knowing who the gifts
come through.
It is essential to learn the true identity of the Giver.
What privilege was hers, though she was utterly
uncomprehending, to have that very Giver sitting before her!
He then introduces the necessity of faith, expressed here
as asking.
With breathtaking succinctness, He preaches the Gospel.
He proceeds in relentless pursuit of her soul.
That's why He came to the well in the first place.
He was waiting for her.

*Heavenly Father, we praise You for a Saviour willing to
pursue only one individual instead of a great multitude.*
*We praise You for a Saviour willing to pursue the ungodly as
opposed to the self-righteous.*
*We praise You for a Saviour willing to work among a rejected
caste instead of a racial elite.*
*We thank You that He stooped so low as to pursue sinners
like ourselves.*
Amen

Jesus answered her, "If you knew the gift of God, and who it is that is saying to you, 'Give me a drink,' you would have asked him, and he would have given you living water."
John 4:10

The combination of words may have been strange.
But the individual concepts are familiar.
They are after all at a well.
And the subject He sustains is the subject of water.
Here He introduces the new subject of His own identity
and purpose.
He declares that if His identity were known she would have
asked Him for water.
Jesus did not introduce the subject of salvation in the
traditional language of that culture.
Instead He linked the spiritual to the concrete and
immediately visible.
Salvation is a thing like water.
Like water it is a thing absolutely necessary for life.
She made a real effort to approach that well and access
that water.
Now He offered water far more necessary and far
more accessible.
A water which could be hers merely by the asking.
But first she must know who He is.
And then she must trust Him.

Father, we trust You.
We trust You because You have sent this perfectly trustworthy
One to show us who You are.
Thank You for the knowledge of this water.
Thank You for the free offer.
And the expense You went to, so that for us it could be free.
Amen

March 26

"Are you greater than our father Jacob?"
John 4:12

Her question of course was rhetorical.
For the second time in the narrative she asks a question
meant to embarrass, a question she was confident she
knew the answer to.
In the long history of human inquiry there may never have
been a question more easily answered.
But it was not the answer she expected!
Jacob was a great man no doubt.
And he was a Patriarch.
But he was also a rascal.
His habit of trying to advance his cause by subterfuge was a
sin which plagued him to old age.
Jacob, perhaps more than any other biblical figure,
dramatically reaped what he had deceitfully sown.
He broke his father's heart through deception.
So did his sons break his own heart.
How was Jesus greater?
In a thousand ways.   .
In every way.
We will only mention one.
Jacob could not love the ugly bride.
Jesus could and did.
Jesus could love the Samaritan Woman.
Jesus could love the Church.
Jesus loves even sinners like you, sinners like me.

Heavenly Father, we thank You for her honest question.
We thank You more for the obvious answer.
We thank You for showing us the greatness of great Jacob's
greater Son.
For Him we praise You. And give thanks.
Amen

**Jesus said to her, "...whoever drinks of the water
that I will give him will never be thirsty again."
John 4:13-14**

This claim is full of boldness.
This promise is fraught with risk.
Bold because it promises so much.
Risky because it is a promise which may be tested.
If we apply to the Lord Jesus for this water and still we
thirst, then the claim is discredited.
Those of us who know Christ may be left thirsting for many
things - physical, financial, social - any number of things.
But we do not wonder who God is.
We do not long to know how things can be made right, how
our sins can be forgiven, what life means, how we can be
sure of heaven.
Those sorts of thirsts we have left behind.
We left all that behind because the water is real.
We thirst no more because the promise is sure.

Heavenly Father, thank You for promises exceedingly great.
Heavenly Father, thank You for fulfillment exceedingly sweet.
Thank You for water which takes away our spiritual
thirst forever.
Amen

"Sir, give me this water..."
John 4:15

The evangelistic progress was rapid to say the least.
First, she ridicules Him for what she takes as bad manners
from a stranger.
Now she asks Him for "this water."
There is no indication at this point that she comprehends
what is happening.
How could she?
She is still operating in the realm of the physical.
She wants physical water to quench her physical thirst.
But the advance from suspicion to trust is dramatic.
She is ready to take what He offers.
She is in the hands of THE MASTER EVANGELIST.
And more than an evangelist.
His piercing words, indeed His whole approach, are a
model for all who wish to bring others into contact with
the living God.
By this time she would have known that she had never met
anyone remotely like Him.
She would soon discover that it was because there never
was anyone like Him.
Nor would there ever be.

Heavenly Father, thank You for sending Your Son to that well.
Thank You for sending Him to our world.
Thank You that He offers us what He offered her.
And thank You for creating within us the desire to receive.
Amen

Jesus said to her, "Go, call your husband, and come here."
John 4:16

We will do well to think back on what must have been her
original theory about His motive.
He initiated the conversation by way of an appeal.
A Jewish stranger speaks personal words in a familiar manner
in a deserted place.
To a despised minority He makes His request.
Her previous dealings with men could have left her with only
one explanation.
His designs, she thought, would have been obvious.
Now He explodes that theory.
First go and call your husband!
No man had ever said anything like that to her while alone.
She is no longer in command.
She is dazed and confused.
Nothing in her experience prepared her for such a request.
The Man was an utter mystery.
And He had only just begun.

Heavenly Father, we praise You for the saving motive
of Your Son.
His aims are ever the highest.
He takes risks, He stoops low, He opens Himself up
to misunderstanding.
All for the saving of poor sinners like ourselves.
Amen

The woman answered him, "I have no husband."
John 4:17

The words were meant to deceive.
No effort could have been more futile.
His name is Truth.
He cannot lie.
He may be lied to, but He Himself cannot be deceived.
He knows who we are and what we have done.
His name is Light and He came to search out the dark places.
Had she known Him truly, she could never have made an
effort so certain to fail.
She may have hoped to excite pity for a poor woman trying to
manage a solitary existence.
But her primary motive was to hide from Him who she
really was.
That was a thing impossible.
He knew her better than she knew herself.
And He was about to make her known across the wide world
for the next two thousand years.

Heavenly Father, teach us the truth about ourselves so
we can tell the truth about ourselves by way of confession.
Heavenly Father, remake us through cleansing and
sanctification so we can tell others what You did by
way of testimony.
In Jesus' Name we ask it.
Amen

Jesus said to her, "You are right in saying, 'I have no husband'; for you have had five husbands, and the one you now have is not your husband."
John 4:17-18

Two powerful and opposing traits are here on display.
The human capacity to deceive and Jesus' ability to penetrate.
Deception is an art which ensnares the artist.
We may carefully arrange true statements and convince ourselves that we have not lied.
But if our aim is to mislead we have lied all the same.
What she declared may have been accurate in a strictly mathematical or legal sense.
But she meant to obscure the true situation.
The truth was she had been a much-married woman.
While a maiden she may have originally believed she could not live without marriage.
Having been disillusioned by many husbands, she now found that she could do without marriage, but she could not do without a man.
The history is ancient.
The experience is contemporary.
There are comparable living arrangements all around us.
What this woman did inadvertently, we would do well to do intentionally.
We must lay our stories out before the Lord.

Heavenly Father, thank You that Jesus knows our story and loves us anyway.
Thank You that He turns mistakes into miracles.
Thank You that He can write happy endings after our sad beginnings.
Amen

April 1

**The woman said to Him, "Sir, I perceive that
you are a Prophet."
John 4:19**

Just before, she had asked a question most easily answered:
"Are you greater than our father Jacob?"
Now she utters one of the great understatements of history:
"SIR, I PERCEIVE THAT YOU ARE A PROPHET!!"
The obvious has begun to dawn on this woman and we are
grateful for it. It was all of grace with her.
In those times when we caught on to the obvious it was also
solely of grace. Grace, grace marvelous grace. Indeed, He is a
prophet, and quite a bit more as well.
We are sometimes surprised by what prophets know, but we
are always shocked by what they know about US.
The King of Aram was told that Elisha knew things the King
said in his bedroom (2 Kings 6:12).
The claims of Jesus were authenticated in Nathanael's mind
when Jesus proved that Nathanael had been observed while
alone (John 1:48-49).
The woman reasoned aright.
But the greatest value a Prophet brings is truth about God.
If we are to know ourselves we must know the character of the
One who made us.
Jesus will tell her of the God who sent His Son to Jews and
Samaritans alike.

*Heavenly Father, we thank You for undeniable
demonstrations.
These demonstrations amount to proofs for fair minds.
For these bold claims and strong proofs from Jesus, Your Son
we praise You.
We would know You better.
We would know ourselves better.
We thank You that this same Jesus, through Your Holy Spirit
can show us everything necessary for life and godliness.
Amen*

"Our fathers worshiped on this mountain, but you say that in Jerusalem is the place where people ought to worship."
John 4:20

People of faith quarrel.
It is a fact which greatly comforts those who have no faith.
"If believers cannot agree upon what is so," they reason, "why should skeptics be expected to embrace firm convictions? If worshipers cannot agree upon a proper mode of worship, why should the non-religious feel obliged to make worship the center of life?"
And when religious folk quarrel to the point of mutual slaughter, is not religious conviction not only a doubtful thing, but even a dangerous thing?
In this manner unbelief fortifies itself.
Jesus had exhibited an uncomfortable degree of familiarity with the woman's private life.
She was keen to change the subject.
It is one thing to discuss religious views as a philosophical subject; it is quite something else to have light shined upon something we hope to remain hidden.
Much better to talk of the historical controversy between Samaritans and Jews!
She was likely genuinely curious about the question she asked.
He would answer her question. But hiding, He disallowed.
He would not allow the conversation to become merely theoretical.
How could He when so much was at stake?
How could He when the thing at stake was her soul?

Heavenly Father, may we learn from You what is needful.
May we lay aside subjects which distract us from the main business. So, show us what that business is.
Grant us an undistracted wisdom in ordering priority and sequence. May we miss not a moment.
Repentance and reformation are at hand.
May we embrace this work for the profit of our souls.
We ask it in Your Son's dear Name.
Amen

"...salvation is from the Jews...true worshipers will worship the Father in Spirit and truth, for the Father is seeking such people to worship him."
John 4:22-23

He does not evade the woman's question.
She would have Him judge between the differing approaches which separated their two peoples.
Very well, He would rule upon the issue.
He does not endorse the ways the Jews had prosecuted their case against the Samaritans.
But the Jews were nearer to truth when it came to the doctrinal aspects of the controversy.
The Jews sinned mightily against the Samaritans, but that did not alter the fact that Samaritan worship was corrupted beyond possibility of approval.
Salvation is from the Jews.
That is, salvation will come to the world from and through the Jews.
But blessedly, in a way that would surprise both Jew and Samaritan, salvation would come first to the Samaritans when the message went out from Israel.
He would send His Apostles to Samaria after Judea.
And salvation was now coming to Samaritans before it came to many among the Jews.
For at that very moment the Saviour was standing upon Samaritan soil.

Father, thank You that You sent Your only Son to
unpromising places.
Thank You that He engaged unlikely candidates.
Thank You that He went forth and broke through.
Thank You in Jesus' Name.
Amen

April 4

"God is spirit, and those who worship him must worship in spirit and truth."
John 4:24

Acceptable worship is not initiated by the creature.
The originating impulse is always from God.
That divine impulse is here expressed through the principles
Jesus sets forth. Since God is Spirit, we fall short if we seek to
worship with the posture of our body and the worth of our
offerings alone. Inward realities matter more to God.
He wants the internal disposition and motivation of the heart
to be warmed by reverence and affection.
To worship God in truth means at least two things.
First, to worship sincerely, not just going through the motions.
Worship becomes our intention and desire, a thing we choose
even if there were no fear of penalty for choosing otherwise.
Second, to worship God in truth means to worship in the true
way, the way God prescribes and requires, according to
patterns of divine disclosure not by way of human innovation.
Creativity is a good thing if it does not produce alternatives to
divine commands. True worship adheres to the physical
arrangement of worship, even the physical substance of it.
But physical conformity is of no value if devoid of spiritual
content. We worship God from the ground up, as spiritual
beings adoring the supremacy of the Highest Spiritual Being.
And we worship God from the inside out, from the deepest
part of ourselves to the deepest places God will take us into
His own heart. This is the place of worship.
This is the place the Son of God was taking one of the most
unlikely prospects in that dark and fallen world.

*Heavenly Father, we praise You for refusing to leave us
without instructions and a Model for this business of worship.
We praise You that You have given us the power to see
worship as attractive and possible.
And so, dear Father we thank You for the Holy Scriptures.
For your Holy Son. For your Holy Spirit.
In Jesus' Name we praise and thank You.
Amen*

**The woman said to him, "I know that Messiah is coming
(he who is called Christ). When he comes,
he will tell us all things."
John 4:25**

The Samaritans also had a messianic expectation.
They expected someone they called "Taheb."
This woman respectfully uses the Jewish designation.
She may have been lacking in biblical obedience.
But somehow, she maintained a lively biblical hope.
She was also now expressing personal faith, "I know..."
she declares.
It was characteristic of the age that almost every person had
some acquaintance with God's dealings with their own nation.
Later this woman would tell her countrymen that this Man had
declared all things to her.
That was her way of saying that He was uncannily accurate in
everything He did declare. In this verse she characterizes
Messiah as one who tells all things.
Although she had only recently realized she had no idea of His
true identity, she was beginning to suspect. We can be sure
that it was not only what He said but the way He said it.
He had spoken with her over the most important issues of life.
By this time she would have felt deeply honored. She may
have even sensed that she was deeply loved. We can be sure
that she had never been treated this way before.
She would have been certain that the person speaking to her
could not possibly be a mere man.

*Heavenly Father, we praise You that You have made Yourself
known by making Your Son known.*
*By Your Spirit's working, whether quickly or gradually, we
too have come to recognize Jesus of Nazareth as the Christ,
the Son of the Living God.*
*We thank You that we stand at the end of that unbroken line of
believers in Jesus stretching back to the First Century.*
*And we thank You that we will stand with them in everlasting
worship around Your throne forever.*
Amen

Jesus said to her, "I who speak to you am he."
John 4:26

The thing Israel's people most wanted to discover was the
Messianic identity.
The people they most savagely disdained were the Samaritans.
So, to whom was the great disclosure entrusted?
The most unlikely candidate imaginable.
This is a narrative impossible of contrivance.
Jesus' words constituted an act of outrageous condescension
which could only have been imagined by God.
What was His name?
Where did He live?
What would He do?
All of this and more was given to a Samaritan woman.
Why is that so shocking?
The Talmud was compiled at a later date than the century our
Lord walked upon this planet. But its teaching was
representative of rabbinic conviction in Jesus' own time.
Three Talmudic quotes:
"Do not speak to a woman in the street, no not to thine
own wife."
"The man who teaches the Law to his daughter plays
the fool."
"Better to burn the Law than to teach it to a woman."
Jesus of Nazareth simply cannot be explained in terms of
cultural and ethnic contexts.
Remember the woman began by consigning the Lord to well-
known stereotypes. He simply would not fit.
HE MUST HAVE BEEN FROM ANOTHER PLACE.
A place beyond the boundaries of human experience.

Heavenly Father, we thank You for these indirect proofs of
authenticity. We know if the account were made up it would be
nothing like this.
Thank You that it happened.
Thank You that the benefit accrues to us.
At a distance of 2000 years.
Amen

Jesus said to her, "I who speak to you am he."
John 4:26

The Lord was mostly reticent and indirect when it came to
boldly proclaiming His Messiahship.
That was partly because of timing.
That was partly because Israel's expectation was so far from
God's intention.
The well in Samaria is the scene of the fullest self-disclosure
of the Messianic identity in the Bible.
The only incident which comes close is the response to Peter's
great Confession at Caesarea Philippi.
Why is that so shocking?
The Jews were discriminated against by much of the world.
The Emperor Claudius would soon expel them from Rome.
But even the Jews looked down upon the Samaritans.
Samaritan men looked down upon Samaritan women.
Why was the woman at the well alone?
Likely because of her reputation.
She would have been cast out by Samaritan women.
She was the lowest of the low.
It was to her that God incarnate chose to identify Himself.
The thing could not have been made up.
Simply because the thing could not have been imagined.

Heavenly Father thank You that You are no respecter
of persons.
Thank You that You do condescend to the lowest of the low.
Thank You that Jesus came to the woman at the well.
Thank You that He came to us.
For that we indeed thank You.
And give You praise.
Amen

...his disciples came back. They marveled that he was talking with a woman...
John 4:27

Shock and dismay are what they felt.
They were likely not a little offended.
Given their cultural attitudes there is no way they could
satisfactorily explain Jesus' conversation with such a woman.
We mark this as overwhelming evidence of authenticity.
It was not contrived because it was not palatable.
Indeed, to the contrary, it was highly objectionable.
A writer cannot invent that which he cannot imagine.
The force of this is lost on those long-familiar with the
Gospel narratives.
We are prone to overlook the outrage Jesus' actions
provoked in the First Century.
Making up this story would have gained the early Christians
no credit with their original Jewish audience.
It would have disturbed the sensibilities of the religious.
The disciples themselves were embarrassed.
This report was published because the Holy Spirit would not
allow local decorum to dictate which parts of Jesus' ministry
could be disclosed.
They wrote it down that way because it happened that way.
We can trust the fearless candor of God's own Word.
We marvel at the fearless ways of God's own Son.

Heavenly Father, we thank You that Jesus risked His
reputation to plead for unworthy souls.
We know He didn't risk His life.
We know He gave His life for those same souls.
For that we offer everlasting praise.
Amen

April 9

So the woman left her water jar and went
away into town...
John 4:28

Here we have no vocal profession of faith as traditionally
formulated. But we are confident the woman was converted.
It's a good idea to look for signs of conversion beyond
the verbal.
The woman exhibits signs in abundance.
First, she embraced new priorities.
She had gone to the well for water, a necessary and non-
negotiable task.
But she leaves her water pot.
The Gospel writer supplies this detail for a reason.
Thirst is an impossible thing to ignore, but somehow, she
manages to do just that.
She is off on a new mission now.
The mission is not self-regarding.
It is OTHER-centered.
She will not hoard this new, miraculous friendship.
She must tell others.
Though they had likely done little good for her, she would
now offer this supreme good to them. They must know of the
unearthly visitor who had come to Samaria.
Her mission is urgent. So urgent she forgot her water pot.
So urgent she forgot to learn His Name.

Heavenly Father, make us to take on right priorities.
Right priorities lead to urgent tasks.
May heavenly necessities overrule earthly necessities.
Grant us the wisdom to identify the water pots in our lives
which distract and delay.
Then grant us the will to leave them behind.
In Jesus' Name we ask it.
Amen

...the woman ...said to the people, "Come, see a man who told me all that I ever did. Can this be the Christ?"
John 4:28-29

She initiated with the courage of a true evangelist.
By this she exhibits proof of authentic change.
She not only left off old priorities, she took up new ones.
She became a witness.
Her conversion was mere minutes old.
As for training, she had none.
Her credibility?
It would have registered negative numbers.
Who was she with her past to speak of the Messiah?
She was willing, and that was enough.
Her urgency qualified her.
The townspeople noted a change.
She arrested their attention.
She was not the same person.
Having been with Him how could she be?
She came to the well morally defeated.
She returns a moral force.
She came to the well a social pariah.
She returns to her town aflame.
She commends not herself but the Man she left at the well.
That Jew who loved Samaritans.
He would love them more than His very life.

Heavenly Father, we thank You for the kind of Saviour who
could affect such a change in such a woman.
We too have been changed.
We would be changed all the more.
Give us a like passion for souls.
Give us a like boldness in witness.
Until everyone knows.
Until the whole world hears of this wondrous Jesus.
Amen

... the disciples were urging him, saying, "Rabbi, eat." But he said to them, "I have food to eat that you do not know about" ... "My food is to do the will of him who sent me and to accomplish his work."
John 4:31-34

Jesus came to show us food we know nothing about.
It was one of the first lessons He taught though the lesson
fell upon the heedless ears of the devil (Matthew 4:4).
His was a heavenly sustenance.
Let the lesson not be lost.
To do the will of the Father.
To accomplish His work.
This was His food and drink.
This was His controlling vision.
Upon this His soul fed.
You are right, Lord.
This is food we know nothing about.
We have long disdained this manna.
It is the leeks and garlic of Egypt we crave.
When He told His parents, He must be about His Father's
business, it was that vision which compelled Him.
Even while expiring upon the bloody spikes, His vision
never dimmed.
As He commended His spirit to the Father the resolve
never flagged.
Here then is single-mindedness at the peak.
This is the path of passion and joy.
We have heard that the Father's aim is to make us like Him.
Does it not make us to tremble?

Father, we thank You that Your Son could not be turned aside
by fond overtures from well-meaning disciples.
Thank You Father for setting us upon this path.
Take us down it Lord, we pray, for Jesus' sake.
Amen

**"Look ...lift up your eyes, and see that the fields
are white for harvest."
John 4:35**

Jesus has food that we know nothing about.
He sees a Harvest we have not yet seen.
That's why He tells us to lift up our eyes and look.
Let us be honest and confess we will never see unless He
opens our eyes.
The amazing thing is that He says this in Samaria, the last
place His countrymen would look for a harvest.
He makes this declaration in the generation which would nail
Him to a cross.
He makes the declaration in a place which has been especially
gospel-resistant for 2000 years.
In that kind of place, indeed in the whole Christ-rejecting
world, Jesus calls our attention to a harvest.
Here we learn that we must hear before we can see.
Here we learn that we are not yet attentive.
That is why we are told to look.
Here we discover that we have been focusing on the
wrong thing.
That's why we are told to lift up our eyes.
No doubt Jesus is a unique Man with a singular vision.
But it is a vision He means to pass along.
He wants us to see what no one else can see.
Only then will we do what no one else can do.

*Heavenly Father, let us see what Jesus shows us.
As we learn to see what He sees, may we do what He does.
May we be guided by His hand.
For His sake we ask it.
And in His Name.
Amen*

"I sent you to reap..."
John 4:38

It is impossible to doubt that Jesus understands His
own vocation.
It is easy to wonder if we know our own.
We have been spared for a reason.
We have been sent with a purpose.
But are we ever fully conscious of it? Rarely, I fear.
To embrace the fact that we have been sent to reap may
seem more alien still.
And yet we have Jesus' own testimony of the same.
Only, of course, if we are serious about the business of
following Him.
Here He arms His soldiers with purpose.
Here we are given a goal toward which we take aim, gain
direction and measure success.
We may not remember volunteering, but we have been
recruited all the same.
Like Moses we may beg off or shrink back.
But the Lord Jesus does not ask our permission.
He merely declares the bare fact.
For this purpose, we are sent.
Let us not forget that we have a Royal Commission.
Let us not forget that He is our King.

Heavenly Father, thank You for ennobling us by a
choice assignment.
May we reach high and stretch forward.
May we attain by faith.
May we become reapers by Your grace and in Your strength.
For the glory is Yours
And all credit forever.
Through Jesus Christ our Lord.
Amen

April 14

Many Samaritans...believed in him ...they asked him to stay... John 4:39-40

Now here is a curious thing.
These Samaritans, hated by the Jews, asked the Jewish
rabbi to stay.
To lodge with them in fact.
To break bread together.
And to fill their days with fellowship.
Just as curiously, He obliges.
In the region of Gadara where demons were cast into pigs the
citizens asked Him to leave.
We are told the Samaritans had become believers because of
the woman's testimony.
Here then is proof.
They do not want Him to leave.
One of the sure symptoms of an unconverted nature is an
aversion to the Holy.
Contrariwise, one sure sign of the New Birth is a desire to
spend time with the godly.
We noted that the woman was converted because her
priorities were new.
Here we cite fresh evidence.
She had become a witness.
And not only a witness but a fruitful witness.
Hers was a converting ministry.

Heavenly Father, we thank You for models.
The more unlikely the models are the more likely we are to
remember them.
Thank You for what this woman did.
Help us to go and do likewise.
In the lovely Name of Jesus we ask it.
Amen

April 15

They said to the woman, "It is no longer because of what you said that we believe, for we have heard for ourselves, and we know that this is indeed the Savior of the world."
John 4:42

If we are ever to mature in our faith, if we are ever to move forward with our Christian lives, there must come a time when we no longer lean heavily on what other people say.
Of course, we trust the Bible because we believe biblical testimony to be the very Word of God.
When we first become believers, it is necessary to be helped along with the aid of those more mature than ourselves.
But baby steps are only acceptable at the outset.
In a very short time the Samaritans attained personal ownership of their faith.
At first their attention was arrested by the new behavior of a woman whose old behavior they knew all too well.
But after they gained a personal acquaintance with Jesus Himself, her influence faded into the background.
Just so, it is a healthy thing for us to taste for ourselves, and discover that the Lord is good.
Our experience will be like the experience of the Queen of Sheba who heard of King Solomon before discovering that the reality exceeded the reputation.
Jesus is greater than anything we have ever heard anyone say about Him. Jesus' impact upon that community near the well transcended all cultural and ethnic barriers. He was the Messiah of Israel but the Samaritans did not call Him Israel's Messiah. They called him the Saviour of the world.
They called Him that because that is who He is.

Heavenly Father, we thank You that the news of Your saving grace through Your Son reached even the Gentiles and over the course of 2000 years has reached us as well.
Those Samaritans proved to be wonderful stewards of their opportunity.
Make us to be faithful stewards as well.
In Christ's own Name we ask it.
Amen

April 16

> **Now there is in Jerusalem ...a pool...called Bethesda, which has five roofed colonnades. In these lay a multitude of invalids... One man was there who had been an invalid for thirty-eight years. When Jesus saw him lying there and knew that he had already been there a long time, he said to him, "Do you want to be healed?"**
> **John 5:2-6**

Here lay a multitude of people with a multitude of afflictions. The spectacle of concentrated misery would have forced many eyes to be averted. Into the sea of this human wretchedness the Son of God walked.
It is important to understand that Jesus did not appear to undo all the suffering on the planet.
He appeared rather to offer residence in a place without suffering. He came to invite us Home.
To prove His authority to make the offer, He banished immediate suffering from those who appealed for relief.
The question Jesus asked may appear at first to be idle, even cruel, but it was far from that.
There is a motive behind every word the Son of Man utters. It is always high, always pure, always for our benefit.
Though the man's desire for healing would have been obvious, it was necessary that the desire be laid before Jesus.
We know that Jesus does not ask questions to learn, but to teach. He knew the man wanted to be healed just as He knew how long he had suffered. But the need must be publicized in all its tragic frustration. The healing was for a sign and so our attention must be caught.
We must never shrink from God's mysterious questions.
They are the forerunner of His mysterious mercies.

Heavenly Father, thank You that Jesus noticed the man in his wretchedness. Thank You that He has noticed us.
Though our problems may not be nearly as obvious, they are there nonetheless.
Thank You that we too may apply for deliverance.
Thank You that we too may know relief.
Amen

The sick man answered him, "Sir, I have no one to put me into the pool when the water is stirred up..." Jesus said to him, "Get up, take up your bed, and walk." And at once the man was healed, and he took up his bed and walked.
John 5:7-9

A large number of later manuscripts declare that an angel troubled the water on infrequent occasions.
Anyone reaching the water immediately after the troubling, was delivered from affliction.
That belief accounts for the crowd near the pool.
It also accounts for the man's explanation.
Our oldest manuscripts do not mention the report of angelic visitations.
The man relates his plight to the Lord Jesus in a manner both pathetic and succinct.
Without dwelling on the problem, Jesus commands the solution. "Pick up your bed and go home."
The miracle came through the command.
Jesus commanded him to do precisely what he could not do.
The power for the impossible came with the sound of the Saviour's words.
Obedience to the command confirmed the wonder.
Augustine said that God gives what He requires and requires what He gives.
Command and obedience.
Both are necessary.
Both are beautiful.

Heavenly Father, thank You for commands which require of us things we cannot do.
Thank You for the enabling power which accompanies those commands.
Father, grant us the obedience which proves the power.
Grant it for Jesus' sake. For we ask it in Jesus' Name.
Amen

**So the Jews said to the man who had been healed,
"It is the Sabbath, and it is not lawful for you to
take up your bed."**
John 5:10

Controversy over Sabbath regulations was a convenient
pretext to wage war upon Jesus.
His enemies loved to major on externals while ignoring the
vital elements of faith.
Expanding Sabbath restrictions and debating the details
endlessly helped deflect attention from the spiritual poverty
which deadened their inner lives.
Sabbath Law was the darling prohibition of scribes,
Pharisees and their sympathizers, something they could
sink their teeth into.
It was so because the legislation was subject to quantification.
The requirement of Sabbath rest lent itself to ongoing
specification and elaboration.
What constituted the maximum allowable exertion on the
sacred day?
Which exceptions and for what reason?
The possibilities were endless.
The qualifications proliferated to a pitiless degree.
Jesus of Nazareth would not be a player.
Let others bind men tight in religious knots.
His vocation would be something quite different.
Something which felt like freedom.
Something which was in fact liberation.

*Heavenly Father, thank You for sending a Man who
could actually keep the Law.*
*Thank You for sending a Man to show us what the
Law really means.*
Thank You for the Man Christ Jesus.
Amen

**...Jesus found him in the temple and said to him,
"See, you are well! Sin no more, that nothing
worse may happen to you."
John 5:14**

Health is not a trivial thing and the Bible nowhere treats it
as unimportant.
It was the precious thing often gifted to men and women by
God's own Son during the days of His visitation.
But physical health is not the ultimate thing.
The blessing is relative and there are higher things to hope for.
Jesus who gave the gift of health to this poor man would now
offer something far greater.
He counsels wisdom.
He advises that there are worse tragedies than poor health.
We remember that healing is a miracle and the miracles in
John's Gospel are offered as signs.
Those healed under Jesus' ministry would be overtaken by
death at the end.
Death overcomes all men and women whether they are able
to manage recovery of health for a time or not.
This side of the grave all healing is temporary.
The greater thing which Jesus offers is the permanent
annihilation of death through faith in Himself.
This is the message He was born to bring.

*Father, we thank You that we have received this Good News
with saving faith.
We thank You that we may ask You for physical healing
in His Name.
We thank You that we already have the permanent and
unending healing that He offers in the place He is taking us.
We thank You in Jesus' name.
Amen*

The man went away and told the Jews that it was Jesus who had healed him. And this was why the Jews were persecuting Jesus, because he was doing these things on the Sabbath.
John 5:15-16

Religion without God is grotesque.
A godless religion is as degrading as it is dangerous.
Those who learned of the miracle had much cause
for celebration.
There was the startling power of the Man who healed.
There was wonderful release of the man who had been healed.
All those cumulative years of unrelieved anguish dammed
up in a reservoir of pain and immobility.
With a word Jesus changes everything.
Power on one side, joy on the other.
What a story!
But there is no celebration.
There is only condemnation.
He had broken one of THEIR rules.
For that He would have to pay.

Father, thank You for this healer of human woes.
Thank You for this breaker of human rules.
Thank You for Your only begotten Son.
May we worship Him joyfully and serve Him faithfully
all our days.
For His own sake we ask it.
Amen

But Jesus answered them, "My Father is working until now, and I am working."
John 5:17

One who has authority to make the Law has authority to interpret the Law.
Here stands One who has the capacity to fulfill the Law.
He would soon bring evidence that He was the One who originally gave the Law.
Jesus claimed the right to cleanse the Temple by calling it His Father's house.
Now He justifies healing on the Sabbath by calling it His Father's work.
He is claiming equivalency of action with the Father.
What the Father does He does.
But who can do what the Father does?
The Father is God.
Precisely.
None can do the Father's work but the Son who shares the Father's Nature.
Jesus follows astonishing works with astonishing claims.
The works validate the claims.
The claims interpret the work.

Heavenly Father, for the words and works of Your
Son we give praise.
Thank You that Jesus heals our sore infirmities.
Thank You that He corrects our poor religion.
May we receive everything He offers with faith.
Amen

April 22

**This was why the Jews were seeking all the more to kill
him, because not only was he breaking the Sabbath, but he
was even calling God His own Father,
making himself equal with God.**
John 5:18

We may credit the enemies of Jesus with this one thing.
They understood the implications of His self-disclosure.
He was endorsing the claim made for Him in the opening
verses of this Gospel.
The Word was God.
And for that they meant to kill Him.
It was a resolve birthed earlier when He cleansed the Temple.
Now they receive fresh impetus for their resolve.
The most urgent thing to understand from our Bibles is why
the Son of Man was willing to die.
But the reason His enemies were willing to kill serves to
augment this most important of Gospel truths.
Man, the creature, is desperately wicked.
If our agenda is upset by God, our inclination is to resist,
not obey.
This is the Lucifer philosophy.
This is the tragedy of Israel in the First Century.
God's own Son appeared.
And He appeared to them as Abel appeared to Cain.

Father, may we always adore and never resist Your Son.
Thank You for sending Him for the everlasting good of
our souls.
May we be done with the sin that makes us doubt the good
He offers.
May we by grace love Him truly and stay close to Him always.
We ask it in His Name.
Amen

> **"...the Son can do nothing of his own accord, but only
> what he sees the Father doing.
> For whatever the Father does, that the Son does likewise."**
> **John 5:19**

What, left to our own devices, could we ever hope to learn
about God?
We may draw accurate inferences from His Creation no doubt.
We may guess something of His great Power, His majesty
and... what else?
Of His moral attributes we could know nothing.
Of His relationships less than nothing.
Unless Someone tells us.
The Son of God not only sees but speaks.
He was sent to speak to us of the Father.
The Holy Spirit was sent to publish and illumine the words
of the Son.
This is necessary because His words are deep, and our minds
are dim.
We could never hope to guess the truth about the relationship
between the Father and the Son.
It is a thing which could only be revealed from the inside.
This is the very thing God's own Son here sets out to do.
What He tells is that there can be no disunity in the Godhead.
The Son does exactly what the Father shows Him to do.
Jesus is the only one who can see the Father's work.
Jesus is the only one who can show the Father's work.
And He shows it by perfect duplication.

Heavenly Father, we have seen and heard.
All because Your Son has acted and spoken in history.
All because Your Holy Spirit has inspired the witnesses
to record. And Father, we have believed.
All because of Your great saving work, our great Triune God.
Amen

"For the Father loves the Son and shows him all that he himself is doing."
John 5:20

We have been told that God loved the world.
Now we are told that God loves the Son.
This revelation is the key to everything.
We do not mean that this revelation is the key to the Trinity, though of course it is that.
We do not mean that it is the key to theology though of course it is that.
We do not mean that it is the key to our spiritual lives though of course it is that.
We mean that it is the key to everything - as in all categories sacred and secular.
It is the key which opens the door to all understanding.
Is the key to our very existence.
The Father's love for the Son is the foundation of all subsequent loves.
Everything in heaven and earth, everything in time and eternity is hidden inside this all-encompassing Reality: The Father loves the Son...

Heavenly Father, thank You for revealing this great truth about Yourself.
We could never have guessed at the hidden realities had You not revealed them.
Thank You so much that Your love for us flows from Your love for Your only begotten Son.
To know this great Trinitarian love it is the highest thing.
It is the greatest gift.
And for that we praise You always and forever.
Amen

**"For as the Father raises the dead and gives them life,
so also the Son gives life to whom he will.
John 5:21**

Gradually, by degrees, the great disclosures by God and
about God unfold.
Appropriately, they are disclosed by God's own Son Who
appeared to tell of the Father.
He cannot tell us of His Father without telling us of Himself.
It is in the character of the Son that we see the character of
the Father.
It is in the work of the Son that we see the work of the Father.
In the first chapter we learned of the role of the Logos in
Creation, the mighty acts which gave form and substance to
the visible universe.
And after substance and form, of course, life.
But life in the universe withers.
Here we learn that the Logos - now called the Son of God -
may give life to those who die.
He gives life not only to those who die, but He gives life to
anyone He pleases.
His is the right of conferral.
His is the right of election.
We call it sovereignty.
And Sovereignty belongs to the Son.

*Father, we thank You that by Your wisdom, authority over life
and death was placed in the hands of Your Son.
And we thank You that by the gracious exercise of redeeming
love, we who were dead spiritually are now alive forevermore.
We will always be praising You for that.
For praise is the true vocation of redeemed sinners.
Amen*

**"...whoever hears my word and believes him who sent me
has eternal life. He does not come into judgment, but has
passed from death to life."**
John 5:24

This verse relates a transformation.
It is an alteration as dramatic as the alteration from
non-existence to being.
It is a transference as extreme as a removal from
earth to heaven.
We know about the passage from life to death.
The passage here described is just as radical, though the
trajectory is opposed. This is the passage from death to life.
With respect to the shared Life of God we are actually
born dead.
"... he who hears My word..."
We understand the hearing of His word to mean the heeding
of His word.
It is that divine word which establishes the vital connection.
It is that word of the Lord which breathes life where before
there was death. It is a heeding which amounts to believing.
And it is a believing that amounts to receiving eternal life as
a present possession.
Heavenly life is a treasure currently experienced and
continuously celebrated.
Jesus also imposes another inescapable conclusion.
Not to believe signals the current experience of judgment.
To be conscious and breathing is no proof that death has
been so far avoided. The spiritually dead still walk.

*Heavenly Father, how we thank You for the words of Jesus
which bring light and life.*
*For us such a thing was solely without merit and even
without expectation.*
*It is a grace we pray now for others who have not heard or
have not heeded.*
For we ask it in the Saviour's own Name.
Amen

"For as the Father has life in himself, so he has granted the Son also to have life in himself."
John 5:26

If we are to learn anything truly about the life of God, it will not come by research or reason.
He must tell us.
If we are to learn anything of proceedings internal and external within the Holy Trinity we will be even more dependent upon the divine tutelage.
It is God the Third Person, the Blessed Holy Spirit, who must keep us from error as we consider these transactions between the Father and the Son.
The reference here is to the Son as Incarnate.
If the Son is to be authentically human something must be surrendered. Obviously, the prerogative of the Son of God not to suffer, the prerogative not to die, is surrendered.
But here we are told that the quality of having non-contingent life, life in Himself, is retained.
No ordinary human being has life in himself.
All human life is contingent.
But this Man is no ordinary human.
This unique human life, born but not created, is not contingent. Jesus of Nazareth has life within Himself.
It is so because it has been given Him by the Father.

Heavenly Father, we do thank You that You have brought us into living contact with this Life-giver named Jesus.
We thank You for the fact of salvation.
We thank You for the way of salvation.
We thank You that we have life.
And we thank You that we have life because You gave life to Him and He gave life to us.
Thank You, Heavenly Father, for this wondrous gift through Your Son Jesus.
Amen

"I can do nothing on my own...because I seek not my own will but the will of him who sent me."
John 5:30

Jesus revealed that He has life in Himself.
But that does not mean He exercises an independent will.
It is to the Father that He ever looks for the living of His life.
As far as words and works go, the Incarnate Son is
wholly dependent.
He looks to His Father in faith.
In the exercise of that faith He is a model and pattern for us.
He faithfully replicates the Father's acts and in so doing He
fully reflects the Father's character.
His own will is lost in the perfections of His Father's plan.
We can only speculate as to how His unfallen nature was
submitted to the Father's authority.
That nature was unfallen, untainted by sin of any kind.
We know that His divine nature was united to the Father in
perfect agreement of will from all eternity.
He would not, indeed He could not, seek anything to
the contrary.

Father, how we thank You that our Saviour walked in such
submission that His will was lost in Your own.
Left to ourselves this is an unattainable standard.
How we thank You that You have not left us to ourselves.
Because Your Son lives in us by the Holy Spirit, all things
are possible.
Evermore grant us this single mindedness.
For it is the thing we seek even now.
Through Your Son we ask it.
Amen

"His voice you have never heard, his form you have never seen, and you do not have his word abiding in you, for you do not believe the one whom he has sent."
John 5:37-38

How alike God's form and voice is to voices and forms we know on earth, we will discover no sooner than the moment we enter heaven ourselves.
We can be sure that God's very form is beheld, and His actual voice is heard in heaven.
How do we know?
Because the original and eternal resident of Heaven took up residence on this poor planet and declared it to be so.
He descended not only to tell of God's form and voice but to show forth and sound out.
To see and believe what He said and showed, is the surest proof of the saving knowledge of God.
That saving knowledge is demonstrated simply by believing Jesus.
There is an enormous distance between formal doctrinal orthodoxy and personal spiritual knowledge.
It is the proximate distance between heaven and hell.
It is the distance between the hypothetical and the actual.
It is the difference between knowing about God and knowing God. To have God's Word abiding on the inside is the peculiar possession of the twice-born.
It is a span bridged by the Cross alone.
The Cross upon which the Prince of Glory died.

Heavenly Father, we thank You that Your Son came not merely to tell us the true meaning of salvation.
We thank You that He came to save us.
By telling the truth He offended those who cherished self-originated spiritual mythologies.
And so they killed Him.
And so He saved us.
And so we praise You for Him.
Amen

**"You search the Scriptures because you think
that in them you have eternal life; and it is they
that bear witness about me..."
John 5:39**

It is possible to prefer the searching to the finding. Missing
the Messiah in the Messianic generation was a tragedy.
To put the Messiah to death in His generation was a crime of
monstrous proportions.
Man may focus on the sign and overlook the thing signified.
How could Jesus' identity be so fiercely resisted when the
Hebrew Scriptures are replete with Messianic references?
First because the Prophets and prophecies of God had always
been resisted. The people spoke of stoning both Moses and
David. Elijah had to hide. Isaiah was likely sawn in two under
King Manasseh.
Secondly, we all more-or-less read the Bible selectively,
majoring on the portions more congenial, shying away from
passages not to our liking.
But there was a third factor influencing Israel's rejection of
her King. The Jewish leaders were profitably enfranchised,
secure within their traditional schools of biblical
interpretation.
Jesus of Nazareth did not conform to the expectations of any
of those traditions. He upset the comfortable equilibrium.
For that He had to die. Instead of revising their expectations
they executed their Messiah.

*Heavenly Father, we thank You that Your sovereignty means
You can cause the wickedest act in history to work to the
advantage of the very sinners who are guilty.*
*Heavenly Father we pray that Your Spirit would help us lay
our prejudices aside when we approach Your Holy Word.*
We are subjective creatures.
Father, grant us objective accuracy in the study of Scripture.
It can only happen by Your Spirit's enabling power.
We ask it in the name of Your wonderful Son Jesus.
Amen

**"...if you believed Moses, you would believe me;
for he wrote of me."
John 5:46**

These words are among the most controversial Jesus
ever uttered.
Here He certifies His prominence in the Hebrew Scriptures.
But, more importantly, He here repudiates the sincerity of
any profession of faith in Scripture which denies His
rightful claims.
Yes, the Law pointed to Him. Indeed, the Law was about Him.
And He was the only one who ever came close to obeying
the Law.
He obeyed that Law and fulfilled it perfectly.
When Moses wrote, Christ was the subject.
He was the greater Abraham who would not abandon
His bride.
He was the greater Isaac who would be delivered up
to sacrifice.
He was the greater Jacob who could love the bride who
was not beautiful.
He was the greater Joseph rejected by his brothers believed
on by the Gentiles.
He was the greater Moses who would not only lead his people
out of bondage but into the promised land.
He was the perfect sacrifice, without blemish, of Leviticus.
He was the Star of Numbers and the Prophet of Deuteronomy
like Moses.
To insist that Moses was believed while Jesus was rejected
was a falsehood incoherent and impossible.

*Heavenly Father, make us always to recognize Your Son
in Scripture.
For when we see Him we love Him, and when we love Him
we worship Him.
We ask it in the Name of this Jesus Who kept the Law we
could not keep.
Amen*

**... Jesus said to Phillip, "Where are we to buy bread, so
that these people may eat?" He said this to test him, for he
himself knew what he would do.**
John 6:5-6

Jesus never asked an idle question.
Nor did He ever ask because He lacked wisdom or knowledge.
There is more to be learned from the questions Jesus asked
than from the answers philosophers give.
We see evidence that Jesus exercised responsible oversight for
those who attended upon His teaching.
He took pains to meet the needs of those present.
Where are we to buy?
Where indeed...
The assumption is that He would never leave them empty.
The certainty is that He Himself will pay the cost.
He is the Source and the Resource.
He will provide where He guides.

Heavenly Father, we thank You as Creator.
We thank You for making us as both physical and
spiritual creatures.
We thank You that our Saviour who came to save us as
spiritual beings was not unconcerned with our physical needs.
We thank You for the wonderful way He uses physical objects
to teach spiritual lessons.
We thank You in Jesus' own Name.
Amen

**"There is a boy here who has five barley loaves and two
fish, but what are they for so many?"**
John 6:9

We may never learn precisely how Andrew came by an
inventory of the boy's provisions until we have the
opportunity to ask Andrew personally.
Did the lad come forward volunteering all he had?
Did Andrew learn what he knew through casual inquiry?
Had he dipped into his store earlier in a first installment
at lunch?
We are confident he was not the only individual in that great
multitude who remembered to bring food.
But he may have been the only one to register a willingness
to part with what he had.
Andrew's question was legitimate.
What good would it do?
By human reckoning nothing would be gained to the crowd by
the acquisition of one lad's meal.
Better that one child at least be fed.
It was not Jesus' practice to reckon by human measure.
The real question is what could be done with so little when
placed in Jesus' hands?
And the appropriate answer is:
"Just watch."

*Heavenly Father, may we be willing to give up everything
we have if what we have is needed to invest in the cause of
this King called Jesus.*
Show us where we are unwilling.
And bring change.
We ask it for His own dear sake.
Amen

Jesus said, "Have the people sit down."
Now there was much grass in the place.
So the men sat down, about five thousand in number.
John 6:10

We are struck by the fact that Jesus refuses to work this
mighty miracle apart from human cooperation.
He gives them something to do.
He requires that they assume a posture of reception.
He will command the loaves and the fish to multiply.
But first He commands the beneficiaries to sit.
There would have been no anticipation or comprehension by
those who were commanded.
The command would have been mysterious to all,
inconvenient to some, and vexing to others.
At the time to depart He commands them to stay.
And five thousand families sat down.
The requirements of God are never irksome to the trusting.
His commands are never arbitrary.
Our inclination to resist signals something rebellious in
ourselves, not something objectionable in God.
Obedience is one way for God to get what He wants.
But if we only knew the end from the beginning we would
know that obedience is also the best way for us to get what
we need.

Heavenly Father, we thank You that we know the reason for
this mysterious and perhaps inconvenient command.
And we thank You for the confidence that Your commands are
for our benefit.
Though we may ask "why" it is enough to know "what."
Amen

Jesus said, "Have the people sit down."
Now there was much grass in the place.
So the men sat down, about five thousand in number.
John 6:10

Remember they don't know yet WHY they were to sit down.
They must have labored mightily under the mistaken notion
that they were being detained.
Of course, they were not being detained.
They were being maintained.
They may have even been entertained.
They were being feted.
They were not merely about to enjoy a meal.
They were about to enjoy a miracle.
5000 men!
Heads of households.
We can only speculate as to the total number.
Most likely it was not less than 15,000 souls.
John calls our attention to the grass.
Here we have the authentic touch of the eyewitness.
John was THERE.
He wants us to know that it was an ideal spot for a picnic.
There was plenty of grass.
This miracle would be definitely comfortable as well as
deliciously filling.
What a Saviour was this...
A Saviour like no other.

Heavenly Father, we thank You for what this miracle proves
about our Saviour's attentiveness to our every need.
Lord if they were weary from listening then Jesus must have
been much wearier from teaching.
And yet He extends the meeting to meet physical needs.
Father, we thank You for a Saviour who troubles and exhausts
Himself in our behalf.
Amen

**Jesus then took the loaves, and when he had given thanks,
he distributed them to those who were seated.
So also the fish...
John 6:11**

This is a verse to make us ponder and adore.
It constitutes a mass miracle with thousands of participants.
It was a banquet no one would forget.
It was a sign to complement the day-long spiritual feast.
It was a sign to prove the authority of the Teacher.
As with the wine in Cana we cannot be sure the exact moment
the miracle took place.
But we can make a good guess.
Unlike the sign at Cana the miracle lay not in transformation
but in multiplication.
The food was already there, provided not by Jesus but by the
unnamed boy.
But the supply was laughingly meager, so meager Andrew
must have hesitated to mention it.
If the multiplication only took place in Jesus' hands the last
served would have waited past midnight for their portion.
No, the multiplication would have taken place not only in the
hands of the disciples but in the hands of those seated and
served as well.
Like the widow's oil and meal in Zarephath the little store
simply refused to be diminished.
Those who waited not only benefited from the miracle, they
participated in the miracle.

*Heavenly Father, we thank You that Your grace makes us not
only recipients but participants.
We thank You for the one who gave, those who distributed,
and those who partook.
Where Your blessings are concerned make us ever and always
to be involved in all three. In Jesus' Name.
Amen*

**Jesus then took the loaves, and when he had given thanks,
he distributed them to those who were seated.
So also the fish, as much as they wanted.**
John 6: 11

As much as they wanted!
This is a delightful formula.
But it is not a common formula in the New Testament.
The clusters of Eshcol may be heavy and thick.
The land of Canaan may flow with milk and honey.
But we are accustomed to associate New Testament piety with
a Saviour who fasts for 40 days and Apostles who carry on
through hunger and thirst (2 Cor.11:27).
To have as much as we want seems a wonderful exception.
The key is to accept gratefully as much as He wants
us to have.
Here He wants His hearers to feast.
There are many components leading up to the miracle.
The first is to offer to the Lord everything we have no matter
how small. That's what the boy did.
The second is to obey.
That's what the multitude did by staying and sitting.
The third is to give thanks. That's what the Lord did.
Then came the surprising participatory miracle, something
only the Lord can make happen for sure.
It was a miracle of the new creation with food appearing not
on bushes and trees but in human hands.
It was a miracle of sustenance.
It was a miracle of refreshment.
It was a miracle to showcase the character and power of Jesus.

*Heavenly Father, may we never by negligence or unbelief
forfeit participation in Your miraculous offers. Teach us to
yield up and give over. Teach us to be grateful after we have
given and before we receive. Bring us into the joy of the "as
much as we want" experiences which You design for us. When
You delight to give, make us delight to receive.
Through Christ our Lord we ask it.
Amen*

**And when they had eaten their fill, he told his disciples,
"Gather up the leftover fragments,
that nothing may be lost."
John 6:12**

Here is a lesson utterly practical and applicable.
The Lord of plenty, though Himself a virtual food multiplying
agent of endless supply, requires conservation.
Abundance never justifies waste.
The magnitude of the miracle was accentuated by the
circumstance that so much was left over.
The abiding proof remained to show that so many were fed
with so little, with much to spare.
Perhaps the abundance was provided to teach that others
should have come who did not.
Perhaps the disciples would be fed for days after, that they
might for days reflect anew.
For whatever reason there was ample proof that provision by
Jesus was not a strain or a stretch.
He provided with ease and with extra. Such was the proof of
His power. Such was the scope of His love.
But there is spiritual import as well.
No fragment of this lesson should be lost.
No implication of any of Jesus' miracles should be lost.
They are signs as well as miracles.
Something great is being provided but something greater is
being taught.
We must never miss what the miracles show about the identity
and intent of this Man who worked the miracles.

*Father, we thank You that Jesus showed us the importance of
saving the fragments.*
*We thank You that when He declared that nothing should
be lost, His declaration was meant for wider and more
spiritual application.*
*Father, we thank You that He would not allow those who
believe and obey His words to be lost.*
Amen

**When the people saw the sign that he had done, they said,
"This is indeed the Prophet who is to
come into the world!"
John 6:14**

To be sure, it was a good thing that the miracles healed the
sick, filled the hungry, and relieved the distressed.
These were undeniable blessings.
But these consequences of the signs were secondary.
The great aim was authentication.
The purpose of a sign is to point somewhere else.
In this case to someone else.
The signs were to enhance credibility.
To bring strong evidence that the One who worked real
wonders made true claims.
Jesus told the disciples that He had food to eat that they
knew not of.
Here He proved that He had food to give that they
knew not of.
This was the desired inference that began to take hold of those
who enjoyed the miraculous meal.
They began to associate the feeding of the 5000 with the
prophecy of Deuteronomy 18.
This was the one of whom Moses spoke.
This was the Prophet who was to come into the world.
The miracle proved He had arrived.
He was already in the world.
They had seen Him.
They sat at His table and were filled.

*Heavenly Father, the table which Jesus sets is the only place
our souls find sustenance.
He has offered us the food which is real and true.
We have been fed by Him and we are forever full.
For that we bless You and thank You.
Amen*

**Perceiving then that they were about to come and take him
by force to make him king, Jesus withdrew...**
John 6:15

Jesus came to be a King.
He revealed the same to Pilate.
But He came to be Heavenly King though resident
upon the earth.
That is something quite different from earthly ideas
about Royalty.
His idea of the Kingdom contrasted from their own.
It was not so much Jesus they wished to enthrone but their
own national aspiration, their hatred of the occupiers, their
ambition for military ascendancy.
In short, they wished to enthrone themselves.
This is the reason He so often commanded that His mighty
acts not be noised abroad.
He knew if His hearers tried to inaugurate the Kingdom before
learning what kind of Kingdom it was, confusion and
disappointment would ensue.
This was the clarification He pressed on Palm Sunday.
This was the correction He explained to Pilate.
This was the reason He withdrew after the feast.

Heavenly Father, we repent of trying to define this
Heavenly King.
Let Him rather define Himself.
And let Him define us, for we have enlisted as His
loyal subjects.
We repent of attempting to impose our personal
agendas on Him.
As if such a thing were possible.
Let Him rather frame our agenda.
And make us eager for orders.
We ask it in the Name of our great King Jesus.
Amen

When they had rowed about three or four miles, they saw Jesus walking on the sea and coming near the boat, and they were frightened. But he said to them, "It is I…"
John 6:19-20

He was pleased to sit often in their boats.
But He didn't need their boats.
It was not His only option for transport.
The boat was theirs, but the Sea was His.
All of Nature belonged to Him.
He created Nature and ruled over it as Lord and King.
The second verse of the Bible tells us that the Spirit of God moved across the face of the deep.
The Sea of Galilee was less than that original Deep but the Son of Man was no less than that Spirit of God in Genesis 1.
Nature assumed its original properties according to His will and Nature would alter its original properties and take on provisional properties according to His pleasure.
He could have changed the properties of water.
He could have changed the properties of gravity.
He could have changed the properties of His own physical constitution and weight.
He could have changed all three, we don't know.
What we do know is that He walked upon the waves.
It was a thing impossible for ordinary mortals.
And by the demonstration He proved that He was far from ordinary.

Heavenly Father, we thank You for the many demonstrations of the Deity of your Son Jesus.
We thank You for the faithfulness and accuracy of the eye-witnesses.
We thank You that the signs were numerous and powerful.
We thank You that they were purposeful.
We thank You that those signs overflowed with meaning.
We thank You that we too have witnessed the signs through what we read.
Amen

"It is I; do not be afraid."
John 6:20

In these few words Jesus addresses the universal human
condition. There is much to be afraid of and there are
many who fear.
Here is the sole and lasting remedy.
He approaches and speaks the comforting word.
It is better to be with Jesus in a dangerous place than to be
alone in apparent safety.
Danger is a test of faith.
Courage is a proof of grace.
We sing of His own dear presence to cheer and to guide.
The song speaks of reality in the present, not a charming
memory now past.
He would be in the boat with them.
He is here in the storm with us.
Though things may be placid now, storms will eventually
arise. We have not yet come to port.
No threat can overtake us apart from His design and purpose.
He will wean us from a carnal safety which clings to shore.
He will inspire the boldness which ventures forth.
The comfort here offered is an accurate index of our true
situation. It is not mere sentiment.
We may see danger approaching.
But look closer.
Is He not near?
Is it not His voice we hear?

Heavenly Father, thank You for sending Your Son to rescue
and comfort.
Thank You that we have heard His voice.
Thank You that we have believed His Word.
We thank You that His presence is real.
We thank You that His peace abides.
And lasts forever.
Amen

"...do not be afraid."
John 6:20

Disciples may ask, "Who is this who commands the waves?"
We may just as well ask, "Who is this who commands
the emotions?"
One can be as hard as the other.
Jesus reigns over both.
He controls the complex forces of Nature.
He also commands the complex forces of our hearts.
He knows us FROM THE INSIDE.
And He cares enough to command us to change.
External words by others, however well intentioned, have not
the power to transform.
Not so with the words of Jesus.
Jesus can deliver on the inside what He demands from
the outside.
He gives what He asks for.
As far as the subjective condition goes, the opposite of fear
is peace.
We must ask Him what He asks of us, and He will provide.
He will deliver from the fear He forbids.
He is, after all, the Prince of Peace.

Heavenly Father, we thank You for the Peace that
Jesus brings.
We thank You that He commands the storm over our head.
We thank You that that He expels the disquiet in our heart.
May we ever yield our hearts to Him.
Amen

May 14

"It is I; do not be afraid."
John 6:20

There is a reason this is the most repeated command in
the Bible.
If we navigate this life we will come upon fearsome passages.
If we are determined followers of the Lamb, the frightening
sequences will not diminish.
They will rather multiply.
Commands contain warnings.
Unbelief is the supreme anti-god state of mind.
And fear is the first cousin of unbelief.
At worst, fear is a denial of the divine attributes.
As if God were not there.
As if God did not care.
There is a reason Jesus identifies Himself before evicting the
fear which had latched on and taken over.
In this exceptional case it was actually the Lord Himself they
had feared.
Once make His presence known, and relief and peace ensue.
Jesus present to protect.
Jesus present to accompany.
Jesus present to empower.
The same Jesus who is with us even until now.

Father, we would reckon upon Your Son's presence in
every circumstance.
May it be a comforting presence.
May it be a transforming presence.
May His presence render us not only stable but useful.
Not only useful but joyful.
For Christ's own sake we ask it.
Amen

May 15

**Other boats... came near the place where they had
eaten the bread after the Lord had given thanks.
John 6:23**

Here is a remarkable thing.
While calling attention to the scene of a mighty miracle John
makes no specific reference to the miraculous nature of the
provision but rather to:
1. Where they did eat.
2. Where the Lord gave thanks.
What was it that hallowed the scene actually?
The fact that Jesus stopped and preached there would have
been quite enough to render the ground sacred.
The fact that they received something from Jesus,
swallowed it, made it a part of themselves would have
been memorable enough.
But John is interested in putting something else across.
He speaks of Jesus thanking God for the meager offering He
was about to multiply.
John refuses to stop reminding us of this.
God the Son thanking God the Father.
God the Second Person addressing God the First Person.
Incarnate Deity praying to Enthroned Deity.
This is the Infinite Communion overheard by
uncomprehending human ears.
It could be possible that the most remarkable thing about the
memory was not the stupendous multiplication of the bread
and fish, but rather the unforgettable experience of HEARING
JESUS PRAY.

*Heavenly Father, we thank You not only for this but for other
examples as well of the Lord Jesus Christ at prayer.
We thank You that when the disciples asked Jesus to teach
them to pray He did teach them.
So Father, help us to pray.
Make us to pray prayers that will be answered.
Prayers like the prayers your Son prayed.
We ask it in His Name.
Amen*

**Do not work for the food that perishes, but for the food
that endures to eternal life,
which the Son of Man will give to you.
John 6:27**

Here we are taught what is, and is not, worthy of our labor.
The New Testament warns us early and often to abandon the
notion that any creature could merit the salvation God offers.
And yet here the "food which endures to eternal life" is put
forward as something worth laboring for.
The apparent discrepancy is easily resolved.
We are told in the same verse that this eternal bread is
something that Jesus will give to us. Give as in "gift."
The matter is settled then in favor of faith over works.
And yet there IS work involved and here Jesus addresses it.
It requires a kind of soul labor, to get the notion of salvation
by human effort out of the way, so that the gift of grace may
be received savingly.
It is the universal default position of fallen intellects
untouched by divine grace or uninstructed by Holy
Scripture, that salvation is something we must earn.
It is always evidence of the Holy Spirit's work when this
prominent feature of man-made religion is once for all
expunged from our assumptions.
And on our side, it feels like a true effort of labor to banish the
thought once and for all.
It is by grace we are saved, and that not of ourselves, it is the
gift of God, not according to works... Except the work that
seeks to cling to that truth against all contradiction.

*Heavenly Father, we thank You for the salvation earned for us
by Another. Had we earned it ourselves we would have no
reason to give thanks for a wage due to us.
But we could never work off such a debt.
May we always work by efforts of clarification and faith to
keep this truth solidly in our understanding.
That salvation has always been and always must be a gracious
gift of Your grace. In Christ's own Name we thank You.
Amen*

Then they said to him, "What must we do, to be doing the works of God?" Jesus answered them, "This is the work of God, that you may believe in him whom he has sent."
John 6:28-29

This is the work of God - that we might believe.
This truth is not one-dimensional.
It is the one work that God sets us to do.
It is a work of irony for it is the work that confesses we can do no work to reform ourselves in God's sight.
No work can advance our spiritual case before a righteous judge in a heavenly court.
But believing, the expression of our own personal faith, can never be solely our work.
Indeed, faith itself is a gift.
It is the gift which proves the mighty work of God's own Holy Spirit within us.
It is a mighty work because it traverses the largest conceivable distance.
The distance from death to life.
The distance from darkness to light.
The distance from hell to heaven.
It is the transference which takes us from God's enmity to an intimate friendship between Father and children.
It is the mighty gulf that God did span.
He is pleased to call it our work.
He is pleased for us to say it is our faith and to declare that we do believe.

Heavenly Father, thank You for working in us that we might work out our salvation, that we might feel this great work of faith being birthed in our hearts by grace.
Thank You in the Name of Jesus who completed Your work for us on the cruel Cross.
Amen

May 18

**So they said to him, "Then what sign do you do, that we
may see and believe you?
Our fathers ate the manna in the wilderness..."
John 6:30-31**

The miracle of the loaves and fish was powerful
and undeniable.
The proof was in the mouths and memories of 5000 families.
But the opposers remained unimpressed.
They had been doing the math.
Moses, they said, fed 3 million for over 40 years.
What Jesus provided was a mere fraction of that.
"What else have you got?" is essentially what they
were saying.
What Jesus did was impossible, God-like and divine.
He would have convinced all but the most stiff-necked.
But these resistant were bent on their own destruction.
One song says, "A man hears what he wants to hear and
disregards the rest."
The song writer spoke truth.

*Father, make us to profit from the light You have shone
on our path.
Make us good stewards of the evidence You provide.
Make it to embolden us that we may illumine the darkness
of others.
We pray it in the Name of Jesus who fed the thousands.
Amen*

"...it was not Moses who gave you the bread from heaven, but my Father gives you the true bread from heaven."
John 6:32

A great many falsehoods were hurled at Jesus through the
course of His ministry.
For the most part He was content to ignore the abuse
without commentary.
But there was one category excepted.
He simply would not allow anything which darkened the glory
of His Father to pass unchallenged.
Though He was loathe to speak to Pilate at the last when Pilate
asserted authority, Jesus corrected the Roman Governor and
declared, "You would have no authority at all unless it was
granted from above."
Here He will not let it be said that the manna was a gift
from Moses.
The manna which fell from above was a gift from His Father.
Necessary as manna was as physical sustenance for the great
multitude in transit, that bread was but a foretaste of the bread
which gives life to the soul.
There is a false bread like that offered by the tempter in
the wilderness.
And there is true bread like that offered by the Saviour in the
Upper Room.
It is essential to discern the difference.
One will give life to our souls.
The other will render us perpetually hungry.

Father, let us not linger at the signs but rather move forward
to what the signs point us to.
Thank You that the ministry of Your Son was prophesied in the
Old Testament. Thank You that the miracles of Jesus signal
blessings in the future.
Thank You that all these confirmations provide solid reasons
to believe.
Amen

**"...the bread of God...comes down from
heaven and gives life to the world."
They said to him, "Sir, give us this bread always."
John 6:33-34**

The context stands in contrast to the interview with the
Samaritan woman, but the principle is parallel.
Jesus is offering something precious but unknown.
The hearers are uncomprehending.
Water and food are equally necessary in the physical realm.
Both are fit emblems of the spiritual reality.
After a brief exchange the multitude of John 6 ask for what
Jesus offers.
She asked for water; they ask for bread.
One obvious sign of spiritual death is the lack of
spiritual desire.
The symptom is disquieting but the reasons are not
hard to find.
We are of the earth, earthly; the bread is heavenly and suited
for heavenly tastes.
Our sins inhibit the savor of heavenly things.
This Man who came down from heaven rehabilitates the
spiritual palate.
We meet Him and wonder why we settled for chaff while
there was wheat on offer.
Jesus comes not only to meet need.
He comes to supply the health of holy desire.

Lord, we thank You for the promises of Jesus.
We thank You that He delivers what He promises.
And we thank You that He paid for everything with
His own blood.
Amen

Jesus said to them, "I am the bread of life... "
John 6:35

The is the first of the great "I ams" of John's Gospel.
The claim is paired with the previous sign.
It was the feeding of the five thousand which certified
authority and authenticated the claim.
The necessity of bread in the old creation is the temporary
pattern which illustrates the permanent truth.
Contrast the two Adams.
It was the eating of fruit in the garden of Paradise which
guaranteed the certainty of death.
It was the refusal of bread in the wilderness of Temptation
which brought forth the possibility of life.
The wilderness manna was the shadow of something.
The Son of Man is the substance.
This is the theme which recurs.
The pattern shows itself in this Gospel and in the whole
of Scripture.
God sent His people manna which would keep them alive
in the wilderness of Sinai.
God still sends Bread which makes alive in this wilderness
of sin.
The bread is a Person.
The Person is God's own Son.

Heavenly Father, we thank You for everything You give us.
Thank You for giving us life...
Most of all we thank You for giving us Your Son, who is the
Bread of Life, and for the life He gives which is,
Life Forevermore.
Amen

**"I am the bread of life; whoever comes to me
shall not hunger, and whoever believes in me
shall never thirst."
John 6:35**

We note variety in the Gospel offer.
Salvation may be represented by more than one formula.
Salvation is a coming to Jesus to receive what Jesus offers.
Salvation is a believing in Jesus for what Jesus promises.
The promise is the essence of truth about Himself.
He is the Bread God gives to ensure life.
What Jesus offers is the profoundest transformation of the
sinner's self, through the partaking of the Saviour's self.
The registry of that transformation may be felt at the level of
desire and fulfillment.
Before, we wanted pardon.
In Jesus we have it.
Before, we wanted assurance that our sins are forgiven.
We wanted to know what God is really like.
In Jesus we behold God Himself come in the flesh.
He fills the empty space in hungry hearts.
He made dramatic promises.
And He is Himself the best fulfillment of His precious and
glorious promises.

*Heavenly Father, You could not give us more than Jesus.
Thank You that You did not give us less.
Amen*

"...you have seen me, and yet do not believe..."
John 6:36

Here is impending tragedy.
Tragedy ultimate and irretrievable.
Once Jesus is beheld Revelation shines forth at a maximum.
There is nothing higher.
No loftier vista could allow us to see further.
There is indeed nothing left to see.
There is only one God.
God has only one Son.
That Son dies only one death and offers only one atonement.
There is no "plan B."
If the Son and His salvation are rejected God has nothing
else to offer.
We behold the summit of divine disclosure in the
appearance of this Jesus.
We behold as well, the sad depth of resistance.
Messianic claims are repudiated.
God sent His only begotten Son.
That Son was rejected.

*Father, thank You forever for sending Your Son to show us
who You are.*
*May Your Holy Spirit ever remove the cloud of sin which dims
and distorts.*
*May we ever behold the King in His beauty and love You all
the more for what we see in Him.*
Amen

"All that the Father gives me will come to me..."
John 6:37

Here is the summit of high doctrine.
Here is the testament of a sovereignty utterly divine.
Salvation is of God!
This is not a truth to be muffled.
Shout it rather from the rooftop.
SALVATION IN JEHOVAH'S HANDS!
This is a Jesus doctrine.
We have the truth from His own lips.
He cannot be mistaken, for who but He could know?
As adamant as the recalcitrance of the rejecters is, it is not a
thing beyond God.
There is a Saviour before us who beckons.
But that is just the half of it.
There is a Father above who compels.
Our fathers called it irresistible grace.
It is the grace which saves.
Jesus will have a people for His own possession for their
faith originates by divine impulse.
All that the Father gives Him will come to Him.
Not one will be lost.

Heavenly Father, we thank You for the guarantee of a grace
which could not be turned aside.
It was the only kind of grace which could save wretches
like ourselves.
In Jesus' Name we thank You.
Amen

May 25

**"All that the Father gives me will come to me, and
whoever comes to me I will never cast out."
John 6:37**

All communion between the Divine Persons of the Holy
Trinity will remain to a degree mysterious to the earth-bound
and finite.
But God graciously condescends.
Though there is much we don't know much has been revealed.
We know that there is absolute agreement, unity and harmony
in the Godhead.
We know that each of the divine Persons may take on
distinctive assignments.
We know that because of essential unity there will be
inevitable overlap.
Here we see compulsion assigned to the Father.
Here we learn that retention is attributed to the Son.
Salvation is a Trinitarian work.
All three Persons are active in the work of securing for the
believer everlasting joy.
And there is no greater wellspring of joy than this.
There is no higher motive for worship.
The Saviour bids us come.
The Father gives us as a gift to His Son.
The Holy Spirit makes the startling transaction known to us
and gives us the desire to forsake self for Jesus.
And here is the assurance that though God propels and
compels He will not expel.
He will in no way cast us out.

*Heavenly Father, we praise You for the Trinitarian work
which brought salvation to each of us.
We thank You for what we have been told.
We would know more.
We thank You for the prospect of an eternity of discovery and
worship as all aspects of our salvation unfold forever.*
In Jesus' Name.
Amen

**"For I have come down from heaven, not to do my own
will but the will of him who sent me."
John 6:38**

All indications of purpose are to be treasured.
When Scripture addresses purpose we get closer to answering
the elusive question, "Why?"
WHY did Jesus leave the confines of His Father's house to
venture forth?
Why would He deign to approach the killing fields below?
Here the inscrutable will of the Father emerged.
He would please the Father.
The Father was never reluctant to save.
The Son was never hesitant to take on the saving errand.
It was the Son's delight to live for the will of the Father.
The Son was willing to die for the same.
That is what saved us, the determined resolve in God which
cost God the terrible price.
The Son came down from heaven to do the Father's will.
Was there ever a steeper descent?
Was there ever a higher motive?
No.
Nor can there ever be.

Father, the mere thought of it takes our breath away.
Where we do not understand we adore.
Thank You for Your determination to save.
Thank You for Jesus' willingness to die.
Thank You forever.
Amen

**"For this is the will of my Father, that everyone who looks
on the Son and believes in Him should have eternal life..."
John 6:40**

What does it mean then to "look on" the Son?
There were many alive in Jesus' generation who looked upon
Him with physical eyes without "seeing" Him in a way which
led to salvation.
Just so there have been millions in the centuries since (and
even in the centuries before!) who saw clearly and savingly.
It means to see Him as God the Holy Spirit was pleased to
reveal Him.
That is, it means to see Him biblically.
We are not to spy Him out by fleshly observation.
We are not to work Him out by human reasoning.
We are not to reconstruct Him by human imagination.
Rather He is to be perceived by the grace of divine revelation;
God showing Himself by sending His Son.
He is seen by what Scripture says and shows.
Seen as foretold by the Prophets, seen as presented in the
Gospels, seen as explained in the Epistles and seen as
promised in the Apocalypse.
It means He is to be seen as the actual Son in relation to His
Heavenly Father, begotten not made, born not created, eternal
not temporal, not merely a son of God but the Son of God,
very God of very God.

*Heavenly Father, thank You that You gave us something
infinitely valuable - eternal life - by causing us to look upon
someone infinitely wonderful - Your very own Son.
We look upon Him with faith.
We receive Him with joy.
We thank You with sincerity.
In His own wonderful Name.
Jesus our Lord.
Amen*

May 28

"...everyone who looks on the Son and believes in him should have eternal life..."
John 6:40

Salvation is motivated by the measureless love of God.
Salvation is secured by the boundless power of God.
Salvation is as permanent as the eternal life of God.
It should not surprise us then that Scripture offers varied formulas for salvation.
In His interview with Nicodemus, Jesus spoke of entry into God's Kingdom as a Rebirth.
Here He equates beholding and believing in the Jesus of the Gospels with the possession of everlasting life.
In both cases He meant the same thing.
Salvation is an ultimate and infinite thing.
It is simple at the point of ignition but widely varied in its implications and applications.
To see Jesus accurately is to have become a favored beneficiary of all the graces of salvation.
To see and to believe is to have received grace in all its saving fullness.
We have Christ's own word for it.

Heavenly Father, we thank You that the initiation was all on the divine side.
We thank You for showing us Christ.
We could never have discovered Him on our own.
We thank You for the gift of saving faith.
Our sinful nature inclined us toward unbelief, but by grace You overcame that resistance and made us willing captives.
For this we will be praising You forever.
Amen

"...and I will raise him up on the last day."
John 6:40

There is nothing more thrilling than the "I wills" and
"I shalls" of Jesus Christ.
There is nothing more precious for the believer.
There is nothing more sure than the "I wills" and
"I shalls" of Christ.
There is nothing more certain for the future.
More certain than the rising of the sun.
More certain than the falling of the night.
And there will be the falling of night upon the Old Creation.
That is part of what Jesus means (ironically) by the Last Day.
And there will be a sunrise upon the New Creation.
That is part of what Jesus means by the raising up.

Heavenly Father, help us grasp the truth that this current
biological life is not ultimate.
Thank You for the Resurrection of Jesus from the dead.
Thank You that His Resurrection guarantees our own
rising up.
Knowing this, let us live this dying life in the light of
that last day.
The day of our rising.
We ask it in the name of the Risen Christ.
Amen

**So the Jews grumbled about him, because he said, "I am
the bread that came down from heaven."
They said, "Is not this Jesus, the son of Joseph, whose
father and mother we know? How does he now say,
'I have come down from heaven'?"
John 6:41-42**

Because the religious leaders were so confident they already
knew, they could never learn.
Because they rejected the truth about Jesus' origin, they were
bound to err with respect to Jesus' destiny.
They measured the Son of God by the gauges of
their traditions.
As if the sea could be measured by teacups.
Divine revelation, not human investigation gives the only true
knowledge of the God-Man.
His human origin was supernatural.
His divine origin was without beginning.
They were wrong to assume they "knew" His Father.
That conceit was their final undoing.

*Heavenly Father, thank You for sending Your Son to show us
who You are.
We would ever know You better by always learning of Him.
We beseech Your Spirit to teach us.
Grant it for His own dear sake we ask.
Amen*

Jesus answered them, "Do not grumble among yourselves."
John 6:43

There is every chance that the words of complaint were
spoken out of normal hearing range.
If so Jesus' knowledge of what they had said was supernatural.
They had, after all, grumbled "among themselves."
And there was irony in their grumbling.
They had argued that the miracle of the loaves and fish was
inferior and unconvincing because Moses fed their fathers
with bread out of heaven.
What's more, that bread fed more people for a longer time.
So they were taking their stand with that Sinai generation who
received the heavenly manna.
They would not stand with this Jesus.
But that Sinai generation was a generation of unbelief.
They died short of Canaan on the near side of Jordan because
they would not obey God and claim the land.
And there was another thing even more telling.
Those wilderness wanderers complained about the manna.
And they were judged for it.
The Jews of the First Century did indeed show a kinship with
their wilderness fathers.
Like those fathers they disdained the bread God offered.

*Lord thank You for offering bread for our souls at untold
expense to Yourself.*
May we take the bread You offer.
May we savor it.
May we be grateful for it.
And may we thank You forever.
Amen

June 1

"No one can come to me unless the Father...draws him."
John 6:44

The Lord Jesus here presents a truth consistently declared in
Scripture and just as consistently explained away by
multitudes of Christians.
It is a hard thing to admit that salvation reposes in hands not
human but divine.
It is a truth which actually brings glory to God the Father.
Therefore, it is a truth which ought not to be resisted.
It is a truth which should not be resisted because it falls from
the Saviour's lips.
It is a truth which should not be resisted because the Holy
Spirit bears witness to the same throughout Scripture.
Salvation is of God.
It is man the sinner who resists.
We resist the thing which best serves our good.
That is why we need to be drawn.
Left to our sinful selves no one would choose salvation.
It is a hard thing to measure the depth of our own fallenness.
We need not.
God has measured it for us.

*Heavenly Father, we thank You that You have indeed
drawn us.*
*Thank You for bringing us into the Kingdom of Your
dear Son.*
Now teach us to believe the truth about the way we arrived.
For we ask it in Christ's own Name.
Amen

June 2

**"No one can come to me unless the Father... draws him.
And I will raise him up on the last day."
John 6:44**

Here is celebrated the sovereignty of God in salvation.
When God saves He saves permanently and forever.
Jesus in this verse not only identifies His Father as the
efficient agent of salvation, He identifies Him as the perpetual
guarantor of salvation.
God finishes what He begins.
Salvation is of no benefit unless it delivers from judgment on
the last day.
The Saviour the Father draws His people to, will raise those
same people on the last day.
We are drawn to the Saviour so He can save us.
This is elementary.
Part of being saved means being raised on the last day.
This follows logically and necessarily.
God who enables at the first ensures to the last.
This is part of what it means for Jesus to be the Author and
Finisher of our faith.
God saves from the first to the last.
Before we heard about the Gospel we were dead in sin.
But God the Father drew us.
One day we will be dead physically.
But God the Son will raise us.
Salvation is something God does.
Indeed, it is something only He could do.

*Heavenly Father, we look back at the great thing Jesus did for
us on the Cross. And we offer praise.
Heavenly Father, we look back at the great thing You did
when You drew us to saving confidence in Jesus' work
on the Cross. And we offer praise.
We look forward to what Jesus will do for us in the future on
the last day.
For the Resurrection of our bodies we thank You in advance.
In the Name of Jesus who died and rose again.
Amen*

June 3

**"Everyone who has heard and learned from
the Father comes to me..."
John 6:45**

This is the second (the first was 3:21) of four verses (the
others are 7:17 and 18:37) in this Gospel which address the
questions "But what about other religions?" and "What about
those who have not heard?"
The four verses taken together rank high on the list of Jesus'
most startling claims.
Here is the test for authentic knowledge of God.
If anyone has heard from God, he will be directed to Jesus.
If anyone has learned of God, he will be taught of Jesus.
Here is the truth in the first verse of this Gospel expanded,
"and the Word was God."
Advance in our knowledge of the Father must come
through the Son.
He has nominated no alternate.
Nor will He ever.

*Heavenly Father, thank You that You wanted to be known so
much that You sent Your only Son to bring the true knowledge
of Yourself.
Thank You for saving knowledge perfectly revealed by a
Messenger perfectly faithful.
Thank You that it is Your plan not only to show us Yourself but
to make us like Yourself.
Lord make us willing and eager for what You require from our
side in that great transformation.
In Jesus' Name we ask it.
Amen*

June 4

**"Truly, truly, I say to you, whoever believes
has eternal life."
John 6:47**

This is among the shortest and most direct of the
Gospel formulas.
The Lord compacts a large promise in a small space.
The promise here is for individuals.
Anyone who believes may rest in the sure and certain hope of
eternal blessedness.
Such confidence cannot be grounded upon either citizenship
or ethnicity.
It is faith which brings assurance that the thing once promised
is the thing now possessed.
Acknowledging the weakness of human judgment, Jesus
begins with the double asseveration: Truly! Truly!
But what is it that must be believed?
Nothing less than Jesus' testimony regarding Himself,
in its entirety.
His Person, His work.
He is the Son of God.
His death on the cross supplies ample payment for sin.
But the benefit accrues only to those who believe.

Heavenly Father, ours is the sin that incurred the guilt.
His is the sacrifice that paid the price.
We praise You for canceled debt and a future assured.
We will fill the eternity gifted to us with
Thanksgiving and Praise.
In Jesus' Name.
Amen

"I am the Bread of Life."
John 6:48

Here then is the reiteration.
He says again what He first declared earlier.
He repeats Himself because some were not listening.
He repeats Himself because some doubted.
He repeats Himself because some disputed.
He repeats Himself because some truths are so wonderful they beg to be repeated.
This truth is in the category called wonderful.
Jesus' first recorded dispute after the public launch of His ministry was over bread.
The venue was the wilderness.
The opponent was the Devil.
The issue was temptation.
Jesus didn't come to give Himself bread.
He came to give Himself as bread.
His Life is the Bread of our lives.
It is the only life in fact, which can nourish our souls.

Father, Your Son is for us the perfect teacher.
We are but poor and sluggish students.
We thank You for His patience.
We thank You for His willingness to repeat the lesson.
We have taken this Bread.
And by it we shall live forevermore.
And while we live we will praise You for it.
In Jesus' own Name we will praise You.
Amen

June 6

**"Your fathers ate the manna in the
wilderness, and they died."**
John 6:49

He highlights the salient factor.
They were missing the obvious.
They noted the quantitative gap in the manna from heaven and
the bread Jesus multiplied.
The advantage was on the side of the manna.
But there was also a qualitative difference.
And that advantage lay on Jesus' side.
Jesus will now delineate the distinction between the manna in
the wilderness and the bread He is offering.
The wilderness manna was supernaturally provided but those
who ate were not supernaturally protected.
The manna did not arrest their mortality.
The common assertion of mortality encroached upon the Sinai
generation as on every other.
He would now explain the shocking difference.

*Heavenly Father we thank You for all the miracles of the
Older Testament.
How often those miracles delivered them then.
How often those miracles dazzle us now.
Thank You that so many of those miracles pointed to
something later and higher.
And not only something but someone.
Someone named Jesus.
In whose Name we pray.
Amen*

"This is the bread that comes down from heaven, so that one may eat of it and not die."
John 6:50

The context is the memory of Moses and the Sinai generation.
The reference is to the sustenance of the long wandering.
Jesus outlines the similarities.
He too offers the heavenly bread.
But He also marks the great distinction.
The manna from heaven and the loaves from the lad's store
pointed to something other and greater.
They pointed to another Bread.
To take in that Bread was to take on a life which could
not end.
Jesus offered the immediate sign to validate the
future promise.
And there is a further distinction.
The adults who ate the manna never arrived at the place they
hoped to go.
Jesus offers the Bread which takes us Home.

*Heavenly Father, we marvel at the wonders You brought forth
in the Old Testament.*
For this greater marvel called Jesus we bow down and praise.
Your people were delivered temporarily.
Your people knew joy for a season.
*For this once for all Deliverer, who brings the joy everlasting,
we praise You.*
We praise You forevermore.
Amen

June 8

**"And the bread that I will give for the life
of the world is my flesh."
John 6:51**

At this point we arrive at the core of the Gospel.
At the core is Substitution.
Someone dies in the sinner's place.
At the core is Redemption.
Someone is handed over so the sinner can go free.
At the core is a gift utterly unmerited.
"I will give" for the life of the world.
The Giver-Redeemer-Substitute teaches in this passage
about Himself.
Here He leaves behind those aspects of the great truth which
are figurative.
He brings us into the realm of the literal.
The giving of His flesh means that He will actually die.
That is how He saves us.
That is what makes Him our Saviour.

*Heavenly Father, thank You that Jesus was clear as to
His intention.
Thank You that He was relentless in His purpose.
Thank You that He died for us.
And by His death we are saved.
Amen*

June 9

**The Jews then disputed among themselves, saying,
"How can this man give us his flesh to eat?"
John 6:52**

We may miss the true sense of Scripture because we do not
interpret literally enough.
But it is also possible to be too literal.
Jesus does not here reference a physical process.
He does not commend cannibalism.
Through the centuries a majority of the confessing church
has interpreted this and other texts to mean that the bread
in the Communion Rite actually becomes the Body of
Christ physically.
But John nowhere calls attention to the Sacraments in
his Gospel.
Since his treatment of the events in the Upper Room is far
more extensive than the other Gospel writers, it is surprising
that he nowhere mentions the Lord's Supper.
Nor is He citing the Lord's Supper here.
He is rather expounding the larger spiritual truth which the
Lord's Supper physically illustrates.
Unless we have the very life of God within us we have no
hope of eternal life.
Jesus came to show us the life of God.
He came to offer us that life, so that we might receive that life
into ourselves, that we might be saved.

*Heavenly Father, we thank You that the salvation You offer is
so utterly personal.
It means the actual life of Your own Son given for us.
It means that same life present in us.
For this precious gift we bow down.
And we give praise.
Amen*

**So Jesus said to them, "Truly, truly, I say to you,
unless you eat the flesh of the Son of Man and
drink his blood, you have no life in you."
John 6:53**

In this amazing succession of verses, we receive a profound
insight into a vital doctrine.
We also see how the Son of God practices apologetics.
By apologetics we mean the defense of the Christian faith.
Jesus refuses to make His point in a way more likely to win
the approval of His questioners.
If anything, His clarification makes His doctrine
less palatable.
Why will He not condescend?
Why does He not relent?
For the simple reason that His challengers are not honest.
There are true believers and disciples listening in to be sure.
But at this specific point the Lord is locked in an exchange
with those who are looking for an occasion to fault Him.
These were grumblers remember (v.41), those who disputed
His heavenly origin (v.42).
They must have felt grateful that His refusal to say something
less provocative gave them just the kind of occasion they were
looking for.

*Heavenly Father, we thank You that Your Son was an unerring
spiritual diagnostician.
He was always able to discern true motives and He gave
answers which addressed the specific condition
of the questioner.
Grant us this same Spirit that we might know and minister
in ways most likely to get at the real causes of unbelief.
For Christ's own sake we ask it.
Amen*

June 11

"...unless you eat the flesh of the Son of Man and drink his blood, you have no life in you. Whoever feeds on my flesh and drinks my blood has eternal life, and I will raise him up on the last day."
John 6:53-54

The point is that Christ must be personally received or there can be no life.
Jesus must be taken to the inside of each one of us or we remain in the realm of sin and death.
The media through which we receive the Life which cannot die is His own Body and Blood.
The irony is that He confers that life by dying.
The only life we have by nature is mortal; we lose a part of it with every passing moment.
When we eat the flesh and drink the blood of the Son of Man we have eternal life as a present possession.
Eternal life means when we die, Christ will raise us up.
He did something for us on the day He died so that He could do something for us on the day we die.

Heavenly Father, thank You that eternal life is something we need never lay down because Your Son laid down His own precious life.
May we know this One who died in our place fully and completely.
May we serve Him unreservedly in His own strength until the day we see Him, our living Saviour, Face-to-face.
Amen

"For my flesh is true food, and my blood is true drink."
John 6:55

We would be hard put to cite another verse in all of Scripture
more likely to inflame controversy than the verse before us.
Of course, it is a truth impossible for unbelievers to receive.
But the various possibilities of interpretation have led to deep
divisions among believers as well.
Our aim has always been to offer simple devotional comment.
It is beyond our scope to produce a theological treatise.
So we offer definition without defense.
Does Jesus mean that His Body and Blood literally and
physically are true food and drink?
He does.
Does He mean that the believer is to eat His Body and drink
His Blood physically?
He does not.
Physical food is for physical sustenance.
The Lord is here referencing eternal life not mortal life.
The transaction He speaks of is spiritual.
The life He speaks of is received by faith.

Heavenly Father, we thank You for giving Your Son to
us as a Saviour.
We thank You for giving Your Son to us as a teacher.
We praise You that by His sacrifice we may have life.
We praise You that through His teaching we may
have understanding.
In His own Name we thank You.
Amen

June 13

**"Whoever feeds on my flesh and drinks my blood
abides in me, and I in him."
John 6:56**

Jesus here provides a clue to the specific meaning of "eats my
flesh and drinks my blood."
He says that whoever does this abides in Him.
This is a theme He will enlarge upon in the Upper Room when
He prepares the disciples for His departure.
At the beginning of the Gospel we saw that God designed the
physical universe as a platform for spiritual correspondence.
He set us in a place of earthly realities, visible and tangible,
to help introduce us to heavenly realities we don't yet see
or touch.
Simply put, He means to teach us permanent spiritual
realities through everyday physical objects, occurrences
and relationships.
Love and marriage, fathers and sons, birth and death, light and
darkness are all illustrative of heavenly truths.
The connection of material food and drink with spiritual food
is one example of that kind of correspondence.
Jesus here takes us to heights and depths.
The doctrines are not simple, and we will remain
uncomprehending unless we linger, study and pray.

*And so, Heavenly Father, we do now linger and pray.
We pray first for understanding.
Let us not only understand what it means to eat drink and
abide but grant us the power to do the same though our fleshly
nature inclines us to wander and leave off abiding.
Grant it Father, according to the Spirit's power for we ask it
in the Son's Name.
Amen*

June 14

**"Whoever feeds on my flesh and drinks my blood
abides in me, and I in him."
John 6:56**

Jesus here introduces the deep subject of mutual indwelling.
We abide in Him.
He abides in us.
To become a Christian is to partake of the nature of Christ.
To become a Christian is to become conformed to Christ.
Jesus abides in His Father.
His Father abides in Him.
This has always been the case.
To become a Christian then means to bc takcn into the very
Trinitarian life.
Soon the Lord will teach those who follow Him of the Spirit's
great work.
It is He, the Holy Spirit, the blessed Third Person of the
Trinity who will bring the Lord Jesus into the believer's life
by His own personal indwelling.
Father, Son, and Holy Spirit are all involved in the vital work
of saving sinners.
We will be taught by and about the Trinity.
And we will do well to listen.

*Heavenly Father, we thank You for bringing us into the reality
of Your own Trinitarian life.
We thank You for the glory of mutual indwelling.
Father, we praise You that by this miracle of salvation we will
always be in Jesus and Jesus will always be in us.
Amen*

June 15

**"As the living Father sent me, and I live because of the
Father, so whoever feeds on me, he also will
live because of me."
John 6:57**

The words will always remain strange in our hearing. But we
must remember that the context of the discussion is the manna
in the wilderness.
And that bread was to be eaten literally.
So Jesus is consistent in His use of literal language.
The manna in the wilderness pointed forward to something
just as the bread and cup on the Communion Table point back
to something.
That something is Someone.
That Someone is Jesus Christ.
He was the Desire of the Nations before His birth.
He is the Hope of the Church after His death.
His Resurrection Life is the believer's meat and drink.
It is the only sustenance heaven offers.
And it more than suffices.

Father, thank You that You are still sending heavenly manna.
We praise You that the manna You offer now is far greater
than the bread the generation of the Exodus fed upon.
Thank You for offering us Jesus who is the Bread of Life.
Amen

June 16

**"This is the bread that came down from heaven, not like
the bread the fathers ate, and died. Whoever
feeds on this bread will live forever."
John 6:58**

The Lord again makes reference to similarities with
a distinction.
He compares what God offered the generation of Moses
to what First Century Israel was being offered in Him.
In both cases the Bread was from heaven.
In both cases the source was from God.
In both cases there was only one Bread on offer.
But there was a distinction, and it was a distinction
already made.
They were dull of hearing, so He makes the point again.
The wilderness manna sustained for a day.
The Bread Jesus offered made alive forevermore.
This is His last reference to eating.
If he does not mean a literal chewing, swallowing, and
digesting what does He mean?
He told them in verse 40.
He means to behold the Son and to believe.
This is what brings eternal life.

*Heavenly Father, we thank You for sending the heavenly
manna to our generation as well.
We thank You that we have eaten His flesh and drunk
His blood.
We thank You that we have beheld the Son and we do
believe in Him.
We praise You for this eternal life we receive in His Name.
Amen*

June 17

Jesus said these things in the synagogue, as he taught at Capernaum. When many of his disciples heard it, they said, "This is a hard saying; who can listen to it?" But Jesus, knowing in himself that his disciples were grumbling about this, said to them, "Do you take offense at this?"
John 6:59-61

Everything Jesus said was true.
But not everything Jesus said was easy.
At this point, even the disciples sympathized with
the grumblers.
They proved it by grumbling themselves.
Capernaum was the town on the north bank of the Sea of
Galilee which became a kind of headquarters for the Lord.
This exchange took place at the Synagogue there.
Of course, His words were hard to understand.
So is all spiritual truth to the carnal mind.
But it may have been easier to understand than to accept.
Jesus asked if what He said caused them to stumble,
thereby proving:
1. He was a wise teacher who well understood
their difficulties.
2. He was a sympathetic teacher who gave them a
chance to air their grievances.
3. He was a patient teacher unwilling to run ahead
and leave them in a cloud of confusion.

*Heavenly Father, may Your Holy Spirit ever make our minds
nimble, our hearts receptive and our wills supple.
Deliver us from that self-regarding pride which dulls the
understanding and stiffens the neck.
Grant it Lord, for Christ's sake we ask it.
Amen*

**"Then what if you were to see the Son of Man
ascending to where he was before?"
John 6:62**

We suggested that the disciples who had begun to grumble
were struggling with understanding and acceptance.
But Jesus' words here suggest a more serious problem.
Some of the disciples may have wondered whether
Jesus even had the authority to teach the things He had
been disclosing.
His question posed a challenge.
Would His ascension, witnessed by those present, certify
His authority beyond all possibility of gainsaying?
Jesus claimed to have come down from heaven.
Would not His visible return to heaven serve to substantiate
that bold claim?
What proof could be more dramatic than that?

*Heavenly Father, make us always to take Jesus at His Word.
May we never allow our difficulty to subvert His authority.
Send Your Holy Spirit, please, to sustain our joyful submission
to our great Saviour's teaching and rule.
Amen*

**"It is the Spirit who gives life; the flesh is no help at all.
The words that I have spoken to you are spirit and life."
John 6:63**

There are few verses in the Bible more full of import and
possibility than the words we have before us.
Indeed, we may apply the lesson taught here to the
interpretation of the just-concluded teaching on eating and
drinking Christ's body and blood.
The suggestion is that mere physical acts are useless.
It is the spiritual operation which counts.
Further, we understand that Jesus' words, difficult as they may
have been to the disciples, are self-authenticating.
That is, they depend upon no greater authority than the
authority of the teacher who spoke them.
The words which Jesus used when He taught about
life were the very catalyst which brought life.
Jesus' teaching is attended by life itself.
His own words are the very media which make life possible.

Father we agree with the hymn-writer.
These are "beautiful words, wonderful words.
Wonderful words of Life."
Thank You that we have been granted access.
Thank You that we have heard the words which birthed faith
in our hearts.
And with faith, life.
Amen

"But there are some of you who do not believe."
John 6:64

From verse 41 onward Jesus was addressing His remarks
primarily to unbelievers.
From verse 60 disciples come into view.
The Lord makes it clear that all who are apparently disciples
are not actually disciples.
Judas is an obvious case in point, but the circle of Jesus'
hearers was likely wider than the Twelve.
Eating the manna in the wilderness did not guarantee
arrival in Canaan.
Eating the Bread at the communion table does not guarantee
arrival in heaven.
Even listening to the words of Jesus which are Spirit and Life
does not make salvation a sure prospect.
Many perish in the darkness.
Some perish in the light.
A person must believe the words of the Lord Jesus before He
can enter into Life.
There is this thing called "faith."
And faith is God's appointed instrumentality to bring the
sinner to forgiveness and everlasting fellowship with God.

*Heavenly Father, we know that we have become Your children
through faith in Your Son.*
*And we know that our faith is not due to our own wisdom
or virtue.*
*Thank You for the desire and power to receive Jesus Christ as
Saviour and Lord.*
Thank You for the gift of faith.
Thank You in Jesus' Name.
Amen

(For Jesus knew from the beginning who those were who did not believe, and who it was who would betray him.)
John 6:64

Unbelief in the generation of the Incarnation was a shocking phenomenon.
Israel in the First Century witnessed a stunning succession of infallible proofs.
Jesus commanded the very elements of nature.
He read the hearts and minds of men.
He exhibited uncanny knowledge of past and future events.
He cast out demons and diseases.
He spoke with profoundest wisdom as of the oracles of God.
And yet...
And yet there were still those who opposed Him to the death.
Shocking to us yes, but Jesus was not surprised.
Jesus knew all along.
He even knew that one would betray Him.

Heavenly Father, let us recognize that unbelief may lurk in our own hearts.
Cause us to doubt our doubts and believe our beliefs.
Grant unto us a robust faith, a growing faith and an enduring faith we pray.
In Christ's own Name we ask it.
Amen

And He said, "This is why I told you that no one can come to me unless it is granted him by the Father."
John 6:65

With slight variation here is the reiteration of
verses 37 and 44.
Simply put, salvation is due to God's decree,
not man's decision.
Salvation lies in the sphere of God's sovereignty
not man's will.
Are we called to decision?
Without doubt.
Is human will engaged when saving faith is exercised?
To be sure.
But the determinative cause lies on the divine side
not the human.
Perhaps Jesus invoked the theme of high sovereignty at this
point because the great crowd had begun to slip away.
His popularity appears to be ebbing.
Was His teaching on the difficult doctrine of eating and
drinking, Body and Blood premature?
Did He make a miscalculation?
Impossible!
Those drawn by the Father would come to the Son.
Those given Him by the Father would infallibly believe.
The issue belonged to God.

Heavenly Father, we have made so many poor decisions.
We have made many a wrong turn.
Often we embraced positions and policies which turned out
not for our good.
So we do rejoice all the more that in the matter of eternal
safety the critical authority belongs to You and not ourselves.
We trust You completely.
And we trust the provision You made for our salvation,
namely the death of the innocent substitute who died for
our guilty selves.
Even Jesus Christ our Lord.
Amen

**After this many of his disciples turned back
and no longer walked with him.
John 6:66**

Behold the serene confidence of the Gospel writers.
They do not hesitate to report even a circumstance which
could be used against Gospel claims.
Apparent defeats are entered into the divine record as
faithfully as actual victories.
The word "disciples" refers not to the Twelve, but to those
who thronged Jesus' ministry in the posture of students
and adherents.
The high doctrine which Jesus preached, His fierce
exactitude as to God's sovereignty in salvation, and the
necessity of partaking His own body and blood, proved
too much for many.
The Gospel makes distinctions between the many and the few.
Many may want salvation, but few accept it on God's
own terms.
To walk on with Jesus, to gratefully receive His teaching, that
is the mark of a Christian.
The "no longer" is ominous.
It suggests that the discipleship was apparent but not real.
A true believer may stray.
But a true believer returns.

*Heavenly Father, we thank You for the truth of Your
unflinching and unfailing Word.
We thank You for the sobriety this verse brings to us.
We take it as a warning.
For our proneness to wander Lord forgive us.
When we incline bring us back before we take one step away
from Your sheltering presence.
For Christ's sake we ask it.
Amen*

**So Jesus said to the twelve,
"Do you want to go away as well?"
John 6:67**

Jesus of Nazareth is fully man and fully God - not in relative
proportion but in a fullness mutual and absolute - two natures
in one Person.
Such is the verdict of Orthodoxy; such is the mystery
of Incarnation.
He came to this planet to show what perfect humanity should
have been and what exalted deity has always been.
Sometimes He functioned in the realm of deity; as when He
worked miracles and read minds.
Sometimes He exhibited true humanity; as when He wept and
when He died.
No words He ever spoke proved His manhood more
than these.
Here is the strange combination of divinity and pathos.
That the Son of God could love and be rejected.
That the Beautiful could be spurned by the unlovely.
It is a fact which ought to astonish and sadden.
Of course, He knew the answer before He asked the question.
Of course, He tested them that they might be proved.
But still we can't help but see here an early hint of that
final abandonment.
As if He were asking,
"My friends, my friends why would you want to forsake me?"

Heavenly Father, here is something which moves us deeply.
Thank You that Your Son became fully human while remaining
wholly divine.
Thank You that His humanity is on full display here.
Thank You that He risked abandonment by His friends so
that we would never risk abandonment by our God.
Thank You Lord, in Jesus' own Name.
Amen

**Simon Peter answered Him, "Lord to whom shall we go?
You have the words of eternal life…"
John 6:68**

Simon Peter often got it wrong.
Here he gets it right.
He zeroes in on the heart of the matter.
We hear the Psalmist's echo:
"Whom have I in heaven but Thee?"
It's not as if there are multiple Saviours.
Modern sensibilities demand that we regard one set of truth
claims as valid as another.
Classic pluralism insisted that the majority not force their
creed on the minority.
But to insist that contradictory statements are equally true
is not pluralism.
It is rather a species of nonsense.
If there is only one God why should it surprise us if there is
only one salvation?
Polytheists and atheists will understandably demur.
Let them.
They ought not to be coerced by believers.
But they will be judged by the one God who is there.

Heavenly Father, You are the only God there is.
Jesus is the only Son You sent.
Jesus is the only Saviour we have.
By this do we know the satisfaction of our souls.
In this we are comforted.
For this we are grateful.
For this we praise You because we could imagine
nothing better.
In Christ's Name.
Amen

**Jesus answered them, "Did I not choose you, the twelve?
And yet one of you is a devil."
John 6:70**

The reference of course is to Judas.
Judas did not take Jesus by surprise.
Jesus knew about Judas all along for the simple reason that
Jesus knew everything all along.
The question remains, "Why?"
The full answer can only be given by Jesus Himself.
Though it is all but impossible not to speculate.
Perhaps because Jesus holds out grace even to enemies.
Perhaps to show that those who side with the devil do not
perish for want of opportunity or information.
Perhaps to forewarn us about false brethren.
Perhaps to comfort us when we are betrayed.
Betrayal is bearable when it brings fellowship with
His own suffering.
As is the Master, so shall the servant be.

*Heavenly Father, we thank You for the infallible
foreknowledge of the Saviour.
We thank You that nothing surprised Him, least of
all our own sin and His own suffering.
We thank You that He trod the path charted for Him
knowing full well what it entailed.
Without His perfect knowledge but with His perfect
example may we do the same.
In Jesus' own Name.
Amen*

After this Jesus went about in Galilee.
He would not go about in Judea, because
the Jews were seeking to kill him.
John 7:1

The reference is terse and to the point.
But to infer that a negative racial characterization was
intended is to miss the point.
The author of these words was Jewish.
The other disciples were Jewish as well.
The Messiah they followed was a Jew, born in Judea,
grown to manhood in Galilee.
The references to Jews in this Gospel are never meant
to cast aspersions.
They rather designate the religious leaders of the nation.
It was the priestly caste who were endangered by Jesus'
preaching and so it was that caste who opposed Him
most violently.
It was their position and power which He threatened.
It was their teaching He exposed as false.
They had the most to lose in worldly terms and for them the
world was all that mattered.
He came from a different world.
He gave up that world to gain this one.
But this world is the one they wanted to hold on to.
For that reason, they were willing to kill Him.
For His part He was willing to die.

Heavenly Father, thank You that Your Son was willing to enter
our world though He knew it meant certain death for Him.
Thank You that He was never surprised by opposition.
We pray that Your Holy Spirit would identify those things we
wish to cling to in opposition to Jesus' plain teaching.
We pray that we could treasure what He says more than
what we hold.
We pray that we would yield to Him in everything for the
joyful privilege of service.
In Christ's own Name we ask it.
Amen

He would not go about in Judea,
because the Jews were seeking to kill him.
John 7:1

But He came to be killed.
That was the purpose of His coming.
That was the reason for His Incarnation.
He took on the mortality of flesh that He might prove His
mortality by dying.
Why then these evasions?
Because He would not die at the pleasure of His enemies.
He would rather die according to the will of His Father.
He would first finish the work He came to do.
No one would take His life from Him.
He would lay it down.

Father, we thank You for the intentionality of Your only
begotten Son.
We thank You that He lived with purpose.
We thank You that He died with resolve.
So sinners like ourselves could live pardoned forever.
In the place where death is a memory.
We thank You in His own wonderful Name.
Who is Christ our Lord.
Amen

**So his brothers said to him, "Leave here and go to Judea…
If you do these things, show yourself to the world." For not
even his brothers believed in him.**
John 7:3-5

Once again we note John's confidence.
He does not hesitate to report the unbelief of Jesus'
own family.
He could not have been unaware of the way the enemies
of Christ would seize upon the circumstance.
"Why should we be convinced, when those who know
Him best remain unconvinced?"
After the resurrection faith would come to Jesus' brothers.
His brother James would become a leader in the
Jerusalem Church.
He would also write the earliest of the New Testament books.
His brother Jude would write another short Epistle.
But at this moment His brothers only desired His absence.
Presumably they felt embarrassed by the greatest honor
in history.
Salvation does not come by way of human advantage.
Their advantage was the earliest and the highest.
Their conversion was the latest and the longest overdue.

*Heavenly Father, let us never despise our great advantages in
having this Jesus revealed to us.*
We know that millions perish without ever knowing His name.
Let us always draw nearer. Let us never wish Him elsewhere.
Thank You for Christ's willingness to show us anything at all.
*We remember those in Jerusalem were shown much and
believed little.*
Thank You that your Holy Spirit opened our eyes to see.
Thank You for the gift of faith.
We do believe.
And we want to see more.
In Christ's own Name we ask it.
Amen

June 30

**So Jesus said to them "My time has not yet come
but your time is always here."**
John 7:6

The Jerusalem festival date they urged upon Him was the
Feast of Tabernacles.
This was one of the three solemn appointments every Jewish
male was required to keep.
It is striking that Jesus tells his brothers the same thing He told
his mother in chapter two.
His time had not yet come.
He meant He must keep to his Father's schedule.
They, on the other hand, were not careful to live with
godly purpose.
They bore no burden of divine mission.
They could go to Jerusalem whenever they pleased.
They wanted Him to precipitate the defining crisis which
would establish His public identity once and for all.
He makes it clear that His presence in Jerusalem will be
determined according to heavenly counsels, not according
to their urging.
We have here a clear echo of His first recorded
words. (Luke 2:49)
Those words were spoken to His parents in the Temple
at age twelve.
They should not expect Him to go where they directed.
He would be about His Father's work.

*Merciful Father, we praise You that the plan You mapped out
for Your Son was for our benefit.
We thank You that He did not listen to His brothers.
We thank You that He listened to You so that we could become
His brothers and sisters by the Spirit's gracious working
in our lives.
Amen*

July 1

**The world cannot hate you, but it hates me because I
testify about it that its works are evil.**
John 7:7

Jesus is actually showing His brothers much grace.
At this point in time those brothers were clearly aligned on the
side of the world, not the Saviour.
The Lord could have just as well said, "The world cannot hate
you because you are of the world."
He chose to be more gentle than that.
What Jesus means is that His brothers would not court danger
by their presence in Jerusalem because there was nothing to
distinguish them from the rest of the crowd.
Jesus, on the other hand, provided a stark contrast not only to
the thronging worshipers but to the reputed leaders.
His teaching was different.
His life was different.
And his credibility was greater.
Therefore, He constituted a threat.
It was a threat His enemies were determined to eliminate.

Heavenly Father, we thank You that Your Son embraced the
risk of danger that we might abide eternally safe.
We thank You in His all-sufficient Name.
Jesus Christ our Lord.
Amen

"You go up to the feast. I am not going up to this feast, for my time has not yet fully come." ...But after his brothers had gone up to the feast, then he also went up...
John 7:8, 10

Did this qualify as deception?
Decidedly it did not.
Their meaning was "Go now."
His plan was to go later.
And when He arrived they would know He was there.
He would not hide it from them.
It would be difficult to hide in any case.
His fame was such that within hours everyone would know He had come to the feast.
We must remember that Jesus speaks to thoughts, not words.
Their meaning was "Go up to Jerusalem during this feast and present yourself for the purpose of decisive confrontation."
That is the meaning of "My time" and "The hour" in John's Gospel.
That moment would come at the Passover Feast not the Feast of Tabernacles.
And that time was not yet.

Heavenly Father, we thank You that Your Son was born "in the fullness of time." (Galatians 4:4)
We thank You that He died "at the right time." (Romans 5:6)
We praise You that it was all for us.
Joyfully, we place our times in Your hands.
In Jesus' Name.
Amen

July 3

But after his brothers had gone up to the feast, then he also went up, not publicly but in private. The Jews were looking for him at the feast, and saying, "Where is he?"
John 7:10-11

Privately He traveled but His presence would not remain
secret for long.
It wasn't merely that He would be noticed.
Even before His arrival He was being looked for.
Looking for Jesus in Jerusalem is a recurrent theme
in the Gospels.
The Magi searched at His birth.
His parents searched when He was age twelve.
But these more recent searchers bore Him no good will.
They searched for Him as Saul searched for David.
They did not have to wait for long.
Soon He would announce His presence in the most dramatic
of ways.

Heavenly Father, let us always seek Your Son for the
best of reasons.
That we may know Him.
That we may serve Him.
That we may worship Him for the rest of our days.
In Jesus' own Name we ask it.
Amen

And there was much muttering about him among the people. While some said, "He is a good man," others said, "No, he is leading the people astray."
John 7:12

We have before noted the serene confidence which allowed John to make known the views of those who opposed the Lord Jesus Christ.
"He leads the people astray..."
The argument sounds weak, but it fortified some to the point where they were ready to kill.
There is an irony here which would be comical were the issue not so life and death serious.
Jesus' opposers were desperate to suppress His claims.
John the Evangelist however does not hesitate to publish the theses of His enemies on the pages of the New Testament.
We might well ask "Astray from what?"
The precepts of the Law?
The preaching of the Prophets?
Decidedly not.
He was leading them out from under the bondage of false teachers and self-serving rulers.
But their masters were not going to let them go without a fight.

Heavenly Father, we thank You for the place your Son
has led us.
From guilt to pardon.
From darkness to light.
From bondage to the glorious freedom of the children of God.
For that we praise Your Name.
Amen

Yet for fear of the Jews no one spoke openly of him.
John 7:13

Fear takes the measure of a man.
Fear is a function of character.
Fear is a gauge of maturity.
If we know what someone fears we know something of what someone worships.
If fear were not important Scripture would not spend so many verses telling us not to be afraid.
The first warning from the mouth of God should have inspired a healthy fear of God on the part of our first parents.
It did not.
All the promises and assurances of God should inspire our confidence in the face of those who seek to shut our mouths and stifle our witness.
Too often we are mute.
Jews in the First Century were slow to hail Jesus in proportion to His true worth for fear of reprisals from their leaders.
Godliness is impossible without the proper allocation of fears.

Lord, make us to fear You as our Creator and our Judge.
Make us to fear nothing else.
Lord make us to love You as our Father and our Redeemer.
Make us to love nothing better.
Thank You that Jesus took our judgment.
He ingested the terror of wrath upon the cruel tree.
Thank You that because of His sacrifice You can indulge Your love for us forever.
Amen

**About the middle of the feast Jesus went up into the temple
and began teaching. The Jews therefore marveled,
saying, "How is it that this man has learning, when
he has never studied?"
John 7:14-15**

Jesus of Nazareth is a phenomenon who can be explained in
only one way.
If He is not the Son of God then He simply cannot be
accounted for.
Even unbelieving Jews of His own generation understood that.
What He taught was not handed down by older human
teachers, because what He taught was known to no
other human.
The Jews taught by tradition.
They cited opinions of earlier rabbis.
Jesus exhibited an electrifying authority which originated in
Himself, "But I say to you..."
God had no other Son.
There is no other explanation.

*Heavenly Father, thank You that 2000 years ago Your Son
came to this planet to teach.
We thank You that after His Ascension Your Spirit was sent so
that His teaching may continue.
Heavenly Father, ever teach us of this Jesus and by this Jesus
we plead.
In His own wonderful Name we ask it.
Amen*

**So Jesus answered them, "My teaching is
not mine, but his who sent me."
John 7:16**

The Jewish leaders longed desperately to categorize Him.
But He defied their stereotypes.
They could trace no identifiable tradition.
He belonged to no Rabbinical School.
There had never been a teacher like Jesus.
Nor could there ever be.
Among mortals Jesus stood alone.
But Jesus was no mere mortal, and His teaching was not
unconnected in an absolute sense.
We contended before that Jesus' authority originated
in Himself.
That is true in terms of a merely human frame of reference.
But everything Jesus said and did was thoroughly rooted in the
Commission given to Him by His Heavenly Father.
Jesus brought the teaching of the One who dictated the
Law to Moses.
Jesus accessed the same source who inspired the Hebrew
Poets and compelled the Hebrew Prophets.
Jesus spoke the very words of the Covenant God of Israel.
That was only natural.
Because Jesus was His only Son.

*Heavenly Father, we thank You that You spoke in many ways
and through many human instruments, especially through the
Holy Scriptures.
We thank You that You have spoken finally, decisively,
sufficiently and comprehensively through Your Son.
Thank You for sending Him to not only say who You are but to
show who You are.
Amen*

**"If anyone's will is to do God's will, he will know whether
the teaching is from God or whether I am
speaking on my own authority."
John 7:17**

This is the second time in John's Gospel (the earlier is
John 6:45) where the Son of Man discloses truth which bears
upon the question "What about those who have not heard?"
His presence in Jerusalem at the Feast sparked division
between those who believed He spoke for God, and those
who did not.
How would they make an accurate judgment?
Jesus, who not only knew all actuality but all contingencies
(the "if...then" cases), declared that the outcome would not
depend on the weighing of evidence alone.
It would depend on the willingness of the sinner to hear from
God at all.
The sad truth is we mostly want from God the ratification of
our own desires.
That is something the Lord Jesus did not come to give.

*Heavenly Father, thank You that we have "known of
the teaching."
Our knowledge, like our faith, is attributable solely to Your
gracious mercy in our lives.
For that we praise You.
And we thank You in Jesus' Name.
Amen*

July 9

"The one who speaks on his own authority seeks his own glory; but the one who seeks the glory of him who sent him is true, and in him there is no falsehood."
John 7:18

The words Jesus spoke were not self-originated.
He was given a commission from His Father.
He discharged the commission faithfully.
The Message from His Father to be delivered to the world was mostly about Himself.
The words the Father spoke about the Son constituted the highest form of praise.
When the ignorant heard those words, they charged the Lord Jesus with groundless self-exaltation.
In fact, it was exactly the opposite.
Jesus declared the truth and was charged with falsehood by men who were themselves consummate liars.
For the Son of God to subject Himself to public slander was itself an act of heroic humility.

Heavenly Father, we thank You that Your Son came to this poor planet to tell the truth about You and about Himself.
We thank You that He never sought His own glory.
He rather sought a way for us to know glory.
Thank You that He accomplished His mission.
May we glorify You with lives of gratitude for Him.
In His own Name we ask it.
Amen

"Has not Moses given you the law? Yet none of you keeps the law. Why do you seek to kill me?"
John 7:19

In a brief space, the Lord exposed two huge sins.
The first sin was hypocrisy.
His antagonists were perpetually parading their solidarity with Moses and the Law given through his hands.
But surely the most solemn among the laws given and the most important to keep was the law against killing.
But they reverenced that law not at all.
In fact, they hoped to break that law as soon as the opportunity presented itself.
The second sin was secrecy.
It was paramount that their agenda remain secret.
But nothing could be hid from His eyes.
It was not doctrinal purity they were after though they would have the public believe that was their chief concern.
What they wanted above all else was to murder the Son of God.

Heavenly Father, we know we are all guilty of hypocrisy in some form.
Lord deliver us.
We know that the strength of sin lies in secrecy.
Lord make us always to confess our sins early and often.
May we renounce the sin we confess.
And may we never go back to what we have renounced.
In Jesus' Name we ask it.
Amen

July 11

"Has not Moses given you the Law?
Yet none of you keeps the law."
John 7:19

By the First Century Israel's Law had been
thoroughly externalized.
It was easy to measure which sacrifices were made.
An observant worshiper might offer more than one
kind of animal.
The same worshiper might bring any number of sacrifices.
But Israel's God had declared, "I desire mercy (compassion)
and not sacrifice." (Hosea 6:6)
It was a simple thing to count the number of lambs brought
to the altar.
It was not so easy to quantify compassion.
We may be able to keep from stealing from our neighbor but
who can be sure he has loved his neighbor as himself?
Jesus more than any other rabbi emphasized the internal
spiritual reality which the Law demanded.
James reminds us that to break the Law at one point is to break
the whole Law.
For Jesus to accuse the religiously conceited of Law-breaking
was a provocation not easily forgotten.
He scarred their pride.
They chafed and conspired.
They would scar His body.

Heavenly Father, we have not kept Your Law.
Some of Your commands we have defied.
Some we have ignored.
Others we have obeyed only half-heartedly.
We thank You for sending One to do what we could not do and
would not do.
We thank You that He then paid the price for
our Law- breaking.
We thank You for Your Son Jesus.
Amen

The crowd answered, "You have a demon!
Who is seeking to kill you?"
John 7:20

By the crowd we understand the opposers among the leaders
attempting to influence the crowd.
They were most threatened by Jesus because He exhibited the
true authority they always claimed but never possessed.
Here they shout two lies in one verse.
The first lie is an audacious piece of hurled blasphemy.
Were the words not published in Holy Scripture they would be
too grievous to report.
Jesus spoke only the words His Father gave Him to say.
His utterance came by inspiration of the Holy Spirit.
To say that a man full of the God's Spirit is filled by a demon
is something very close to the unforgivable sin.
The second lie is hidden in the hypocrisy of
affected innocence.
"Who sought to kill Him?" they asked.
But the questioners knew the answer best of all.
They themselves were the aspiring killers.
And on a day not too distant they would succeed.

Heavenly Father, we are ashamed that such words were
spoken by our human race on our fallen planet.
Guard our lips we plead from anything which would ever
dishonor Your Son.
Let us cherish Him in our hearts, praise Him with our words
and exalt Him through our lives on every day You
grant us here.
We ask it in His Name, who is Jesus our Lord.
Amen

**Jesus answered them, "I did one work,
and you all marvel at it."
John 7:21**

The reference is to the healing of the lame man beside the
pool in Chapter 5.
Jesus does not mean "marvel" in a positive sense.
He is reproving not congratulating.
He means simply, "Why does it offend you so that I did a
good thing on the Sabbath?"
Adhering to a complex assortment of Sabbath restrictions
had become the test of public piety in First Century Israel.
Jesus refuses to play their game.
The sad state of affairs actually signaled the triumph of
legalism over true godliness.
He was perfectly obedient without being the least
bit legalistic.
He was moved by an impulse of love not law.
This brief text exhibits two instructive phenomena.
The creature is rebellious enough to be offended at
the works of God.
God is patient enough to allow it.

Heavenly Father, we yield You our hearts.
Fashion them according to Your pleasure.
Make us to love the things deemed lovely by You.
May we abhor that which offends You.
What we are asking is that You make us like Your Son Jesus.
In whose Name we pray.
Amen

July 14

**"... you circumcise a man on the Sabbath... are you angry
with me because on the Sabbath I made
a man's whole body well?"
John 7:22-23**

The law of God is consistent, coherent and wholesome.
The legalisms of men are erratic, contradictory
and destructive.
Legalism assumes that men are made for law and
not law for men.
Jesus understood that the whole purpose of the Law was
to promote the Good.
These critics would frustrate any good not authorized
by themselves.
The requirements of God are liberating.
The rules of men are burdensome.
The Sabbath was meant not only for the honor of God but also
for the health of women and men.
Jesus brought honor to God and health to women and men
every time He healed.
Jesus' opposers should have known that a man who could heal
God's people could also interpret God's Law.
But they knew nothing.
They were too full of themselves to know anything of God.

*Heavenly Father, may we not only know Your Law but may we
know what Your Law means and how it is to be applied.
May we understand Law by interpreting it through a grid of
grace and love.
May our application of Your truth always build up and never
break down.
For we ask it in Jesus' Name.
Amen*

July 15

**"Do not judge by appearances, but judge
with right judgment."**
John 7:24

The Lord Jesus here enlarges upon the counsel His Father
gave the Prophet Samuel as he examined the sons of Jesse.
Fallen creatures like ourselves are forever judging according
to outward appearance alone.
Unaided by grace we have not the capacity to do otherwise.
The Lord Jesus, on the other hand, is the searcher and
knower of hearts.
He SEES.
But how to obey this commandment?
Three things are needful.
First is the Law of God as the perfect standard.
Second, the Son of God as the perfect model.
Thirdly, the enabling presence of the Holy Spirit imparting
the competence for right judgment.
Of these three those who opposed Jesus recognized
only the first.
And for them it proved to be not nearly enough.

Heavenly Father, give us eyes to see thoroughly.
Grant us the understanding to judge rightly.
Make our hearts to deal mercifully.
That we might be like Your Son Jesus.
In whose Name we pray.
Amen

July 16

**Some of the people of Jerusalem therefore said, "Is not this
the man whom they seek to kill?"**
John 7:25

This is one of the greatest recorded questions in the Bible.
Indeed, this is one of the great questions in all of history.
It is a question full of sad ironies.
It is a question which bears witness to a crushing tragedy.
Think of it.
There once walked upon our planet a Man who could heal
the sick.
A Man who gave sight to the blind and made the lame to walk.
A Man who could restore dead children alive to their
grieving parents.
Who would want to kill a man like that?
The depravity of humankind is almost as astonishing as the
idea that God would become a man in the first place.
When God came into the Garden of Eden our first parents
hid, so He would not find them.
When the Son of God came to Israel they killed Him so He
could not pursue them.
It is a terrifying thing for an unrepentant sinner to face a
holy God.
For those sinners the murder of God's only Son became
an attractive option.
Here then is depravity on a grand scale.
Here is tragedy to make Israel weep.

Heavenly Father, we are a foul and fallen race.
We are complicit in the death of Your Son who died
for our sins.
Cleanse us from this guilt by His own blood.
Renew us to holiness by Your own grace.
For we ask it in His own Name.
Amen

"Is not this the man whom they seek to kill? And here he is, speaking openly, and they say nothing to him!"
John 7:25-26

EVEN THOUGH they try to kill Him, still His ministry is bold.
He may travel to the Festival by stealth, but He will not minister by stealth once He arrives.
EVEN THOUGH they want to kill Him, still they do nothing.
And why are we told this?
Chiefly for two reasons.
First, for the sake of the historical record.
This was the actual state of affairs in Jerusalem during the Feast.
Second, to contrast the courage of the Lord Jesus in the face of danger with the cowardice of those who conspired against His life.
They are plotting an epic crime.
The crime of the ages.
So far they cannot find the courage to transform wicked desires into wicked actions.
But their day will come.
The day which is more like midnight.

Heavenly Father, how we thank You for the boldness
of our Saviour.
Thank You for His private piety.
Thank You for His public preaching.
Make us to be bold like Him.
Bold as a lion without fear.
Make us to be innocent like Him.
Spotless as a lamb without blemish.
For Christ's own sake we ask it.
Amen

July 18

"Can it be that the authorities really know
that this is the Christ?"
John 7:26

The great crowd posed a great question.
The question was more complex than it appears on the surface.
They knew the leaders of their religion wanted to kill the
miracle worker from Nazareth.
So they were hard-put to account for His continued ministry
and free movement with such powerful forces against Him.
Could it be possible that their hesitation meant they were
revising their opinion?
Could He possibly be, after all, who He claimed to be?
There was ample weight to support the conclusion.
No physical infirmity was so great that He could not heal it.
No demonic hold was so strong that He could not break it.
No theological objection to what He taught was so compelling
that He could not refute it.
And the refutation came with astonishing wisdom compacted
into the merest brevity of words.
The multitudes adored Him.
At least some were convinced that He was the Davidic King.
It is also just possible that some among them knew Him to be
the Promised One and for that very reason they wished to
eliminate Him as a rival to their own prominence.
Such a thing is almost too wicked to imagine.
But such a thing proved really to be true.

Heavenly Father, thank You for the many convincing proofs.
Thank You for the fulfillment of the prophecies.
Thank You for the quality of the ministries.
Thank You for the gracious words and powerful deeds.
Thank You that He was indeed the Christ.
Thank You that He remains Israel's True King.
We look not for another.
When He comes it will be the same Jesus.
For that we praise You.
And say, Amen

July 19

"But we know where this man comes from, and when the Christ appears, no one will know where he comes from."
John 7:27

The Lord was opposed by a viciously intransigent form of unbelief.
The unbelief of First Century Judaism was fortified by a tissue of dogmatically held myths.
The first myth was that no one would know where the Messiah came from.
Scripture was clear that in terms of human origin He would come forth from Bethlehem.
The second myth was that they knew where He was from.
Most assuredly they did not.
Had they known they would have fallen down in worship.
As to His heavenly origin they had evidence aplenty.
To that they turned a blind and prideful eye.
There is no blindness like willful blindness.
No light in history shone brighter than His.
No blindness in history sank deeper than theirs.

Heavenly Father, thank You for sending Light through the Man Christ Jesus.
Thank You that Your Holy Spirit has shined that light on blind sinners like ourselves.
Thank You for giving us eyes to see.
Thank You for giving us a will to believe.
We wish to thank You forever
for heaven's greatest treasure.
Your Son
our Saviour
in whose Name we pray.
Amen

"But we know where this man comes from, and when the Christ appears, no one will know where he comes from."
John 7:27

This verse highlights a number of false assumptions on the part of Jesus' opponents.
But first we note again the calm security displayed by the Gospel writer.
He was not afraid to publicize the position of those who rejected Jesus' claims.
He had no hesitation to share reasoning which allegedly kept many from believing.
Of course, the stated reasons were not always the true reasons.
They were embracing a man-made tradition when they insisted no one would know where the Messiah was from.
The Prophet Micah was clear Messiah would arise from Bethlehem, King David's own city.
We can be sure that they knew where Jesus was born just as they knew the prophecy of Micah.
But it suited their purpose to emphasize the Lord's connection to Nazareth on some occasions while here insisting that His origins were mysterious.
Of course, His true origin was a mystery to them for the simple reason that they would not believe.
His origins were heavenly not earthly.
He had come forth from His Father.

Dear Father, we thank You that the Lord Jesus' heavenly origin is so overwhelmingly obvious.
We know no one ever spoke like Jesus.
We know that no one ever did the things which He did.
Thank You for giving us ears to hear and a heart to believe.
Thank You for His willingness to leave the high place He lived, to be born and to die in the low place we live.
Amen

So Jesus proclaimed, as he taught in the temple, "You know me, and you know where I come from. But I have not come of my own accord. He who sent me is true, and him you do not know."
John 7:28

Jesus knew better than they themselves what His enemies understood and what they did not understand.
It was not that proofs were lacking or that Jesus' credentials were inadequate.
The real problem was that these people simply did not know God.
The god they knew was man-made, a product of their own self-originated fantasies.
In brief, their god was an idol.
When Jesus' words and actions did not conform to their ideas, they rejected Him.
Not only did they not understand who Jesus was, they didn't understand themselves.
Idolaters seldom admit they are idolaters.

Heavenly Father, teach us to worship the God who made us, not the gods we have made.
Teach us to worship You, the one true God through Jesus Christ Your Son.
For we ask it in Jesus' Name.
Amen

"I know him, for I come from him, and he sent me."
John 7:29

Self-knowledge is a critically precious possession.
Without it we have no sure identity.
The evil one assaulted the Lord Jesus at the point of identity
from the beginning.
The last thing Jesus hears in Matthew 3 are the words of His
Father: "This is My beloved Son..."
The first thing He hears in Matthew 4 is the voice of the
tempter: "If you are the Son..." prove it on my terms.
Jesus knew who He was and whose He was.
Because He knew who He was, He knew what He had to do.
Because we also know who He is, we know who we are,
because we belong to Him.
Upon this our identity is established and our destiny
is secured.

Heavenly Father, we praise You for adopting us so that You
could give us a new name.
We praise You for causing us to be born again so You could
impart to us a new nature.
Thank You that both the name and the nature come to us
through Your Son.
By Your abiding grace and Your Spirit's power may our
identity as believers in Your Son be always manifest in our
words and in our walk.
For in Your Son's Name we ask it.
Amen

So they were seeking to arrest him, but no one laid a hand on him, because his hour had not yet come.
John 7:30

Here is displayed the mysterious interface between the sovereignty of God and the iniquity of man.
God will prove His love for sinners by sending His Son to die.
Sinners will prove their hatred of God by seeking Christ's death.
Their hands strained to bind his hands.
But their hands were bound by omnipotent restraint.
Jesus would not be spared indefinitely.
But neither would He be killed prematurely.
Jesus' hour was appointed and would soon approach.
His Father was Lord over the "what."
He was also sovereign over the "when."

Heavenly Father, thank You that You are Lord over days.
Thank You that the events of our lives were foreordained.
Thank You that the great event called salvation was planned.
Horrible as it was, we thank You that the hour came for Your Son to die on the cross.
Wonderful as it will be, we thank You that the hour will arrive for Your servants to arrive in heaven.
All because of Jesus.
Amen

**Yet many of the people believed in him. They said,
"When the Christ appears, will he do more signs
than this man has done?"**
John 7:31

Some threatened Him.
Others trusted Him.
It is a pattern which persists to this day.
This is the companion verse to verse 27.
There the Lord's Messianic claims were doubted because
of false assumptions about His origins.
Here His claims are validated because of His
miraculous works.
As the works were authentic, so must the claims be.
At the personal level - the level of healing and relief - the
level of blessing and provision, the works of Jesus of
Nazareth exceeded Messianic expectation.
The conclusion was inescapable.
He was either the Messiah or someone greater.

*Father, we thank You that though some pursued Him unto
death, others believed Him unto life.*
May we always trust and follow.
No matter what others say.
Amen

**...the chief priests and Pharisees sent
officers to arrest him.
John 7:32**

The Chief Priests and Pharisees were antagonists
in normal times.
The Priests ironically were the more secular.
The Pharisees prided themselves on religiosity.
The Priests believed the Romans should be accommodated.
The Pharisees regarded Roman occupation as an abomination.
But on this point, they were united:
Jesus of Nazareth was a menace to be neutralized.
There is always a constituency for the status quo.
And Jesus upset the status quo.
The Roman presence may have been inconvenient or
something worse.
But the rival factions had learned to cope.
The Nazarene was proving untamable.
He threatened an arrangement made comfortable enough.
So they sent officers to seize Him.
They had settled on a plan.
They would remove the threat permanently.

Heavenly Father, the enemies of Your Son are united.
So may His friends be.
May we be joyful and willing contributors in the service of the
Crucified and Risen King.
Make it to be so dear Lord.
In the Name of Your Son Jesus Christ.
Amen

**Jesus then said, "I will be with you a little longer, and then
I am going to him who sent me. You will seek me and you
will not find me. Where I am you cannot come." The Jews
said… "What does he mean by saying, 'You will seek
me and you will not find me,' and,
'Where I am you cannot come'?"
John 7:33-36**

The enemies of Christ sought to lay hands on Him.
He felt obliged to point out that the success of such a venture
was a matter beyond their control.
One day He would return to His Father.
One day He would be in a place they could not touch Him.
From first to last Jesus was always concerned to emphasize
that He was delivering Himself up.
No one would take Him unawares.
Indeed no one could take Him at all unless He allowed
Himself to be taken.
In terms of His being out of reach, of course He was speaking
about the ultimate reality.
In the near future He would allow them to take Him.
That was one of the purposes of the Incarnation.
God would allow His Son to come within killing distance
of Man.

*Heavenly Father, we thank You that Jesus was in
control of His own life and death.
We thank You that He would not allow Himself to be
taken before the appointed hour.
We thank You that when that hour came He gave
Himself willingly.
We praise You that He is now in a place His enemies
cannot touch Him.
We thank You that in that place, by Your side, He
makes intercession for us.
Amen*

July 27

**On the last day of the feast, the great day, Jesus stood up
and cried out, "If anyone thirsts, let him
come to me and drink."**
John 7:37

The Feast is sometimes called the Feast of Tabernacles,
and other times, the Feast of Booths.
It called to mind the transit huts of Israel in the desert.
The point was to emphasize the dependence of God's
people upon their God, and the sufficiency of God's provision.
The Eighth and last day was called The Great Day.
On that day water was poured out and the people
prayed for rain.
Thus, the correspondence of the Lord's words to the
visual spectacle.
The ritualists would have deemed His cry disruptive.
He disturbed the solemnity of their ceremony.
But He had to call attention to Himself.
For He Himself was the fulfillment of all Israel's feasts,
prophecies and hopes.
To miss that was to miss everything.

*Heavenly Father, we thank You that Jesus was willing to
die for us.*
*He was willing to put Himself in potentially embarrassing
positions for us.*
*We thank You that He was willing to upset the religious
decorum of Israel.*
All for the sake of our salvation.
Amen

July 28

**On the last day of the feast, the great day, Jesus stood up
and cried out, "If anyone thirsts, let him
come to me and drink."
John 7:37**

We are each of us pilgrims in transit after all.
Compared to where we will be, we dwell in huts.
We settle for less than we could have by faith.
We settle for less than we will have by grace.
We thirst for something more.
The Lord Jesus offered the same water to the orthodox
observers that He offered to the Samaritan outcast.
Both classes thirsted but only one class was aware of
their need.
If we are to have the water that cleanses we must apply to
Jesus definitively once for all.
If we are to have the water that refreshes we must apply to
Him daily.
There is no other water.
There is no other Fount.

*Heavenly Father, we thank You that Your Son thirsted on
the Cross.
We thank You that He gave up physical water and physical
life that He might give us spiritual water and spiritual life.
Show us how to always drink deeply from Him, who is our
everlasting Fount.
Amen*

**On the last day of the feast, the great day, Jesus stood up
and cried out, "If anyone thirsts, let him
come to me and drink."**
John 7:37

Jesus stationed Himself along the parade route and chose a
critical moment to cry out.
That moment would have been solemn.
The interruption would have been stark.
The drama would have been high.
By human standards what He did would have caused not only
consternation but embarrassment.
The Gospel is seldom decorous.
Jesus stood up and cried out.
Some who confess a willingness to die for the Faith are not
willing to be embarrassed for the Faith.
Jesus never shirked nor shrank.
He shouts to us as we go through the motions of our religious
or irreligious lives:
"Come to Me and drink ..."

*Heavenly Father, thank You for all that Jesus was
willing to do.
Thank You for all He achieved through the exercise of that
indomitable will.
Grant us we pray, a kindred will.
Make us available.
Make us able.
Make us to avail.
By Your Spirit's Power.
In Your Son's Name.
Amen*

**"Whoever believes in me, as the Scripture has said,
'Out of his heart will flow rivers of living water.'"
John 7:38**

John tells of the connection of water to Jesus' ministry in
every chapter up to now.
Water is necessary for life, for refreshment, for cleansing, for
irrigation, for navigation.
Water is necessary to quench fire.
The necessity of water in the physical world is the apt
correlative to what Jesus offers in the spiritual world.
We were given water for all things of practical purpose,
but we were also given water to teach us about many
things eternal.
All thirst, but few know that it is this Lord Jesus Christ they
thirst for.
The water Jesus gives, and the water Jesus alone gives, can
satisfy the thirst of a parched heart.
The water Jesus gives makes the dry land to flow
with rivers.
The one who drinks may also dispense.
That is what it means for rivers of living water to flow out
from the center of our being.
What a thought!
What a Saviour!

*Heavenly Father, all our spiritual thirsts have been quenched
by the bringer of this Heavenly Water.
May those of us who drink share freely.
That others who thirst may know and be satisfied.
In Jesus' Name we ask.
Amen*

July 31

The officers then came to the chief priests and Pharisees,
who said to them, "Why did you not bring him?"
The officers answered, "No one ever spoke like this man!"
John 7:45-46

Jesus had already proven that He would not die on anyone
else's schedule.
Nor could He be detained.
It was a terrifying thing for Jesus' enemies to know He
was at large.
More frightening still to know that armed officers would recoil
at His mere manner of speech.
Jesus' words carried an unprecedented potency.
Even among the unconverted His words repulsed armies and
frightened empires.
He spoke with authority.
Even the authority of Incarnate Deity.
No hint of fear or uncertainty could be detected in His speech
or His demeanor.
There was none like Him.
None before.
None after.

Heavenly Father, thank You for sending such a One.
The very earth under our feet is ennobled because He once
walked upon our planet.
We thank You that even unbelievers were awestruck.
Help us to proclaim this awe-inspiring Jesus with faithfulness.
That the unconverted might believe by His grace.
Amen

August 1

The Pharisees answered them, "Have you also been deceived? Have any of the authorities or the Pharisees believed in him?"
John 7:47-48

Here the enemies of Jesus offer a defense of their own
position which marks a new low in the history of
absurd reasoning.
Jesus offers substantiation of His claims by speech
unprecedented in terms of profundity.
Jesus offers substantiation of His claims by miracles
unparalleled in terms of impossibility.
The Pharisees argue that those claims must be bogus because
no one in their group had yet believed.
Against the mighty works of the Nazarene they entered the
plea of their own infallibility.
At the end they brought the same argument to Pilate.
Strikingly absent is any evidence of a true knowledge
of God.
Such knowledge leaves the sinner prostrate in the dust.
True knowledge of God is a powerful incentive for humility.
No wonder these "leaders" failed to recognize the Son of God.
They were too busy worshiping themselves.

Dear Heavenly Father, we are appalled at the reasons put
forward to justify unbelief.
Father, make us not to feel superior to these Pharisees lest we
fall into their own trap.
But we know we have worshiped a superior God because You
alone are God.
We know we have received the true Saviour because Jesus
alone is Your Son.
We are humbled that You would receive the worship of sinful
creatures like ourselves.
We are amazed He would ransom us with His own blood.
And so, we bow down and praise You.
We worship You in His holy Name.
Amen

August 2

**Nicodemus...said to them,
"Does our law judge a man without first giving him a
hearing and learning what he does?"
John 7:50-51**

We may be grateful that at least one sane voice was raised
against the madness.
We may thank God that not all Israel's leaders opposed
Israel's God.
Nicodemus was both Ruler and Pharisee.
The fact that he appealed for Jesus' body with Joseph of
Aramathea after the Crucifixion gives good hope that he had
come to faith.
Precisely when he believed we cannot say.
But here he raises a protest against the consensus of
the wicked.
He was likely a believer already.
The Chief Priests and Pharisees could not have known the
specific beliefs of all among their number.
It would not have mattered if they had known.
They would have lied anyway.

*Heavenly Father, guard us we pray against the arrogance
of unbelief.
We have no native faculty to protect us from error.
It is only by grace that we could ever learn truth.
Thank You for dispatching Your own Son to teach us truth.
Thank You for the truth that He laid down His own life
to save ours.
Amen*

August 3

They replied… "Search and see that no prophet
arises from Galilee."
John 7:52

Here one false argument is added to another.
Ignorance is joined to arrogance.
The two make a compatible pair as arrogance cannot be long
sustained without ignorance.
The Priests and Pharisees had not seen the obvious because
they had not weighed the evidence.
With eyes shut tight they bid others search.
They boasted of real scholarship and genuine piety.
They possessed neither.
Elijah and Elisha, mighty Prophets in an earlier age, were both
from that same general region of Northern Israel called Galilee
in Jesus' day.
Like Jesus they were opposed by rulers.
Like Jesus they stood for truth.
Jesus' career perfectly matched the biblical pattern
long established.
His message was that of a Prophet.
His ministry was that of a Priest.
His manner was that of a King.

Heavenly Father, how we thank You for this Jesus.
Thank You that He is Prophet, Priest and King for our sakes.
Thank You that, shockingly, He is also the Lamb
sacrificed for us.
To this spurned Prophet we give praise.
For this slain King we give thanks.
And we bow down.
Amen

August 4

**The scribes and the Pharisees brought a woman who had
been caught in adultery...they said to him, "Teacher, this
woman has been caught in the act of adultery."
...Jesus bent down and wrote
with his finger on the ground.
John 8:3-4, 6**

The vast majority of textual experts insist that this story did
not originate in this place in John's Gospel.
They offer sound evidence from the earliest Greek
manuscripts.
But even if they are right, that is no proof John did not write
the account.
Far less would it prove the event never took place.
CS Lewis was not only a Christian apologist but also one of
the world's great literary authorities.
He contends that there can be no doubt that this was an actual
event reported by an eye witness.
He argues thus because of the detail that Jesus wrote on
the ground.
We are not told what He wrote, why He wrote or what the
gesture meant.
At no time in the ancient world, argues Professor Lewis, did a
writer of fiction ever insert an uninterpreted detail.
Very common in modern literature, yes, but never done in the
imaginative literature of the past.
And so, we can be sure the thing really happened.
And so, we watch and wonder.
There is loving wisdom here.
There is matchless grace.
See now how the King of Mercy reigns.

*Heavenly Father, make us always to trust this sacred deposit
called Scripture.
May we rest upon these Truths, count upon them by faith,
prove them in application, and profit by them in memory.
For Christ's sake, the living Word we ask it.
Amen*

August 5

...they said to him, "Teacher..."
John 8:4

Here is play acting at its extreme.
Jesus' enemies, Scribes and Pharisees chief among them, in no
way regarded Jesus as their Teacher.
They were certain He was an impostor.
He must be an impostor because He exploded their most
cherished myths.
He especially exposed the myth of their superiority.
He performed mighty miracles which they could not begin
to duplicate.
He stood in the tradition of the Prophet Elijah.
They were as impotent as the Priests of Baal.
Here then is hypocrisy at its most rank.
Here then is deception at its most futile.
As if they could deceive HIM!
They tried to seduce by flattery, One who knew all men.
But He could not be taken in.
He was the infallible judge of all hearts.

Heavenly Father, deliver us from the sin of hypocrisy.
Let us approach You with an open and honest heart.
Especially since You already know our hearts.
Especially since You alone can mend our hearts.
Make the Lord Jesus to be our Teacher-Master truly.
For we come to You in His Name.
Amen

August 6

**"Now in the Law, Moses commanded us to stone such
women. So what do you say?" This they said to test him,
that they might have some charge to bring against him.
Jesus bent down and wrote with his finger on the ground.
John 8:5-6**

He appeared not to hear them, but of course He did hear.
He heard not only their words but their thoughts.
And He was well aware of their motives.
It is not without reason that we are told that He wrote upon
the ground.
It is not without reason that we are not told what it was
He wrote.
We know that the Law was originally graven on tablets of
stone by the finger of God.
We may wonder if anyone - disciple or detractor - drew near
to see what the writing was.
In this life we will never know what was written.
Heaven will doubtless reveal the mystery.
But we know what He said.
And His words would strike them like a bolt of lightning.

*Heavenly Father, we praise You for John's faithfulness to
record the words and deeds of your Incarnate Son.
We praise You for the Holy Spirit's faithfulness to inspire an
accurate record.
We thank You that by Your Providence these words have been
preserved for us.
We thank You that for now we have been told all we need
to know.
In Jesus' Name we thank You.
Amen*

> **...they said to him, "Teacher, this woman has**
> **been caught in the act of adultery.**
> **...Moses commanded us to stone such women.**
> **So what do you say?"**
> **This they said to test him...**
> **John 8:4-6**

They did not care what Jesus thought any more than they
cared what Moses wrote.
Though they maintained that they were the true interpreters
of Moses.
We might well ask if the woman was taken in the act, where
her partner was and why he was not arraigned.
Adultery is no solitary act, and so why was one alone
condemned and not two?
His foes hoped to set Him at variance with the Roman
authorities as they retained the right of capital sentence
for themselves.
They would trap Jesus into a choice which would either
offend the Jews or provoke the Romans.
They knew that God's Law was set aside by Romans.
What they did not know was that they opposed One who
would judge both Romans and Jews.
It was He alone who gave the Law.
It was He alone who kept the Law.
It was He alone who could temper Law with Mercy.

Heavenly Father, we thank You that Jesus kept the Law we
could not keep.
We thank You that He took the punishment He didn't deserve.
We thank You that He offered mercy we don't deserve.
For such a Saviour we offer praise.
For such a Saviour we give thanks.
Amen

August 8

...he stood up and said to them, "Let him who is without sin among you be the first to throw a stone at her."
John 8:7

The response is adroit.
But it is more than that.
To say the words are profound is to understate.
The words are unearthly, god-like and divine.
The words radiate power.
The words turn tables.
Here is truth to convict the hypocrite.
Here is mercy to woo the sinner.
Here is wisdom to confound God's enemies.
Here is a grace to fortify God's friends.
How could a man so young display insight so deep?
He must have been the Son of God.
No other explanation will do.

Father, thank You that Jesus unmasked the self-righteous.
Thank You that Jesus delivered sinners from death.
Thank You that He does the same today.
Amen

August 9

**And once more he bent down and wrote on the ground.
But when they heard it, they went away one by one,
beginning with the older ones, and Jesus was left alone
with the woman standing before him.**
John 8:8-9

Once more the text gives evidence of an eyewitness account.
We are told that the older left first.
Perhaps because longer memories surfaced more
numerous sins.
Perhaps because wide experience told them they
were beaten.
It is likely that Jesus referenced sin of the same kind that
brought the woman to judgment.
They may have been afraid that Jesus would name names and
cite instances.
One sure symptom of hypocrisy is a greater willingness to
claim mercy for self than for others.
The combined wisdom of religious scholarship was no match
for the Galilean carpenter.
They would kill her to trap Him.
But they were foiled.
They were tangled in their own snare.
He spoke as the solitary witness to truth.
And when He spoke His challengers retreated, to a man.
He was unconquerable.
He was incomparable.
God's own Son was what He was.

Lord, for the preservation of this text we thank You.
The uncommon wisdom of Jesus makes us marvel.
The depthless mercy of Jesus makes us adore.
We bow down, and we offer praise.
Amen

August 10

But when they heard it, they went away one by one…and Jesus was left alone with the woman standing before him.
John 8:9

This is the relic from Eden which abides.
It is that vestige which somehow survived the Fall.
From the center of our being it beckons.
It can be suppressed or ignored but it cannot go unnoticed.
We mean the mysterious thing called conscience.
It makes morality possible among unrenewed creatures.
It is evidence which shows we retain God's image.
Even these wretches eager to shame and to kill still
possessed a conscience.
Their conscience was buried under the weight of hypocrisy.
So Jesus went down deep.
His words pierced the stony shell where conscience
lay hidden.
Mighty words to accomplish a mighty thing.
Words to confront and convict.
Words to rescue and restore.

Father, we too are convicted by this same Jesus.
Teach us to speak His words.
Teach us to do His work.
We have no higher ambition.
Indeed, none is possible.
Amen

Jesus... said to her, "Woman, where are they? Has no one condemned you?" She said, "No one, Lord." And Jesus said, "Neither do I condemn you; go, and from now on sin no more."
John 8:10-11

What relief to escape the condemnation of the ungodly!
What encouragement to receive forgiveness from God's own Son!
By His own terms Jesus alone could have cast the first stone.
Just as He could have cast the last stone.
But He would not.
He alone was without sin.
He alone could extend grace.
And grace He did dispense in abundance.
His grace is sufficient for all who apply to Him for forgiveness.
Earlier He was found alone with the Woman of Samaria.
Now He was left alone with a woman taken in adultery.
The first woman left without water.
This second woman would leave without wounds.

Heavenly Father, we praise You for lavish grace offered in rich abundance.
We have sinned extravagantly and continually.
And so, we need extravagant grace and continual forgiveness.
Thank You Father, for giving us just that in Jesus your Son.
In whose Name we pray.
Amen

August 12

"...go, and from now on sin no more."
John 8:11

Law without grace deadens.
Grace without responsibility cheapens.
And the grace God provides is not cheap.
Grace is made possible by the payment of a price unutterable.
We mean the ransom by blood offered up by God's only
begotten Son.
The giver of grace was the purchaser of grace.
Grace exacts an obligation.
We are not ransomed for the sake of pardon alone.
Our redemption is meant to free us from sin's power as well
as sin's penalty.
We are freed so that we may sin no more.

Heavenly Father, how we thank You that grace removes
the penalty for past iniquity.
How we thank You that grace provides power for
future righteousness.
We offer praise for all we are offered in Christ Jesus
our Lord.
Amen

**Again Jesus spoke to them, saying, "I am the light of the
world. Whoever follows me will not walk in darkness..."
John 8:12**

Genesis 1 tells of light created.
John 8 tells of the Light uncreated.
John explores the theme as early as the fourth verse of
this Gospel.
In Him was life and that life was the light of men.
Those who study, experiment, and explore, seek to shed light
in spaces yet undiscovered.
Jesus came to reveal what God had always known.
We would never have discovered anything God had not
elected to reveal.
We see the light shining from Jesus' deeds and words.
That light is not derived.
It is rather self-originated.
It comes from no source but Himself.
Drawn to the light we follow.
And the more we follow the light, the more light we see.
It is one proof of the authenticity of the bold claim.

*Father, we have light enough to believe, light enough to
follow, light enough to rejoice.
Lord, evermore give us such light.
Thank You for the light which found us.
Thank You for the light we find in Christ Jesus our Lord.
Amen*

August 14

**"...Whoever follows me will not walk in darkness,
but will have the light of life."
John 8:12**

You don't have to be a Christian to know that something
is wrong.
Wars rage, poverty abounds, lies are the rule rather than
the exception.
Iniquity, in other words, abounds.
But understanding the cause of human iniquity without
light from the Creator of humankind is impossible.
Effecting a cure for the brokenness is harder still.
We need light from above.
The Old Testament teaches that the way of the wicked
is darkness.
The inspired writer goes on to imply that the wicked know
they stumble but over what, they know not. (Prov. 4:19)
We walk in darkness of course when we flee the Light.
It is sin - offense against God - which is the source of all ills.
And the root of sin is unbelief, trusting self over against
our Maker.
For the transgression of refusing to put ourselves in God's
hands the offended party (we mean God Himself) offers a
shocking remedy.
He sends His only Son within reach of the wicked.
That was one way the Light of God would shine.

*Heavenly Father, we were in darkness and You brought
us out.
Thank You for creating light so we could see the world.
Thank You for sending the One who is Light so we could
see heaven.
Thank you in Jesus' Name.
Amen*

August 15

**So the Pharisees said to him, "You are bearing witness
about yourself; your testimony is not true."**
John 8:13

Jesus is no less the Light of the world because He says so
Himself. There are Three Persons in the Godhead whose
testimony is unanimous and unvarying.
That being so, the witness of the Son can never be solitary or
exclusive. The combined testimony of the Prophets also lends
credence to Jesus' claims. Those claims are startling in their
immensity to be sure. To unbelieving ears they seem
extravagant, to a degree most extreme.
But Jesus had to tell the Truth, and that meant telling the Truth
about Himself. He had His Father's commission after all. He
would identify Himself in the world, offer Himself to the
world and give Himself for the world. The claims of the Lord
Jesus which sound exaggerated to human ears are actually
modest compared to the inexpressible reality.
Human speech can only describe God's greatness, it can never
measure it. Human speech is a finite thing though it has been
exalted to its highest degree by inspiration.
By inspiration it becomes the Word of God.
Jesus could not but speak God's Word.
He is the Light of the world.
That is the truth.
And it is the truth He came to tell.

*Heavenly Father, we thank You that Jesus never shrank from
speaking truth about Himself. He knew it would bring
condemnation from some. He knew it would bring salvation to
others. Thank You for saving us through the truth found in
Your Son Jesus.*
Amen

August 16

"You judge according to the flesh; I judge no one."
John 8:15

The meaning is this: "You size up others depending solely
upon the distorted perception of a fallen nature.
My own judgment labors under no such disadvantage.
You make your evaluations alone, unaided by no resource
outside yourself.
I make no independent judgment.
I call upon all the resources of the Eternal Godhead.
My Father is my Partner and My Guide.
Because He is infallible, so are My judgments infallible.
Your judgments are fleshly and from below.
My own are spiritual and from above.
Where you contradict Me you do necessarily err.
Because I only say what my Father says.
When you oppose Me you oppose God Himself."

*Heavenly Father, thank You for sending us a Saviour as true
and as infallible as Your Son.*
May we rush to His side.
*May we always be found on His side in all matters of
controversy and doubt.*
*For we ask it in His matchless Name
who is Christ the Lord.*
Amen

They said to him therefore, "Where is your Father?"
Jesus answered, "You know neither me nor my Father."
John 8:19

They might well ask, "Where is your Father?"
To be sure the Father was not to be found in their own
religious system.
It was a system twisted into a monstrosity unrecognizable as
the faith of Abraham and the Prophets.
On the last night of his biological life the Lord Jesus Christ
told one of His disciples, "He who has seen me has seen
the Father."
This band of interrogators were already hardened conspirators.
Soon they would become hardened killers.
They studied every aspect of Jesus' life and ministry and
noted no hint of the divine.
They perpetually missed the obvious and the overwhelming.
The reason is plain.
Their sin blinded them.
And their darkness was profound.

Heavenly Father, thank You for opening our eyes.
Thank You that through no virtue, desert, or merit of our own
You caused us to behold the light of a blazing glory.
Use us we pray.
Help us to help others to see the Light who made the world.
This Light who came into the world.
To save the souls of the blind.
Amen

August 18

**He said to them, "You are from below; I am from above.
You are of this world; I am not of this world."
John 8:23**

It is possible for a good person to account for wickedness.
But a wicked person can never account for goodness.
Unaided flesh cannot understand spirit nor can the earthly
understand the heavenly.
Lack of sufficient data is not the problem.
What is wanted is a full transformation of character.
The earthly aspect must take on the heavenly.
Jesus lived and died to make just such an apparently
impossible thing happen.
He came to die as a sinner condemned, so that sinners could
live as righteous people redeemed.
His incarnation, death, resurrection and ascension made the
way and lit the path between heaven and earth.
No one else could have done it.
No one else would have done it.
That was the work His Father gave Him to do.

*Heavenly Father, thank You that Your Son taught us, then He
showed us the character of those who are authentic subjects of
the Heavenly Kingdom.
He then took us in His arms and brought us personally into
that Kingdom.
All the while trailing blood.
All the while shedding grace.
Amen*

"...unless you believe that I am he you will die in your sins." So they said to him, "Who are you?" Jesus said to them, "Just what I have been telling you from the beginning."
John 8:24-25

Jesus of Nazareth claimed to be God's only Son and Earth's only Saviour.
Believing those claims is what we mean when we use the word "believer."
The unbelievers interrogating him were experts on those claims.
They did not ask the question out of curiosity.
They were baiting Him, hoping that a fresh iteration of His claims could provide more evidence to be used against Him.
He refused to repeat what they already knew.
He assured them that His story had not changed.
From the beginning, His testimony concerning Himself was consistent.
He warned them.
He was the only shelter God provided for sinners.
To die without that shelter would mean ruin for the soul.
They would forfeit something irreplaceable.
They would lose something they could never get back.

Heavenly Father, thank You for sending the Saviour into the world.
Thank You for giving us faith in the name of Jesus Christ the righteous.
Use us to bring others to faith we pray.
That they might not die in their sins.
Amen

"When you have lifted up the Son of Man, then you will know that I am he..."
John 8:28

Here the Lord Jesus speaks of His Cross.
He speaks *of* the cross, but He speaks *to* the Remnant.
By the Remnant we mean those Jews who would be converted
by that ultimate demonstration of God's love and God's
judgment at Calvary.
Alas they would number but a fraction of Israel's
total population.
But the Lord was also speaking of those who would know the
truth of His claims, but be hardened still more by the refusal to
admit error and receive forgiveness.
Christ's final agony was attended by a thick cluster of
public miracles: the darkness at noon, the rocks and veil both
rent, the multiple resurrections, and ultimately the Empty
Tomb all served to authenticate His claims.
When Peter charged the crowd with the murder of a Man
approved by God, they cried out "What shall we do?"
(Acts 2:37).
But others insisted the Disciples stole the body.
They insisted yes, but they knew it was a lie.
He was lifted up and the sky darkened.
It seemed midnight at midday.
They had to know it was Israel's own Messiah they had killed.

Heavenly Father, we thank You for the many great proofs of
Jesus' great claims.
We thank You that He troubled Himself to the point of torture
to make His claims believable.
We have seen this Jesus lifted high on the Cross.
We know He is your only Son and our only Saviour.
And so, we cry for pardon and blessing in His Name.
Amen

August 21

"...for I always do the things that are pleasing to him."
John 8:29

Jesus' claims are ultimate.
They express the upper limit of all we believe to be true
about God.
For one truly human to make such claims is beyond
all imagining.
Here we arrive at a kind of Everest.
Nothing exceeds this declaration in terms of
spiritual grandeur.
Indeed, it is the one achievement that redeemed creatures
should desire most.
We were never meant to share the essential attributes of
God's Son.
None of us will ever be the Light of the World or the Way
the Truth and the Life.
None of us is eternal and preexistent.
But by Death, Resurrection and the disposition of the Holy
Spirit we are offered a share of Christ's moral attributes.
We are offered the holiness without which no one can
see God.
And here Jesus gives one definition of what holiness is.
To always do those things that please the Father.
Think of it!
There could be no greater goal or aspiration.
Indeed, nothing greater can be conceived.

Heavenly Father, how we thank You that the Lord Jesus lived
to show us a Perfect Example.
We thank You too that He died to give us a Perfect Power.
May we follow His example.
May we draw on His power.
May we live for His approval.
That we may always do things pleasing to You.
Amen

So Jesus said to the Jews who had believed him, "If you abide in my word, you are truly my disciples..."
John 8:31

This is Jesus' way of saying, "It will not always be this easy. It's going to get rough."
For Jesus to distinguish a true disciple necessarily implies there are false disciples.
Few begin fewer continue.
A disciple follows and learns.
What is it we learn?
We learn to stay close and to finish.
We learn to be like the one we follow.
Anyone may draw close to Jesus with his feet while the heart is estranged at a distance.
In some seasons it may be materially or socially advantageous to be a Christian.
At such times false disciples abound.
But difficulties will inevitably arise.
And difficulty has a winnowing effect.
Difficulties DEFINE.
False disciples begin to fade.
True disciples keep to the path.
True disciples continue to follow.

Heavenly Father, we would be true disciples.
Thank You for sending Your Son.
Thank You for sending Your Spirit to bring us to Your Son.
May He keep us close.
We know the path leads through the cross.
We know the path leads us to a crown.
May we keep to the path.
May we meet at the throne.
For Christ's sake we ask it.
Amen

August 23

**"...you will know the truth, and
the truth will set you free."
John 8:32**

This is the one of the most thrilling sayings ever to fall from
the Saviour's lips.
It's neither easy nor necessarily wise to rate the perfections
Jesus offers when He speaks.
But this promise must rank high on any list of
memorable words.
Freedom is a beautiful word in any language.
Freedom is a precious possession for any nation.
It is the word once shouted at the barricades.
It is the goal most fought for in the battles.
It is a prize to die for.
Which is precisely what Jesus did.
He didn't die for His own freedom.
He was already free.
He died to end the slavery of the underserving.
He died to free us from sin and death.
This is truth.
And if we are to be free we must believe it.

*Heavenly Father, it is possible to grow comfortable
as slaves.
It is possible to savor the leeks and garlic of Egypt
more than the manna which falls in the desert.
Make us to loathe the slavery of sin.
Make us to relish the freedom which Jesus gives.
For Christ's own sake we ask it.
Amen*

August 24

**They answered him "We are offspring of Abraham and
have never been enslaved to anyone.
How is it that you say, 'You will become free'?"
John 8:33**

These Scribes and Pharisees held a slanderously low opinion
of Jesus Christ.
It was an opinion born of bigotry out of touch with the facts.
They held to a correspondingly exaggerated view of their own
national experience.
Their prejudice could only be sustained by distorting history
out of all recognition.
The Children of Israel were slaves in Egypt for nearly four
hundred years.
They were conquered and deported by Assyrians in the 8th
Century B.C. and conquered and deported by Babylonians in
the 6th Century B.C.
They were then conquered successively by Persians, Greeks,
Syrians, and Romans.
Far from being unconquered and free, Israel had been a
plaything of Empires for the better part of a thousand years.
No one can be wrong about Jesus Christ and right about
everything else.
To be wrong about the greatest and most obvious thing makes
it inevitable that other errors will follow.
They rejected Jesus' true claims while boasting falsely about
their own.

*Heavenly Father, may Your Spirit always grant us a true
estimation of Your Son.
We know that right belief about Him brings a blessedness
which abides through eternity.
We know that believing falsely about Him brings
irreparable woe.
So make us always to know Him accurately, savingly, and
joyfully, we pray.
In Christ's own Name we ask it.
Amen*

**Jesus answered them, "Truly, truly, I say to you, everyone
who practices sin is a slave to sin."
John 8:34**

The Lord Jesus refuses to score cheap debating-points off
those foolish enough to engage Him in argument.
He could have easily exploited the weakness of the absurd
contention that they had never been slaves. Instead of
referencing slavery in Egypt or captivity in Babylon (not to
mention the Roman occupation), the Lord took them to the
deeper and more urgent consideration.
There is irony here.
One of the reasons Jesus' ministry was rejected was because
the Messianic expectation centered on political deliverance.
It was spiritual deliverance the Lord came to offer.
The true Messiah was delivered over to judicial murder
because of a false expectation.
Here His opponents claim that they need no deliverance
because they know no captivity.
Jesus pointed out that they were held in the bondage of sin.
Pride is the king of sins.
The arrogance of their pride engendered the ignorance of
their history.
Jesus had come to offer them freedom from their perpetual
and settled habit of sinning against the Heavenly Father.

*Dear God, we thank You that we have been delivered from
sin's cruel bondage by the Sacrifice of Your Son.
We would be the willing and delighted servants of the One
who made us free.
Make it to be so now, we ask it in Christ's own Name.
Amen*

"The slave does not remain in the house forever; the son remains forever. So if the Son sets you free, you will be free indeed."
John 8:35-36

This is a deep saying and more than one implication flows from the Saviour's words.

The Scribes and Pharisees prided themselves on being Sons of the Kingdom.

Jesus insisted that in point of fact, they were slaves to sin.

Jesus, the true Son and Kingdom heir, had come to conquer sin and abolish sin's dire consequences, something far beyond the power of His opponents to accomplish.

Moreover, Paul likened what could be achieved by Law to Abraham's relationship with Hagar the slave girl. (Genesis 16, Galatians 4)

The Law was associated with Hagar and Ishmael, slavery, and the flesh.

A relationship to God by faith was associated with Isaac, the son of promise.

The Scribes and Pharisees, who were slaves to sin, could not free themselves (much less others) by administering more Law.

Jesus, the true Son of Promise, brings the true freedom which can only be accessed by faith.

The freedom the Son offers brings us into a loving relationship with God and delivers us from slavery forever.

This is freedom indeed.

Heavenly Father, thank You that the awful ransom price for our freedom was paid by Your Son.
We exult in the freedom Christ died to give us.
May we live as redeemed and grateful creatures.
And may we be done with the bondage of sin forever.
Amen

August 27

**"I know that you are offspring of Abraham; yet you seek
to kill me because my word finds no place in you."
John 8:37**

Here the Lord grants His enemies the biological connection to
Abraham by way of physical descent.
But He repudiates any claim of spiritual kinship.
Ishmael and Esau shared their grandfather's blood.
But they inherited no vestige of the great Patriarch's
noble character.
Here He unmasks their highest goal and fondest desire.
It was the liquidation of the Son of Man.
The Pharisees had no room for Christ's words because they
had no room for God.
For Jesus spoke nothing He had not heard from His Father.
His opposers were not animated by fear of God.
They were driven along with murderous intent by envy, hatred
and fear of displacement.
They worshiped idols of their own fashioning.
Idols which looked suspiciously like themselves.
The Lord Jesus bore no resemblance to Scribes
and Pharisees.
And so they esteemed Him not.

*Heavenly Father, we thank You that our Saviour
not only knew You perfectly but He knew men and
women thoroughly.
He knew our thoughts and motives.
He knew our words and actions.
He knew our hidden depths.
We thank You that He was never fooled by hypocrisy.
We thank You that He never ran from controversy.
We thank You that He knew the fullest extent of our iniquity.
And He saved us anyway.
Amen*

**Jesus answered them, "…you do what you
have heard from your father."
John 8:34, 38**

In this passage Jesus' diagnosis of those who oppose Him
takes a dramatic turn.
He declares those challenging Him to be children of the devil.
Are we to infer that the Lord Jesus is saying that all
unbelievers are Satan's children?
That would be reading too much into it.
It is certainly true that all unbelievers have been deceived in
one way or another and the devil is the author of deceit.
But the Lord reserves his harshest condemnation for those
who make themselves his implacable public enemies.
And these wretches qualify.
Momentarily they will ramp up their own condemnation and
shower him with the vilest abuse.
What does the devil do?
He accuses. That's what the word "devil" means.
He opposes. The word "Satan" means - adversary.
The men of John 8 are doing what the devil does for one
simple reason.
Like begets like.
They are his children.

*Heavenly Father, left to ourselves we would grow more and
more like the Evil one.
Thank You that You have not left us to ourselves.
Thank You that by adoption You gave us Your name.
Thank You that by the new birth You gave us Your nature.
Cause us we pray to become more like Yourself by making us
to walk by faith in Your Son.
For it is in His Name we ask it.
Even Jesus Christ our Lord.
Amen*

August 29

They answered him, "Abraham is our father."
Jesus said to them, "If you were Abraham's children,
you would be doing the works Abraham did..."
John 8:39

Flesh and blood guarantee precisely nothing.
It is spiritual kinship, the shared connection to God,
which is critical.
As to family pedigree the Scribes and Pharisees
were impeccable.
They were in fact Abraham's physical descendants.
But the position they occupied before God was at the opposite
pole from the great Patriarch.
According to Jesus it is character, not claims, which certify the
true family alliance.
If a man's deeds contradict his words we must always look to
the deeds as the true index of identity.
They were heirs to the true religion.
But they were "Esaus" who despised their inheritance.
They wandered far from the true faith.
Esau stopped short of killing Jacob.
These false brethren would stop at nothing.

Heavenly Father, thank You for making a way for us to
become Abraham's spiritual children by Your own
elective grace.
Thank You for granting us the character of great Abraham's
greater Son Jesus by the gracious work of your Holy Spirit.
May that same Spirit grant us a life lived up to the nobility of
our own heritage.
In Jesus' Name we ask it.
Amen

**"...but now you seek to kill me, a man who has told you
the truth that I heard from God. This is not what
Abraham did. You are doing the works your father did."
John 8:40-41**

At the beginning the Lord Jesus divulged the true family
lineage of Israel's religious leaders.
Now He reveals their true motive and goal.
Nothing is hid from Him.
The opposition of His enemies is final and ultimate.
It was bound to end this one way.
After they chose the side of their father the devil, it could not
be otherwise.
The devil's aim is death.
His method is deception.
First he deceives.
Then he kills.
In this case it was the Pharisees themselves who
were deceived.
And before they would die themselves they would kill others.
They would bring death to their nation by bringing death to
their nation's King.

*Heavenly Father, by faith in great Abraham's greater Son
make us to do the work of Abraham.
Don't let us believe a lie because we know that susceptibility
to a lie is a form of judgment.
Having learned the truth, may we be faithful in bringing the
truth to others.
By telling the truth, we pray that we would rescue many
from death.
We know that this is what the Lord Jesus did.
We know that this is what we want to do.
Amen*

**Jesus said... "You are doing the works your father did."
They said to him, "We were not born of sexual immorality.
We have one Father - even God."
John 8:39, 41**

Again Jesus explains their behavior by their spiritual ancestry.
They retort by descending to the lowest level recorded in New
Testament history. The low point of all histories.
It's easy to miss but important to remember that their words
were not primarily a defense. They assumed the offensive.
We are reluctant to spell out what they were implying because
it was blasphemous.
But since the accusation was admitted into Holy Scripture we
discreetly and reverently offer comment. The emphasis is on
the "we." The insinuation was "We are sure WE did not enter
the world because of illegitimacy but we have no such
assurance about YOU."
They meant it as the strongest form of insult. And so it was.
And though they may have aimed what they said at Jesus and
His mother only, they spewed the toxin over the full
Trinitarian range. They insulted the Heavenly Father who
commissioned the Son and sent Him into the world.
They insulted the Holy Spirit, who effected that mysterious
and chaste overshadowing upon the Virgin Mary.
It was that overshadowing which added humanity to divinity.
It was that overshadowing which brought God into the world.

*Heavenly Father, we are amazed by Your mercy.
We are filled with awe by the forbearance that held You back
from immediately destroying the planet upon which such
words could have been uttered.
We blush because we are human and these were human words
of insult hurled at Your impeccable and only begotten Son.
Forgive us O Lord for low words springing from low thoughts.
We would ever think high thoughts of Your Son.
We would always speak the noblest words to Your Son and
about Your Son. Because He is the noblest we have ever
encountered. He is the highest that could be conceived.
And so we praise Him. And so we pray.
Amen*

September 1

Jesus said to them, "If God were your Father, you would love me, for I came from God... I came not of my own accord, but he sent me."
John 8:42

The Lord's teaching at this place surfaces at least two critical truths.
First, no one's spiritual state can be reckoned by mere profession alone.
Anyone may say that he is a child of Abraham or a child of God.
That does not make it so.
There must be more.
A profession is evidence to be sure, but it is not sufficient evidence.
There must be a conformity of life consistent with the profession.
In other words what the professor does must substantiate what the professor says.
Second, when God saves He saves the whole person.
God does not give a believer the gift of faith while leaving him sterile with respect to the affections.
Anyone who truly believes in God the Father will truly reverence His Son.

Dear Gracious Heavenly Father, thank You for this precious gift of faith.
We do truly believe.
Make our performance to always match our profession.
Make our lives to adorn the doctrine we hold sacred.
That's the way it was with Jesus.
And that's what we wish it to be with ourselves.
For we pray in His Name.
Amen

> **"Why do you not understand what I say?...**
> **You are of your father the devil...**
> **But because I tell the truth, you do not believe me."**
> **John 8:43-45**

In this searing passage the only infallible physician of souls
renders a diagnosis.
The diagnosis is dire.
The diagnosis is devastating.
Here the Lord asks and answers his own question.
He asked that he might teach.
He asked that we might learn.
Why could Israel's self-exalting leaders not comprehend truths
so convincingly argued and so powerfully attested?
Arguments accompanied by miracles.
Why did they stubbornly resist the irresistible?
Because understanding and faith were no part of their nature.
Because they were children of the devil.
They had no more regard for truth than did their
spiritual father.
They rejected the Gospel because they loved the lie.

Gracious Father, we are blind.
You made us see.
We are by nature children of wrath.
You adopted us as Your own.
Thank You that Jesus was punished as if He were guilty
of our sins.
Thank You that we are rewarded as if we were possessed
of His righteousness.
Oh, our Father, we cannot imagine it.
But we do believe it.
In Christ's Name we praise.
Amen

**"Whoever is of God hears the words of God. The reason
why you do not hear them is that you are not of God."
John 8:47**

This is the fifth of five verses (3:21; 6:45; 7:17; 8:37) which
explode the myth that there are countless true God followers
in the world who yet will not follow Christ.
Christ speaks only what He hears from His Father.
His words therefore are the very words of God.
To reject His words is to reject God.
Those who come against Christ in this chapter claimed to
worship the God of Israel.
They did not.
They were painstakingly religious.
But it was not the religion spelled out in the
Hebrew Scriptures.
Who then did they worship?
They worshiped a God fashioned in their own image.
They adhered to a religion of their own devising.
In a word, they were idolaters.
They would have vehemently rejected the label.
But that's what they were nonetheless.

Heavenly Father, never allow us to pretend.
Never allow us to deceive ourselves into thinking we are
worshiping You when we are only pleasing ourselves.
Thank You for showing Your character and sharing Your
nature by sending Your only begotten Son to die in our place.
Thank you for Jesus.
In whose Name we pray.
Amen

September 4

**The Jews answered him, "Are we not right in saying that
you are a Samaritan and have a demon?"
John 8:48**

The words could not have been more hateful.
No condemnation of such words could be too severe.
Scripture tells us it is possible to grieve the Holy Spirit.
It must have grieved the Spirit of God to inspire the words to
be recorded. It would have grieved the Gospel author sorely to
write them down.
It is important to remind ourselves at this point, that the term
"Jews" is not a reference to race. John is himself a Jew.
He invariably refers to the prominent and representative
religious and political leaders of Israel as "the Jews."
A double insult is leveled by them in this instance.
Both Jesus' physical ancestry and His spiritual energy
are smeared.
The Samaritans were of mixed Gentile and Jewish heritage.
Once more they insulted the Lord's mother. While granting
that his mother may have been a Jew they were insinuating
that his father was not. The spiritual insult was clear enough.
They could not deny that Jesus' ministry exhibited a certain
supernatural power.
But they accounted for this by insisting that the power came
from the devil.
The Gospel writers were so firm in their commitment to report
what actually happened, that they did not shrink from offering
verbatim accounts of the vilest personal attacks upon the Lord.
It was the devil who animated the attackers.
And here lies the great irony.
Demons accused the Righteous of being demonic.

*Heavenly Father, may we always speak lovingly and
worshipfully of Your Son. It makes us want to worship Him
more because He took such shameful offenses on our behalf.
We know that even to our own day those offenses persist.
May we counter them with love, truth and Gospel power.
That the world may know about Jesus our Saviour and Lord.
And that knowing, they may believe.
Amen*

"...if anyone keeps my word, he will never see death."
John 8:51

Was there ever a promise more bold, more extravagant
than this?
It is a theme which will receive fuller elaboration at the grave
scene at Bethany.
To this point Christ startled by what He said about Himself.
Now He startles by the promises He makes to His followers.
For the Christ rejecter, death is a terminus, the place of
ultimate finality.
For the one who keeps Christ's word, death is a point
of transit.
For the believer death is a place he passes through, not a place
he passes to.
And the passage is so swift that it is a place he never sees.
It is a thing which approaches.
Then it is gone.

Heavenly Father, we thank You that death cannot touch us.
It is a vanquished thing, held at bay, then banished by Christ's
own blood and righteousness.
How we do praise You our Father, for the death of death in
the death of Christ.
Amen

"Now we know that you have a demon! Abraham died, as did the prophets, yet you say, 'If anyone keeps my word he will never taste death.'..."
John 8:52

Jesus spoke by the Holy Spirit.
These insisted He spoke by a demon.
Not all are agreed upon a definition of the unforgivable sin.
But we can be sure it looks something like this.
Jesus' words provoked a fresh round of blasphemy from
His enemies.
Jesus promised to protect His followers from death.
But Abraham and the Prophets died.
His enemies could not conceive that Jesus was greater than
Abraham and the Prophets.
But what if He were?
Abraham ascended from a lower place to a higher place.
Jesus came from the highest place to a lower place.
He would sink even lower in death.
Abraham and the Prophets had no choice but to die.
Jesus need not die as He had no sin.
But He chose to die to set prisoners free.
By His own death He would exempt His followers from
death's cruel bondage.
That's what He promised.
And that's what He did.

Heavenly Father, we are amazed that our Saviour persevered
through such insults.
We thank You that He died that we might live.
We praise You that He was bound that we might go free.
Amen

September 7

**"Are you greater than our father Abraham, who died?
And the prophets died!
Who do you make yourself out to be?"
John 8:53**

Jesus did not claim that He Himself would not see death.
He made the claim for His followers.
But the scoffers cross-examined Him as if He made the claim
for Himself.
For the second time in this Gospel someone asks Jesus
whether He is greater than one of the patriarchs. The woman
of Samaria asked Him if He were greater than Jacob.
But the questioners in this chapter are not sincere.
They didn't really want to know because they thought they
knew already. They refused any bit of evidence which did not
serve to confirm their prejudice, whether it was the power of
His miracles, the authority of His preaching or the wisdom of
His answers.
Everything He said and did pointed to who He claimed to be.
He was the Davidic King and the Desire of the Nations.
He was the Jewish Messiah and the Lamb of God who takes
away the sin of the world.
He was the fulfillment of the Law and the subject of
the Prophets. He was God's only Begotten Son.
That's who He made Himself out to be.
Because that's who He was.

*Heavenly Father, we thank You that the Lord Jesus never
exaggerated His claims.
Indeed, His claims could not be exaggerated because He is
Incarnate God in the highest.
And we thank You for opening our eyes and granting us the
grace to believe what He said about Himself.
In His own Name we thank You.
The Name of Jesus Christ our Lord.
Amen*

Jesus answered, "If I glorify myself, my glory is nothing. It is my Father who glorifies me, of whom you say, 'He is our God.' But you have not known him. I know him. ...and I keep his word."
John 8:54-55

Jesus knows that, not only to His enemies, but even in the hearing of any pious Jew unfamiliar with His words and works, what He says about Himself sounds like an outrageous boast.
He defends Himself by calling God as His witness.
He points out that if His testimony were uncorroborated by God it would be empty.
But His testimony is supported in heaven.
He came from heaven to bring heaven's message to earth.
If He did not say what God said He would be unfaithful; in fact, He would be a liar.
In bearing faithful witness the Lord Jesus not only identified Himself but He identified those who accused and opposed.
Jesus said what He said because He was bringing God's personal message to Israel and the world.
Those who attacked that message said what they said because they didn't know God.
They were of a different spirit.
They were of a lower world.

Heavenly Father, the words of Jesus find resonance in our hearts.
We believe this is Your doing.
We believe You put Your words in His mouth.
We believe You gave the gift of faith to our hearts.
For that we bless You.
And offer eternal praise.
Amen

September 9

**"Your father Abraham rejoiced that he would see my day.
He saw it and was glad."
John 8:56**

Saw Christ's day when?
During the generation of Abraham's biological life 2000 years
earlier no doubt.
Saw Christ's day how?
Abraham saw Christ's day in a vision.
When God appeared to Abraham we believe it was God the
Second Person Abraham saw.
We believe Abraham saw Jesus' day in promise.
God appeared to Abraham and promised that he would
be a blessing to all families.
The fulfillment was not exhausted by the birth of Isaac.
The fulfillment came through the birth of Jesus.
Abraham saw Jesus' day in the visitation.
When heavenly visitors stopped at Abraham's tent in
Genesis 18 we believe that two of the three were angels.
The third was the preincarnate Son of God.
The Scribes and Pharisees boasted of their connection
to Abraham.
But Jesus actually KNEW him.

*Heavenly Father, thank You for showing Your Son
to Abraham.
Thank You for sending Your Son into the world.
Thank You for showing Your Son to us in this Gospel.
We have seen Him, and we believe Him.
And we praise You for it.
Amen*

September 10

**So the Jews said to him, "You are not yet fifty years old,
and have you seen Abraham?"**
John 8:57

Because of this verse some have speculated that Jesus looked
older than his actual age.
He was a young man in his early 30s and yet they said that He
was not yet 50.
We simply infer that 50 was an easy round number for them
to mention.
We need not read anything more into it than that.
They doubtless congratulated themselves upon a common-
sense rejoinder to what they believed was an outrageous boast.
Little did they realize that the claim was true.
Their closed minds and bigoted rejection of everything Jesus
said made it impossible for them to comprehend the little
things, much less the larger things.
And the Lord Jesus was in the process of claiming much
larger things.
At this juncture He was about to make the largest claim of all.
After all, He was the Divine Logos who was in the beginning
with God.

*Heavenly Father, we praise You that Your Son took a real
human body and became a real human being.*
*We praise You that though He created time He subjected
Himself to the effects of time and exhibited the marks of age.*
*We are grateful that as Incarnate God he remembered events
which took place before His human birth.*
We thank you in Jesus' own Name.
Amen

September 11

**Jesus said to them, "Truly, truly I say to you,
before Abraham was, I am."
John 8:58**

The message of this Gospel is never hidden.
Jesus of Nazareth, the eternal Logos, is and always has been
undiminished deity.
The Son of God He is to be sure. But He is also God the Son.
The Gospel writer says this about Jesus in chapter 1 verse 1.
In this verse Jesus says it about Himself.
When Moses stood before the burning bush He asked God to
identify Himself by name.
Moses knew that the polytheistic Pharaoh would demand to
know the name of the God who commanded him to release the
Hebrew slaves.
God declared His name to be "I am."
Jesus here addresses three questions.
He is establishing the grounds upon which He could grant
immortality to His followers.
He is justifying His claim of personal intimacy with a
Patriarch who lived in the distant past.
And He is answering the question asked in verse 25.
They demanded to know who He was.
Well now He has told them.
His voice spoke to Moses from the flaming bush unconsumed.
He is none other than the Covenant God of Israel.
"I am" is His name.

*Heavenly Father, we praise You for all the great truths
Your Son revealed. Truths we could never have guessed at.
Truths we would never have discovered on our own.
He revealed our own nature to us as fallen creatures
and sinners.
He revealed Your own nature to us as Creator and Father.
Lord, we thank You that He revealed His own identity to us
as God the Redeemer.
We have believed His word and are saved by His Name.
For that we praise You forever.
Amen*

September 12

So they picked up stones to throw at him,
but Jesus hid himself...
John 8:59

The chapter begins with Jesus rescuing a woman from stoning.
The chapter ends with Jesus rescuing Himself.
They did not throw the stones to chase Him away.
They meant to kill Him.
In their minds he had spoken blasphemy.
He identified Himself with the ineffable name, a name too
holy to be uttered among the pious.
A name impossible to be appropriated even by angels.
And now a Galilean carpenter solemnly claimed the name
for His own.
By their reasoning punishment by death became a
sacred necessity.
In the near future He would accommodate them.
He would not always hide.
Soon He would stand still while they bound Him.
That was one of the chief reasons He came down
from Heaven.

Heavenly Father, we thank You for the courage and
candor of Jesus.
We know that Moses approached You in the bush.
And we know You approached us in the flesh through
your Son.
And so we praise You for the Incarnation.
In Jesus' own Name.
Amen

> **...he saw a man blind from birth.**
> **And his disciples asked him, "Rabbi, who sinned,**
> **this man or his parents...?"**
> **John 9:1-2**

It is a human thing to inquire after causes.
We are especially curious about the causes of suffering.
We hope that the more we learn the more we may be relieved.
It is a proper thing to submit questions to God who alone can
infallibly account for causes.
But it is never wise to limit God's options in the accounting.
The disciples gave Jesus two choices.
He chose neither.
We are finite creatures with limited understanding.
By nature we imagine a restricted number of possibilities.
God is the infinite Creator, boundless in knowledge and
unlimited in possibilities.
He knows all realities and contingencies.
God does not have to guess.
He need not imagine.
He simply knows.
Jesus the Son of God appeared to disclose the things of God.
His answer in this case would reach beyond the range of
human reckoning.

*Heavenly Father, we thank You that the Lord Jesus received
our questions and tolerated them.*
*We thank You that He answered the questions which
needed answering.*
*We ask You to stretch our minds and hearts to understand,
to accommodate and to love the answers He gave.*
We ask it in His own Name, who is Christ the Lord.
Amen

**"Rabbi, who sinned, this man or his parents,
that he was born blind?"
John 9:2**

There is something puzzling about the way the question
was framed.
The idea that a child may suffer for the transgressions of the
parents is common enough in Hebrew thought.
But in what sense could an unborn child have sinned?
Had the question come from Paul the Apostle, that great
theologian and systematizer of the Christian faith, it would not
surprise us.
It was Paul who outlined the deep doctrine of Original Sin, the
assertion that all Adam's descendants were represented by him
in such a way that all actually participated with him in the
first transgression.
It is not likely that such a degree of doctrinal sophistication
inspired the disciples' question.
Still less likely that the disciples allowed for a pre-existence
affording the possibility of sinning before birth.
Like the origin of sin itself, the reasoning behind the question
retains a certain mystery.

*Heavenly Father, we thank You that You know the answer to
all questions. We thank You that You will answer our
questions either in time or eternity. We are troubled by
questions touching upon the reason for suffering and the
extent of suffering. We thank You that Your Son entered into
our suffering. We thank You that He Himself is such a large
part of the answer. And we thank You in His Name.
Amen*

**Jesus answered, "It was not that this man sinned,
or his parents, but that the works of God
might be displayed in him."
John 9:3**

The suffering had something to do with God's glory. God's
work was made manifest - which amounts to His glory.
By human reckoning it sounds like a cruel trade off.
The man languished through sightless years so that in one
blazing moment others might see the glory of God displayed.
And what did they see?
They saw an impossible deliverance by an
improbable Deliverer.
They saw something they never before had seen.
Would the man have felt sufficient compensation for all
those days of darkness?
Only he can say.
But we may be confident that 2000 years of compensation
have more than sufficed for that man.
He was touched by Jesus in a moment on earth.
He will be with Jesus forever in glory.
God compensates His children in ways incomprehensible to
those outside the circle of suffering and mercy.

*Gracious Lord, we know that if we live long enough we will
see suffering.
We pray that we will see Your glory through the suffering and
in the suffering.
That Your works may be made manifest in us.
Through Christ the Deliverer we ask it.
Amen*

September 16

**.. he spit on the ground and made mud with the saliva.
Then he anointed the man's eyes with the mud...**
John 9:6

Nothing could be more counterintuitive than rubbing mud in a
man's eyes to help him see.
It was an act akin to Elijah's flooding the altar with water
before prayer set it ablaze.
We may speculate as to Jesus' motive in choosing the opposite
of human methodology to achieve the optimal divine result.
He may have wanted to show that the healing He wrought was
a thing wholly of super nature.
So He employed means dramatically opposed to
ordinary nature.
It may be that He wanted to demonstrate His entire mastery
over the created order.
He who originally invested the commonplaces of nature with
the properties we associate with them can in a moment invest
those same commonplaces with new and opposing properties.
Such is the creative power of His will.
It may be that He chose such an unlikely methodology to
render the miracle the more unforgettable.
For unforgettable it surely was.

*Gracious Father, thank You that there walked upon this planet
a man who could fashion the ordinary elements of nature into
extraordinary forces of mercy.*
Thank You that that man was Your only begotten Son.
*Thank You that by a deeper Mercy You made Him
our Saviour.*
By his own Name we pray.
Amen

September 17

**.. he spit on the ground and made mud with the saliva.
Then he anointed the man's eyes with the mud...
John 9:6**

We have noted that the methodology is counterintuitive.
By counterintuitive we mean that which is opposed to human
inclination and expectation.
Nearly everything Jesus said and did was counterintuitive.
We don't notice it because we are so familiar with the details
of His life and ministry.
Because we know the stories we expect Him to do the things
He says and does.
But we must stop to consider how shocking His words
and deeds were to the generation which originally heard
and witnessed.
At one level we should not be surprised.
He came to show us the Father. His Father once shrank an
army to win a battle.
That He is otherworldly is wholly consistent with His nature.
He is after all, from another world.

*Heavenly Father, we thank You that Jesus told us of
His divine origin.
We thank You too for manifest evidence of His
heavenly nature.
He would not live His life as an ordinary man.
Thank You that He came to impart to us that same
extraordinary life.
For we thank You in that same extraordinary Name.
The Name of Jesus.
Amen*

September 18

**Then he anointed the man's eyes with the mud and said to
him, "Go, wash in the pool of Siloam."
John 9:6-7**

The Lord Jesus had options to heal without delay or process.
He refused to exercise those options.
Means and instrumentality were often His chosen way.
A touch of mud and an act of obedience were the channels of
power in this case.
The man's obedience became an integral part of the miracle.
The blind man must do a certain thing in a certain place if he
is to finally see.
Jesus rarely worked in a vacuum.
He chose to display His power in the context of
human participation.
He set a goal and He assigned a role.
His instructions were clear.
In this way He dignifies us as partners.
He can do anything without us.
Yet He elects to accomplish much through us.
This is for us a form of exaltation.
This is for Him an act of mercy.

Heavenly Father, for such mercy and exaltation we bless You.
We thank You that Your Son stooped low to raise us high.
We thank You that He infused common things with
uncommon power.
We praise You that He healed the blind on this planet.
Make us like Him Heavenly Father.
Make us help others to see.
Amen

So he went and washed and came back seeing.
John 9:7

Seldom has so much matter been compacted into so few
words. He went and washed and came back seeing.
Savor the glory of it!
Rubbing mud in the eyes of the blind was not the only
counterintuitive thing the Saviour did.
He commanded the poor man to go away.
Such commands seem a consistent part of the divine habit.
God seems always to be sending His servants somewhere else,
to a place He will meet them, a place He will bless them, a
place He will use them.
This sending away is always for our own good as was the case
with the blind man.
He could have been insulted that mud was rubbed in his eyes.
He could have retorted, "You put it in; you wash it out."
He could have felt cruelly inconvenienced by being ordered to
another place.
How was he to know where the other place was?
He was, after all, blind.
Was there not a nearer place to wash?
He responded in none of these contrary ways.
He obeyed immediately and without questioning.
His was the obedience of faith.
And great was the reward of that faith.

Heavenly Father, may we listen for Your commands.
May we hasten to a swift obedience.
May we exercise a complete faith.
May we enjoy a comparable reward.
In Jesus' Name we ask.
Amen

**The neighbors and those who had seen him before as a
beggar were saying, "Is this not the man who used to sit
and beg?" ...Others said, "No, but he is like him."
John 9:8-9**

John is concerned to highlight that class of miracles he
calls signs.
Those miracles were of a public and irrefutable variety.
Miracles which made it impossible to account for apart from
an act of God.
The man was a beggar well known to the public.
The disability which forced him to beg was also well known.
His transformation was a sensation.
As with all sensations rumor abounded.
It was the goal of some to explain the thing away.
And so, the mistaken identity theory was noised abroad.
The power of darkness is formidable.
It deploys the plausible lie to oppose the obvious light.

*Heavenly Father, we thank You that Jesus did not perform
magic; He rather worked miracles.
We thank You that His miracles exhibited a divine power
which divested human sufferers of besetting weaknesses.
We thank You that there was evidence and testimony.
We thank You that there was consensus and agreement.
We believe the mighty acts of our Lord.
And we know that one day we will see the vindication
of our faith.
For this confidence we thank You our Father.
In Jesus' Name.
Amen*

September 21

**Now it was a Sabbath day when Jesus made the
mud and opened his eyes.
Some of the Pharisees said, "This man is not from God,
for he does not keep the Sabbath."
John 9:14, 16**

True religion is easily corrupted.
Corrupt religion is false religion.
False religion confuses worship and multiplies victims.
It preys upon true adherents.
Persecution is its stock in trade.
This was the case from the first generation when the brother
who worshiped falsely slew the brother who worshiped aright.
The Pharisees had confused themselves with the Almighty.
They could not imagine themselves to be mistaken because
God makes no mistakes.
By amendment and modification, by addition and alteration
they transformed the Law of Moses into a distortion of their
own creation.
When Jesus corrected their distortions, they judged Him a
transgressor impossible to forgive.
And so, they would arraign God's Son before their tribunal.
Israel's religion had been turned upside down.

*Heavenly Father, deliver us from the sin of
overestimating ourselves.
Make us to abide humbly in Your presence with a humility
which befits fallen creatures.
Help us to be severe in our estimation of self and charitable in
our regard for others.
Through Christ our Lord we ask it.
Amen*

**...the Jews had already agreed that if anyone should
confess Jesus to be Christ, he was to be
put out of the synagogue.
John 9:22**

This unholy opinion was not a rare delusion among the few.
They counseled together and came to an agreement.
Jesus could not possibly be the Christ.
He did not fit their specifications.
The synagogue culture proceeded determinedly
toward the abyss.
Those who confessed Jesus of Nazareth as the Jewish Messiah
were to be expelled from the Jewish synagogues.
It was not enough to reject Jesus.
Those who followed Him must be hounded and chased away.
Persecution is a metastatic sin.
It begins with social exclusion.
It progresses toward murder.
Within a generation the Christ-followers would
face martyrdom.
Again, we note the policy of Cain who slew his own brother.
His brother's offense?
He had chosen the way of true worship.

*Dear Lord, we ask in the Name of Jesus that You make us
true and authentic worshipers.
We know we court opposition.
Strengthen us for that battle we pray.
We thank You for the prospect of abiding in a noble tradition.
Let us then stand.
And let us exult in the joy of a commitment both faithful
and opposed.
We ask it for Christ's own sake.
Amen*

September 23

**So for the second time they called the man who had been
blind and said to him, "Give glory to God.
We know that this man is a sinner."
John 9:24**

The Pharisees were careful always to practice public piety.
Skilled in the art of religious talk, they classified Jesus as a
sinner who displeased God.
But they tread on dangerous ground.
They were forced to concede that something mighty
had happened.
Something which could be attributed to God alone.
Something which called for praise.
Still, Jesus must be a great sinner they reasoned.
He had to be a sinner because He was not of their caste.
He did not keep their rules.
Their arrogance, of course, was suffocating.
"We know..." they boasted.
So confident they were that they knew.
But they knew nothing.
And their ignorance was invincible.

*Heavenly Father, make us always aware of our great
tendency toward pride.
May Your Holy Spirit identify the Pharisee in each of
us and drive him out.
We confess our ignorance and long to be taught by You
moment by moment.
Teach us then we pray.
For Christ's sake we ask it.
Amen*

September 24

"...How did he open your eyes?"
He answered them, "I told you already, and you would not
listen...Do you also want to become his disciples?"
And they reviled him...
John 9:26-28

Though the play is a tragedy there is humor here.
Nothing could be more absurd or contrary than to suggest
that the Pharisees wanted to become Christ's disciples.
It could be that the question asked by the blind man was
merely naive.
But we doubt it.
It is more likely that the sarcasm was intentional and meant
to sting.
Whatever his intent he enraged them.
Their response was swift and harsh.
They reviled him.
They had to discredit him in any way they could.
He was, after all, proof against their thesis.
As such he was a threat.
And so, as an enemy he must be opposed.
But abuse is a burden far more happily borne than blindness.
It must have seemed a light thing for a man whose eyes had
been opened.
For now he could see.

Heavenly Father, thank You for opening our eyes.
Thank You for making it possible to see our sin, Your grace
and Christ's love.
Thank You that we see all those things in the Cross.
No amount of reviling could ever make us regret that.
In Christ's Name we thank You.
Amen

September 25

"We know that God has spoken to Moses, but as for this man, we do not know where he comes from."
John 9:29

God did speak to Moses.
In fact, He spoke to him about this very Jesus.
Moses wrote:
"The Lord your God will raise up for you a prophet like me from among you, from your brothers − it is to him you shall listen..." Deuteronomy 18:15
How did Moses know that?
He knew because God told him.
Who was Moses writing about?
He was writing about Jesus.
It was a fact the Pharisees refused to acknowledge.
To follow the evidence where it led was for them a dreadful option.
To concede the heavenly origin of this Healer was a prospect too painful for contemplation.
If Jesus brought a message from heaven, then their own message, so different from His own, must be from another place.
In the last chapter they tried to contrast Jesus with Abraham.
Here they use a similar strategy in the comparison to Moses.
But it was a strategy doomed to fail.
Jesus alone was the Son who could keep the promise made to Abraham.
Jesus alone could keep the Law given through Moses.
To Him the Law and the Prophets had pointed.
It was a truth overwhelmingly obvious.
It was the truth they called a lie.

Heavenly Father, before this Son of Abraham we bow down.
To this keeper of Moses' Law we offer praise.
We know who He is.
And we worship Him as Saviour and Lord.
Amen

September 26

The man answered, "Why, this is an amazing thing!
You do not know where he comes from,
and yet he opened my eyes."
John 9:30

Training is always desirable, but training is not
always necessary.
An untrained soldier may prove his worth on the battlefield
by his courage.
Courage and conviction more than compensate for
lack of training.
This soldier is newly enlisted.
The longer the debate lasts the more bold he becomes.
He sees their faces for the first time and he sees their
hypocrisy for the first time.
So he strikes like a tiger.
The battle is now fully joined.
He fights on the side of the Nazarene.
He is aflame with the logic which he wields as a weapon.
His points are artfully arranged but his audience is deaf.
The leaders of Israel have their heels dug in.
He will not penetrate their unyielding arrogance.
They are resolved to resist all evidence and entreaty.
The man born blind had been subjected to
blindness unwillingly.
But Israel's leaders relish the darkness.
Their blindness is self-induced.
Their commitment to unbelief is a settled thing.

Heavenly Father, we register once more our commitment to
Jesus our King.
Our love for Him and our loyalty to Him is also a
settled thing.
Thank You for making the choice easy by Your grace.
Left to ourselves we too would have loved the darkness.
But now we will love the One who is light.
And we love it that He has made us to see.
Amen

September 27

"Never since the world began has it been heard that anyone opened the eyes of a man born blind."
John 9:32

No one word can encapsulate all Jesus said or did.
Many words may approximate some fragment of the reality.
The assessment of the newly healed man calls forth one such word.
Unprecedented.
No one had ever healed one blind from birth.
But there never was one like Jesus of Nazareth.
There never could be such another again.
This was the problem the Jewish leaders stumbled over.
They believed their own categories to be exhaustive.
But this Jesus fit no entry in their catalog.
They regarded Him as their most recent threat.
But He was no mere novelty.
He was the Original.
He was the Logos.
He was in the beginning with God.

Heavenly Father, we thank You for the unique ministry
of our Saviour.
We know there never was another fully human and actually
divine in the same person.
We know that He is incomparable beyond all analogy.
Thank You for disclosing Yourself in Him.
We know we will never see all there is to see in His wondrous
person, His profound words and His amazing works.
Thank You for showing Him to us in Your Word. Thank You
that one day He will show Himself to us in Your heaven.
In His glorious Name we pray.
Amen

September 28

"If this man were not from God, he could do nothing."
John 9:33

The man born blind was not a theologian.
He had no formal religious training as far as we know.
Plus, he was one against the many.
Still he held his own against Israel's religious elite.
His inference was a simple one, but it was difficult to gainsay.
If Jesus were not of God He could do nothing.
And all over Judea, Samaria and Galilee Jesus was
doing plenty.
He did all that was required, lacking nothing.
For one born blind, the man saw much.
He weighed the evidence and rendered the verdict.
It took no unusual genius to plead the obvious.
Jesus Christ was a messenger sent from God.
The professional religionists resisted the irresistible.
Their eyes were closed to what the common people saw.
Jesus is Israel's own Messiah.
Jesus is God's only Son.

Heavenly Father, we thank You for manifest tokens which
substantiate bold claims.
We are amazed that those claims were resisted by many.
Root out in us sins which cause us to resist as well.
We want to honor Him.
We want to be the servants who do His bidding.
Grant it Father.
For Christ's sake we ask it.
Amen

September 29

**They answered him, "You were born in utter sin, and
would you teach us?" And they cast him out.**
John 9:34

They could not defeat his argument, so they attacked
his pedigree.
Having been vanquished by the beggar in public debate the
enemies of Jesus resort to personal attacks.
His mother's virtue was denied, and his legitimacy questioned.
They could not answer his challenges, but they could
insult him.
Plus, they could throw him out of the Synagogue.
Which is precisely what they meant to do.
That is the import of the words, "They cast him out."
The man by his faithful truth telling was made an outcast.
Their ancient cruelty, so devastating at the moment, clothed
him with an everlasting distinction.
It is a distinction we honor to the present day.
His expulsion was his promotion.
They were not worthy of his company in any case.
What fellowship has light with darkness after all?

*Heavenly Father, we thank You for the blind
man's faithfulness.*
*We thank You for the way his faithfulness then
benefits us today.*
We know that truth often requires a solitary demonstration.
*We know that standing for truth is costly and few are willing
to pay the price.*
We thank You for this man's sterling record.
We are the better equipped for having known it.
Amen

September 30

**Jesus heard that they had cast him out, and having found
him he said, "Do you believe in the Son of Man?"
John 9:35**

Jesus so often refers to Himself in the third person.
Why the third person?
The reasons may be varied.
Some reasons we may never discover.
But the majesty and dignity of Jesus' offices are hard to
capture in a personal pronoun.
He is the Son of Man.
He is the Son of God.
The Gospel is a profound thing with broad implications.
Conversion may be a complex thing psychologically, socially
and spiritually.
But realities broad and profound may be simply put.
Jesus' summary is remarkable for brevity.
He comes straight to the point.
Do you believe in the Son of Man?
The answer to that question matters supremely.
It is a matter of eternal life and eternal death.

*Heavenly Father, thank You for specific and
personal revelation.
Thank You that Your Son came to this planet and
asked searching questions vital to our future.
Thank You for sending the Holy Spirit to convict
us and convince us.
To make Him lovely to us.
Thank You that You made us believers.
We hear the question Jesus asks.
We answer, yes, a thousand times.
We believe in the Son of Man.
In fact, we pray in His Name.
Amen*

He said, "Lord, I believe," and he worshiped him.
John 9:38

This is that rare instance of specific worship offered
personally to the Incarnate God.
In the Gospels we see it first from the Magi who worshiped
the Infant Christ in Bethlehem.
The Magi came to worship when they brought Him gifts.
The healed man stayed to worship because he received gifts.
Not merely the gift of sight but also the gift of insight.
Much religious activity may pass for worship, but biblical
worship adheres to a high standard.
When Israel was called to worship they were commanded to
love God with the entire being: heart, soul, mind, strength.
Worship is the offering of the whole self to God in adoration.
Worship is the reflection of God's attributes back to Him
in praise.
Worship is the registration of availability to God.
This man did not learn the rudiments of worship by study.
He was inspired to worship by a spontaneous and
grateful affection.
Once we begin to understand what Christ has done for us we
begin to worship.
Worship, in fact, becomes inevitable.

Heavenly Father, if we worship we will pray.
And we want to offer ourselves to You in sincere
worship continually.
We know You have shown us far more than the Lord Jesus
showed that man.
One thing You have shown us is the worship of that
once-blind man.
May we become more worshipful by consistent practice.
May we worship according to biblical pattern with a
spiritual motive.
For Christ's sake we do ask it.
Amen

October 2

Some of the Pharisees...said to him, "Are we also blind?"
John 9:40

The question was far more likely to be rhetorical than sincere.
That a Pharisee could overlook something was a thought
which occurred to no Pharisee.
Still less would it occur that they could not see because they
were blind.
Their system accounted for everything.
Little wonder that their posture was one of perpetual
self-congratulation.
But their system could not account for Jesus.
He was the monumental exception.
If their traditions and calculations were correct He could be
nothing more than an upstart and an impostor.
But their calculations were not correct.
The Messiah God sent was someone far different from the
Messiah they wanted and expected.
We will truly worship when we turn aside from what we wish
to see and fix our eyes upon what God is showing us.
Until we see that, we will see nothing at all.

Heavenly Father, thank You for sending Your Spirit to
open our eyes.
We would never have seen Jesus had you not revealed
Him to us.
To us He is lovely.
To us He is essential.
Left to ourselves we would have seen nothing.
But You have made us wise unto salvation.
And for that we praise You.
In Jesus' own Name.
Amen

October 3

Jesus said to them, "If you were blind, you would have no guilt; but now that you say, 'We see,' your guilt remains."
John 9:41

No one will be condemned over something he never knew.
It is not darkness which brings us to judgment.
It is rather rejecting light which brings us
under condemnation.
Even those who live and die beyond the pale of Gospel
witness have light. (Romans 1)
They have the light of nature which shows the universe to be
governed by something enormously powerful.
They have the light of conscience which shows that we are
judged by Someone ineffably righteous.
Those lights are enough to convict but not enough to convert.
Those who grope under lesser lights will be brought to less
severe judgments.
It is only the special revelation of God's Word that can
convert the soul unto salvation.
Those who see by that light enjoy a special privilege.
They also court a special danger.
To reject a privilege so high is to sustain the greatest guilt
of all.
That sin, the Pharisees committed enthusiastically and with
genuine relish.

Heavenly Father, how we thank You for the light of
Your Word.
How we thank You for sure and certain knowledge of our
Saviour Jesus.
We know that to whom much is entrusted much is expected.
May we render You a stewardship proportionate to privilege.
In Jesus' wonderful Name we ask it.
Amen

October 4

"...he who does not enter the sheepfold by the door but
climbs in by another way, that man is
a thief and a robber."
John 10:1

There is more than one competing voice clamoring to
be heard.
Many in their turn offer some version of salvation.
Since they offer different solutions by different paths
they cannot all be right.
Somebody is mistaken.
Or somebody is lying.
How are we to recognize the One Authentic Voice?
Scripture is emphatic that there is one path which leads home.
One path which we discover through One Shepherd who goes
before and beckons.
All others are by-paths which lead to destruction.
The great task is not to find the true path but to trust the
true Shepherd.
His identity is well known.
His human name is Jesus.

Heavenly Father, we thank You that we have been led to the
true Shepherd.
We thank You that we have been led by the true Shepherd.
Cause us by Your grace always to hearken.
We know that because of Him we are on the true path.
We know that by Your grace we will soon be truly home.
Amen

October 5

"But he who enters by the door is the shepherd of the sheep...The sheep hear his voice, and he calls his own sheep by name and leads them out."
John 10:2-3

Israel was from the beginning the chosen flock of God.
Jacob and his sons were herdsmen, but they were also themselves sheep, belonging to the great Shepherd-God who protected, provided and guided.
Jesus, God's own Son, was the ultimate Shepherd of Israel.
He was great Jacob's greater Son.
All that the Law, the oracles, and the Prophets did for Israel would be done by Him and more.
Indeed, the Law and Prophets pointed to Him and were fulfilled in Him.
The gate and the way are emblematic of the truth God disclosed to His people.
Truth about sin and righteousness, truth about the world and the devil, truth about God and ourselves, was never self-evident.
True doctrine was never a thing which could be guessed at or worked out by human ingenuity.
Fallen creatures were always in need of a guide - someone who would lead them safely to the truth.
God was faithful to send such a Shepherd.

Heavenly Father, thank You that the True Shepherd knows our name.
Thank You that He called our name and changed our nature.
Thank you for teaching us His Name.
The Name in which we pray.
The Name of Jesus.
Amen

October 6

**"...he calls his own sheep by name ...and the sheep follow
him, for they know his voice."
John 10:3-4**

There is a mutuality here which is wonderful.
It is a mutuality celebrated already in the Hebrew Scriptures.
I am my Beloved's and He is mine.
His banner over me is love.
That is what the Old Testament says.
But it is also a theme continually celebrated in the
New Testament.
I belong to the Saviour.
My Saviour belongs to me.
He is MY Saviour.
I am HIS child.
He is MY King.
And I am HIS adoring subject.
He calls only the sheep who belong to Him.
The sheep respond only to their owner and true Shepherd.
The whole arrangement is supernatural to the core.
It is a wonder wrought by the power of God.

*Heavenly Father, thank You that we are new creations by
virtue of Your merciful grace.*
*Thank You that You have adopted us by virtue of Your
overruling love.*
We are Yours completely.
*And we want by a grateful obedience to manifest the practical
out-working of that privileged status.*
For Christ's sake we ask it.
Amen

"...the shepherd of the sheep...The sheep hear his voice... the sheep follow him, for they know his voice. A stranger they will not follow..."
John 10:2-5

Here is a sequence both instructive and profound.
And it explains much.
Low as a sheep may be in the natural order of things there is something within him which knows.
He knows the difference between a true and false Shepherd.
What is true in animal existence is truer still in the higher spiritual plane.
The True Shepherd calls with the authentic voice of God speaking true words about God.
How can a sheep discern?
Not because sheep are clever.
Only because the God who calls from without also works a work from within.
He has given the sheep a new nature.
He has made the sheep His own.
The heart of the true sheep recognizes the voice of the true Shepherd.
It is a work wrought by the Sovereign God.

Gracious Father, thank You for implanting in us a new nature.
Thank You that the new nature knows the true voice.
Thank You for sending Your Son to call out to us.
We praise You for the grace to hear and to follow.
In the name of our Shepherd Jesus we pray.
Amen

This figure of speech Jesus used with them, but they did not understand what he was saying to them.
John 10:6

It is a striking thing that nearly 2000 years ago the
Gospel writer alerted readers to be careful to note the
use of metaphors.
John will sometimes editorialize for the sake of clarity.
He is a writer inspired and controlled by the Holy Spirit,
who is the ultimate editor.
He was also an eyewitness.
How much he understood at the moment we do not know.
That he understood by the time of the writing is clear enough.
It is also clear that the Lord often used figures of speech.
We do not always interpret the Bible literally.
It is better to say that we always interpret Scripture plainly
since both Testaments are replete with figures of speech.
Jesus did not expect any mature listener to think He meant
that His followers were wooly animals who could not fend
for themselves.
But the analogy is entirely apt.
There are some notable correspondences between ourselves
and sheep.
And not all of them are flattering.

Heavenly Father, thank You that the biblical writers took
pains when they wrote to call our attention to the needful.
Help us to take pains as we study that we may gain all the
profit You intended for our good.
For Christ's sake we ask it.
Amen

October 9

**So Jesus again said to them, "…I am the
door of the sheep."
John 10:7**

John declared that the Lord employed figures of speech.
He referred to His followers (and we may apply the
reference to the church) as "sheep."
Now He calls Himself the "door."
It was not true in the literal sense of course, but it was true in
the sense of practical application.
In the Ancient Near East most sheep-folds were simple,
inexpensive arrangements.
They were often constructed in a circular configuration with
an empty space serving for the door.
Inside that space the shepherd would station himself.
They could not get out, and the predator could not get in,
without going over the shepherd.
The Door PROVIDED an entrance into the haven within.
The Door PROTECTED from any dangers without.
Jesus of course does both.
He grants entry into the place of protected rest.
He places Himself between danger and His sheep.
He is the door of the sheep.

*Heavenly Father, we thank You for bringing us to the place of
rest through Your Son.
We thank You for protecting us in a place of safety by
Your Son.
He is everything to us.
Make us in everything to be faithful to Him.
In Christ's own Name we ask it.
Amen*

**"I am the door. If anyone enters by me, he will be saved
and will go in and out and find pasture."
John 10:9**

"I am the door."
The most recent "I am" declaration is here repeated.
The sheep-fold is a place of protection not restriction.
The Christian life is not a prison.
It is rather the way to find true freedom.
In Jacob's vision he saw angels entering and exiting heaven by
something like a ladder.
At the end of John 1 the Lord linked Himself with that ladder.
In this chapter He declares that He is the door to salvation.
Jesus is emphatically the way to heaven.
Jesus is the way in to that state Christians call salvation.
Since salvation is the ultimate benefit, knowing Christ is the
ultimate blessedness.
Sheep go into the fold via the door to rest in safety.
Sheep go out by the door to seek pasture.
God's true sheep go in and out by the door called "Christ."

Heavenly Father, all we know about Your Son is wonderful.
And we want to know so much more.
We love this picture of Christ as the door.
Thank You for taking us through the door called Christ to the
place called salvation.
Every day we discover richer pasture and deeper meaning
through the one who is our Shepherd and Saviour.
Amen

October 11

"I came that they may have life and have it abundantly."
John 10:10

To be sure every word handed down from above is a treasure.
But words which disclose purpose are especially to be prized.
God's only Son became earth's only Saviour for
many reasons.
Here the Lord supplies one of the reasons for His appearing.
Of course, He came to die.
Humans die; God cannot die.
Jesus took on our humanity that He might take on
our mortality.
But He took on our death that we might take up His life.
He came that we might have life.
And not just any life.
In another place Jesus tells us that life does not consist in an
abundance of possessions.
When He speaks of abundance here, He makes no reference
to the material.
He speaks rather of the abundance and quality of the spiritual
life which is the joy of the saints in heaven.
He died to give us His very own resurrection life.
That means something far above the biological.
It means a life indestructible and unending.
He died to give a life which cannot die.

*Heavenly Father, we have tasted this abundant life and we
have been abundantly satisfied.*
*We know that there is more to come, and we know that it will
be wonderful.*
*We praise You that Your Son gave up His own life that
we might gain the abundant life only He can give.*
It's a gift that never ceases to overwhelm us.
And so, we never cease to thank You.
Amen

October 12

"I came that they may have life and have it abundantly."
John 10:10

Life is a divine invention.
God thought of it.
He created it.
He sustains it.
He governs it.
Death, though universal, is the aberration.
Death is the deviation from the original arrangement.
What is the abundant life?
It means the green pasture.
It means the still water.
It means what all people need and what the wisest
people want.
It means the best gifts from the best Shepherd.
But it also means something we have not yet
fully experienced.
Indeed, it means something we can scarcely imagine.
Here we see through a glass darkly.
Eye has not seen, and ear has not heard; it has not even
entered into the human heart what that abundance will
be in its fullness.
But we have the foretaste.
And for now, the sweetness suffices.

Father, may we know the fullness of what Jesus
came to give.
That the Son of Man might have the recompense
of His wounds.
Amen

October 13

"I came that they may have life and have it abundantly."
John 10:10

Our first parents were evicted from the place of
first abundance.
Their sin cost them their Eden.
God would not endure their presence in the place
originally prepared.
They left the place of abundance and life on the inside to
enter the place of difficulty and death on the outside.
But they didn't leave everything behind.
When they evacuated they took with them this promise:
the Seed of the woman would crush the head of the serpent.
God would also send His Son to the place of exile.
In the Garden of Eden, God issued a warning.
In the place of exile, God delivered a Promise.
It was a promise about life.
The Second Adam retrieved more than the first
Adam forfeited.
The abundant life Jesus offers through His death will be more
than the Paradise Adam lost through his sin.
The glory of Redemption will be greater than the glory
of Creation.
It has to be.
It came at a far dearer price.

Heavenly Father, we thank You that Jesus offers us abundance
through His own willing poverty.
We thank You that He offers us life through His
voluntary death.
We thank You in His own Name.
Amen

October 14

"I came that they may have life and have it abundantly."
John 10:10

None of us has lived life as God originally intended.
Only Adam and Eve enjoyed that high privilege.
We have lived all our lives inside a body which is dying.
Even after the new birth it is a body which inclines us mightily
toward sin.
God warned about death if the fruit was eaten.
Our first parents did not die immediately when they
swallowed the fruit.
But they knew they were dead.
They knew because they felt the difference between the life
before and the death after.
When someone dies our first impulse is to cover him up.
After they sinned Adam and Eve covered themselves up.
When Jesus came to the Cross the soldiers took the covering
from His body.
Then they hung Him up to die.
There is something momentous here.
He died for us.
Now we may live for Him.

Heavenly Father, having come to Jesus, teach us to go in
and out to pasture.
Bring us into the abundance and make us to abide.
Never allow us to wander like the Prodigal.
Never let us deny like Peter.
You restored them.
We ask You to keep us.
We ask You in Jesus' Name.
Amen

October 15

"I came that they may have life and have it abundantly."
John 10:10

Nothing is more common than life and death.
And nothing is more commonly misconstrued.
Jesus came not only to give life but to correct false notions
about life.
He did that by manifesting His own life and death to
the world.
He did that by exhibiting and imparting His own
Resurrection life.
He lived a perfect life.
No one had ever done that.
He died an atoning death.
No one had ever done that.
By living such a life and dying such a death He attained a
deathless resurrection.
No one could ever do that.
Unless of course we could somehow participate in Christ's
own death and resurrection.
But it is this very participation He offers.
It was the whole point all along.
He does not merely give His life; He shares His life.
He did not appear merely to correct our lives.
He came to confer His own life.
This is the abundance promised.
This is the abundance offered.
This is the abundance we have and will receive.

Heavenly Father, we know that the Atonement wrought by the
Saviour was not one dimensional.
We know that by His death and resurrection Jesus achieved
many things.
We want to thoroughly understand those things.
We want to consciously appropriate those things.
We want to accurately proclaim those things in
our generation.
For Christ's sake we do ask it.
Amen

"I am the good shepherd..."
John 10:11

Though we may have romantic and idyllic notions, a
shepherd's life is remote from us.
It would have been a common enough vocation in the Ancient
Near East.
But we may pass our entire lives without ever knowing the
name of even one shepherd much less getting to know a
shepherd personally.
We should be aware that a shepherd's job was always
laborious, often lonely and sometimes dangerous.
The hallmark of a good shepherd was constant vigilance.
Though we may know little of sheep or shepherding, of all the
"I ams" none is more obviously consistent with what we know
of the Lord's character than this identification
with a Shepherd.
We cannot provide for ourselves.
He feeds us.
We cannot protect ourselves.
He defends us.
We cannot find our own way.
He guides us.
He heeds.
He feeds.
He leads.
Indeed, He must be the Good Shepherd.
There has never been a better.
Nor could there ever be.

Heavenly Father, this is our greatest comfort in life.
This is our greatest hope in death.
We belong to a Good Shepherd.
He cares for us.
He will never abandon us, not now, not through all eternity.
Amen

**"I am the good shepherd. The good shepherd lays
down his life for the sheep."
John 10:11**

The Shepherd analogy is spoken by the Saviour, inspired by
the Spirit and written by the Apostle.
As such it is true and is profitable for instruction, doctrine,
correction and training.
But the analogy, like all figures of speech, has its limitations.
We cannot push the thing at all points.
Sheep are tended to meet the consumptive requirements of the
shepherd, his employer or his market.
They may often yield wool. They may once provide meat.
But this teacher who calls Himself the Good Shepherd regards
His sheep with a dramatic difference.
It is not that He takes risks and may possibly die for them.
The plan was always that He would definitely die for them.
He will never wear garments of their wool.
But they will be clothed in His righteousness.
Ultimately the analogy is turned upside down.
Why will He do this? Because He loves them.
He loves them not as a pet, and not as a man loves a warm
coat or a good meal as a sheep might provide.
He loves them as a man loves a child, or a spouse, or a friend.
That love is the chief feature of His goodness.
That love is the chief reason we call Him good.

*We are amazed Heavenly Father, that our Shepherd went
through with it.
We praise You that He laid down His life for us.
Fill us with His love, that we might love others sacrificially.
Fill us with His love that we might love You worshipfully.
Let Him love through us or we might not be able to love at all.
In Christ's own Name we ask it.
Amen*

"No one takes it (my life) from me, but I lay it down of my own accord. I have authority to lay it down, and I have authority to take it up again. This charge I have received from my Father."
John 10:18

There is something about the subject of "God" that inspires the making of myths. Sadly, there are Christian myths as well as pagan myths. There persists among a few, the mistaken notion that one Member of the Godhead had to be persuaded by another Member. As if there could be disagreement.
As if God were reluctant for sinners to be redeemed.
As if the Father were persuaded by the Son's offer to sacrifice Himself.
Or, as if the Son were reluctant to give up His life but knew He must so the Father would relent.
These notions are false, betraying profound ignorance of the Triune God.
There never was reluctance among the Three Persons regarding the plan of Redemption. There is a blessed, perpetual unity within the Godhead. There was no contradiction between Jesus' perfect freedom and His Father's perfect will. He wanted what the Father commanded, and the harmony is explicit here.
Neither could Jesus' hand be forced by any earthly power.
Jerusalem's sin in demanding the execution of Jesus was real.
The sin of complicit Rome was likewise real.
Their respective roles were monumentally evil.
But overriding all was a plan gracious and full of mercy.
Nothing compelled Jesus.
Nothing except the compulsion of His own omnipotent love.

Heavenly Father, we thank You that each person of the Godhead was active in the salvation of sinners like ourselves.
We praise You for the combined perfections of divine attributes.
We thank You that omnipotence joined with omniscience motivated by a love that brought us from death to life.
For all these things we praise You.
And we bless Your Name. Amen

Many of them said, "He has a demon..." Others said, "These are not the words of one oppressed by a demon." John 10:20-21

There were few mild or moderate opinions about Jesus of Nazareth.
His words and deeds left little possibility for middle ground.
Israel was divided.
Many among the common folk believed Him to be the Son of God and the Saviour of the world.
The religious elite insisted He was either a fraud or something worse.
The opinions were as divergent as the destinies of those who held them.
Adam and Eve erred by believing the serpent over the Lord.
Many in Israel erred by attributing to the Lord the attributes of the serpent.
"Err" is but a weak word to characterize the monstrosity of their charge.
But the second view expressed in our verse is the correct one.
Do demons really possess such wisdom?
Were the powers of hell being marshaled to bring mercy and relief?
Was the devil capable of expressing such love?
Was this Jesus not the sanest of men?
Jesus' enemies, like Adam, were taking the side of the serpent.
They no longer distinguished the voice of the devil from the voice of the Lord.
Israel had gone mad in opposing God's Son.

Gracious Father, we are appalled that those who read the Law and the Prophets could go so far astray.
We see that these men turned Your very mercy against You.
Grant us the grace always to recognize the truth which set us free and made us whole.
Grant us the grace to never dishonor Your Son.
In whose Name we pray.
Amen

October 20

At that time the Feast of Dedication took place at Jerusalem. It was winter, and Jesus was walking in the temple, in the colonnade of Solomon.
John 10:22-23

The glory of the Incarnation is here.
We see it embedded in the details.
It was an appointed time all Jews celebrate.
It was a definite season all people note.
It was in the famous city.
It was the most famous building in the famous city.
It was in a specific part of that building.
Fables are vague as to particulars.
History is exacting.
And eyewitnesses supply facts.
Anyone who happened to be in that place at that time would
have seen God walking as man.
God Almighty, come in the flesh, accessible to five senses,
observable in three dimensions.
Was there ever a more favored people?
Was there ever a more propitious moment?
Israel, the time of your visitation did come.
O Israel, O Israel!
He came to you...

Heavenly Father, we thank You that Your Son became
truly human.
We thank You that He visibly entered an observable time in
our world's history.
We thank You that He came to Jerusalem to die in our place.
We thank You that it really happened.
We thank You that it really matters.
We thank You in Jesus' Name.
Amen

October 21

Jesus answered them, "I told you, and you do not believe.
The works that I do in my Father's name
bear witness about me…"
John 10:25

Jesus answered them.
Of that we can be sure.
But the wonder is that He continued to bother.
He had faithfully answered their faithless questions all
along the way.
And He answered not with mere words.
The words alone were unforgettable.
But His deeds were thunderous.
And He calls the deeds to witness.
Had He never said a word they should have known His
identity by the proof of His acts.
But it was not answers they were after.
They were hoping for missteps and errors.
Their aim was entrapment.
But in this they remained disappointed.
He never once erred.
Indeed, He could not err.
Missteps and errors were not His domain.
He was, after all, the Son of God.

Heavenly Father, thank You that Your Son offered many
convincing proofs.
Thank You that He endured the opposition of sinful men.
We believe His witness.
And we bow down.
Amen

**Jesus answered them, "I told you, and you do not believe.
The works that I do in my Father's name
bear witness about me…"
John 10:25**

Early in the Old Testament we learn that the Spirit of God will
not always strive with a man.
If truth makes a certain kind of heart hard, then added truth
can make that same heart harder.
At some point truth resisted becomes a liability not an asset.
These resisters and rejectors reached that point quite early in
Jesus' Messianic career.
But still they pressed Him.
His words without His works would have convinced the open-
minded, for no man spoke like this Man.
The works alone without the words should have proved
irresistible to any fair judge, so great were the
works themselves.
But Christ's enemies were far from fair.
Fairness found no place in their makeup.
They were judges corrupted to an unimaginable extreme.
They forever resisted the great works combined with the
great words.
Their condemnation, then, was proportionately great.
They were privileged with the light of Christ's own presence
while so many languished at great distance in thick darkness.
Their condemnation was proportionate to privilege.
Israel's great opportunity.
Israel's great tragedy.

*Heavenly Father, we deserved darkness, but You sent light.
Let us always follow the light to the place where the path
shines brighter still.
Make us to believe and follow always the Light of the world
who took the name Jesus.
Amen*

October 23

"...you do not believe because you are not among my sheep. My sheep hear my voice, and I know them, and they follow me."
John 10:26-27

Salvation, we have noted, is a complex phenomenon.
It was never a one-dimensional reality.
Salvation issues forth from factors both human and divine.
There are contributions from the human side to be sure.
But the initial and critical movement lies on God's side of the equation.
That we are privileged to hear the Gospel at all is something determined by God's sovereignty.
Many lived and died without hearing.
Here Jesus gets at the root of things.
There are deeper reasons some believe and some do not.
The true sheep have partaken of a nature they were not born with.
How did they come by that nature?
They received it from God.
He imparts it, and the originating impulse is not human but divine.
Faith is a thing wrought by Almighty God.

Father, we do humbly confess that heaven is a gift from You, unearned by us.
We did not trust Christ because we were more wise or more worthy than those who turned away.
We trusted Jesus because You gave us a nature which caused us to know our true Shepherd.
We could not help but trust Him.
Because He is our Shepherd and we are His sheep.
And so, we yield up to You everlasting praise.
Amen

"My sheep hear my voice...and they follow me."
John 10:27

We know from the Gospels that thousands heard with physical ears the audible voice of the Incarnate God.
We know from the same Gospels that no very great percentage of those hearers followed.
What point then is the Saviour driving home?
In this verse "hear" is a term great with meaning.
Hear means to recognize.
Hear means to embrace.
Hear means to resolve.
Hear means to begin.
Hear means to persevere.
In a word, "hear" means to "heed."
The hearing makes a difference.
What we hear is a beckoning, an invitation to follow on.
And so, this verse leaves us with a challenge.
Have we really heard?
We have heard only if we have followed.

Heavenly Father, by Your grace we have heard Christ's voice.
By Your Spirit's enabling we mean to follow.
Help us Lord to bring others with us.
For Your glory and for their good.
And for our joy.
In Christ's Name we ask it.
Amen

"I give them eternal life, and they will never perish, and no one will snatch them out of my hand."
John 10:28

There has long been a controversy among the godly and scholarly over this question.
Can a believer, once secure, be finally lost?
If there were no verses appearing to support both sides there would be no controversy.
While recognizing the passages which bring warning, we believe that the weight of evidence lies on the side of the believer's safety.
This verse speaks to the question.
And the words are emphatic in one regard.
If a believer can be ultimately lost, then Jesus Himself must lose him.
This we know to be a thing impossible.
No one shall pry the believer from his Saviour's grasp.
Least of all the believer himself.
We have this on Jesus' own authority.
We believe Jesus to be in the business of saving not losing.
Thus, we rejoice in the certainty of a salvation which issues forth from One so mighty to save.

Heavenly Father, we thank You for the memory of our salvation at the beginning.
We thank You for the enjoyment of our salvation now.
And we thank You for the hope of our salvation throughout all eternity.
All glory to You, heavenly Father.
And to the Lamb.
Amen

October 26

**"My Father, who has given them to me, is greater than all,
and no one is able to snatch them
out of the Father's hand."
John 10:29**

Thus, is our assurance more than doubled.
God the Son, Omnipotence enfleshed, holds us in the palm
of His hand.
What greater guarantee of everlasting safety could we
possibly need?
Indeed, it would be difficult to imagine any greater guarantee.
And yet, amazingly, that is precisely what we are given.
Jesus here adds assurance to assurance.
There is a Covenant between the Father and the Son to
provide salvation.
Since the Covenant is eternal we may infer that the salvation
is eternal as well.
So the Covenant is also meant to preserve salvation.
After we are made secure by the Saviour's strong grasp it is as
if God the Father places His own hand over the hand of Jesus.
That being so, two of the three divine Persons are
safeguarding our eternal inheritance.
Paul the Apostle will later write of a sealing by the
Third Person.
Pondering any truth about the Trinity always takes us
to the depths.
We are not likely to fully grasp the concepts with our heads.
But we are meant to feel their comforts in our hearts.

*Heavenly Father, Your Son went to the trouble to save us.
He also took time to give us grounds for assurance.
As we have been greatly comforted, so also we do
greatly praise.
In our Saviour's Name.
Amen*

"I and the Father are one."
John 10:30

Jesus never offers the brute, frontal declaration:
"I AM GOD."
But this verse comes close.
Of course, He was God and He is God.
But the New Testament approach is to convict by evidence
both massive and cumulative.
Evidence from words and deeds.
Evidence from circumstance and testimony.
Evidence from fulfilled prophecy.
And yes, evidence from claims like this one.
But the claim is not absolutely direct.
Jesus did not say to the Samaritan woman,
"I am the Messiah."
He did say "I who speak to you am He."
Slightly indirect, but with the equivalence of a bold formula.
How can someone appear humble and self-effacing while at
the same time claiming to be God?
It would be impossible to imagine if it were not a part of the
historical record.
It would be impossible unless there actually was someone who
could be both God and humble at the same time.
It would be impossible for anyone but Jesus.
Jesus explodes our categories.
Jesus shows us how it's done.

Heavenly Father, we thank You that Your Son did not merely
tell us what You are like.
Though that alone would have been a gift of surpassing worth.
But He did much more than that.
He showed us who You are by showing us Himself.
We see Him, we know that He is very God of very God.
When we see Him we can do nothing less than worship.
Amen

October 28

**The Jews picked up stones again to stone him. ...
(they said) "It is not for a good work that we are
going to stone you but for blasphemy, because
you, being a man, make yourself God."
John 10:31-33**

Of course, this is not the first time such a thing happened.
Before Jesus had identified Himself with the holy and
unutterable "I am."
On that occasion He as much as said, "I am the God who
made Covenant with Moses."
Now He says that He is One with the Maker of Heaven
and Earth.
One with the Father Israel prayed to.
He was claiming to be God.
If the claim were not true, He was subject to stoning
under the Law.
If He really were God, He deserved to be worshiped
according to right.
The men who picked up stones reached their verdict quickly.
These Jews were right to conclude that Jesus was
claiming deity.
They were wrong in accusing Him of blasphemy.
The irony is that His accusers were the true blasphemers.
These men had seen God in human form.
And now they were preparing to murder Him.

*Heavenly Father, the indignities heaped upon Your Son must
have been painful for John to write down.
They are certainly painful for us to read.
We are sobered to know that those who hate His claims are
still abroad in our generation.
We know if we say what He said those who hated Him
will hate us.
May our witness be true and our purpose resolute.
Make us truly willing to suffer for Him who died for us.
In Christ's own Name we ask it.
Amen*

October 29

Jesus answered them, "Is it not written in your Law, 'I said, you are gods'? If he called them gods to whom the word of God came - and Scripture cannot be broken - do you say of him whom the Father consecrated and sent into the world, 'You are blaspheming,' because I said 'I am the Son of God'?"
John 10:34-36

Jesus' answer to His would-be executioners was as artful as it was subtle.

Although the God of Israel reserved the attribution of divine identity to Himself alone, it was true that Scripture sometimes referred to those with prerogatives of governance and arbitration as "gods."

Angels, princes and judges were so designated at times.

And so the Lord quoted the Psalmist.

Jesus' argument was as follows:

If those with minor roles were called "gods" how could it be blasphemy for the unique and only begotten, who received the Father's saving commission, to call Himself the Son of God? Their case was weak.

But their reasoning had never been objective.

They were looking for a pretense for murder.

Jesus' self-revelation unfolded little by little.

His strong claim to a divine identity was becoming clearer.

The clearer it became the more convinced they were that they had found the pretense they were looking for.

Heavenly Father, false religion was looking for one reason to crucify Your Son.
We have found many reasons to worship Him.
Thank You for disclosing them to us.
We know there are many more.
Amen

October 30

"...Scripture cannot be broken..."
John 10:35

In the short space of five verses the Lord of glory brings forth
two unyielding dogmas.
The first is a candid disclosure of an exalted identity.
"I and the Father are one."
The second has to do with the authority which authenticates
the identity.
"Scripture cannot be broken."
The crisis of the world is a crisis of authority.
If God has spoken, then His Word must be true.
If His Word is true, then what He says must be trustworthy
in every sense that matters.
If God has not spoken, then we are all adrift in a sea
of conjecture.
Our soul has an enemy who wages war with the weapon
of doubt.
"Did God really say...?" he hissed to Eve in a Garden
of delights.
"If you are the Son of God" he challenged Jesus in a
wilderness of fasting.
"If you are the Son of God" his servants scoffed to Jesus
on the Cross.
For Jesus, the verdict of Scripture settled everything.
For Scripture cannot be broken.

*Heavenly Father, in Scripture we see how the Divine Son
died for us.*
In Scripture we see how to live for Him.
*Thank You for Your infallible word which we believe and
which we cherish.*
In Jesus' Name.
Amen

October 31

**Now a certain man was ill, Lazarus of Bethany,
the village of Mary and her sister Martha.
John 11:1**

The name and address are important.
When we regard pain as an abstraction, philosophy
becomes a possibility.
When we experience pain as a sufferer, theology
becomes a necessity.
By John 11 suffering made its way to one specific address.
A mortal illness entered the dwelling of Jesus' dear friends.
Pain was no more an abstraction for them.
It was a home where the Saviour had been refreshed.
Now His friends were afraid.
We may resist the teaching that God refuses to exempt His
intimates from suffering.
But it is a truth everywhere attested.
Abel was murdered, Joseph was made a slave, Daniel became
an exile.
Job was the best man under heaven but it's hard to think of a
way he did NOT suffer.
Lazarus was Jesus' much-loved friend.
And this friend was sick unto death.

*Heavenly Father, we know that suffering is no necessary
sign of Your disfavor.
We know that pain makes us realize our insufficiency.
We thank You for this record of distress on the part of
Jesus' friends.
We know that still at a distance of 2000 years it holds
many lessons for us.
And we thank You that we too are Jesus' friends.
Amen*

November 1

So the sisters sent to him, saying,
"Lord, he whom you love is ill."
John 11:3

There is no overt request.
The sisters merely relay information.
They leave off pleading.
But they have a friend they do not need to ask.
Though the urgency is muffled the import is plain:
"Come quickly Lord, he is dying."
Mary and Martha rely upon the universal obligations of love.
Those obligations are obvious.
Anyone who can help should help.
They report to Jesus that Lazarus is sick.
They remind Jesus that Lazarus is loved.
That should be enough.
Loved by Jesus!
Could there be a better advantage than that?
They will discover the advantage to be something far different
than what they had expected.
They will discover a benefit far greater than what they
could hope.

Heavenly Father, we know that You know everything.
And yet still there are things we long to tell You.
We are grateful that You love to listen.
We cry out to You in our distress.
We are confident in Your steadfast love.
And so, we thank You in Jesus' Name.
Amen

November 2

**But when Jesus heard it he said,
"This illness does not lead to death..."
John 11:4**

Because Lazarus does in fact die we may well wonder
about the meaning.
A few verses after He declares that the illness is not
terminal, He reveals that Lazarus has died.
There is no contradiction, and Jesus is not confused.
These verses measure a space of two days.
Jesus does not require news from Bethany to discover
what has happened.
Nor does He require on-site inspection.
He simply knows.
He means something like this:
This story will not end in death.
Death will not detain Lazarus long.
Death will not have the final say.
Death is a one-way street.
But Lazarus will come back up this street.
This story is not about the death of Lazarus.
The story is about Lazarus' Friend.
Lazarus' great Friend who is greater than death itself.

*Heavenly Father, we thank You that Jesus knows how
things will end.
We thank You that Jesus can change the way things will end.
We know that Jesus is in control.
He encourages us by declaring the end from the beginning.
Amen*

November 3

**"...It is for the glory of God, so that the son of God
may be glorified through it."
John 11:4**

Any mystery in this passage persists in exact proportion to our
unfamiliarity with the chief theme.
The main subject is not Lazarus or his family.
The subject is not Lazarus' demise and his deliverance.
The primary theme is not even Jesus and His power, though
that motif must always be prominent throughout.
No, the real topic is GLORY.
The glory of God and of Jesus Christ, God's Son.
A subject is glorified when a new discovery brings credit
to the subject.
Death is the just wage of man's sin.
Resurrection is the sure proof of God's grace.
It is a thing which requires not only good will but great power.
Jesus' mission in Bethany proves both.
Those present beheld glory.
Glory as of the only begotten of the Father.
Full of grace and truth.

Heavenly Father, we know so little of glory.
We need to be taken to school.
We thank You that Scripture is our school and Jesus is
our teacher.
May we be diligent students.
And may we seek Your glory all our days.
For Christ's sake we ask it.
Amen

November 4

**So, when he heard that Lazarus was ill, he stayed
two days longer in the place where he was.**
John 11:6

Here is a curious thing.
Christ's delay was opposed to all human inclination.
And it was intentional.
If we measure the distance between Galilee and Bethany, we
see that even if Jesus began His journey immediately, He
would have arrived after Lazarus died.
It is possible Lazarus was dead by the time the Lord received
the health report.
But still He tarried.
Why?
Almost certainly for more than one reason.
Possibly for reasons we may never be able to fathom.
At least one motive for the delay presents itself
quite plausibly.
Jesus would not have wanted to leave the false impression
that He tried but failed to arrive in time.
The Lord Jesus Christ was never hurried and never late.
His ministry constituted a combination of perfections.
Included among those perfections was His timing.
Plus, He may have wanted the full reality of Lazarus' death
to sink in.
That would have helped to press home the full reality of
his resurrection.

*Heavenly Father, we thank You for all the advantages we have
over Lazarus.*
We know how his story ended.
He never knew in advance.
*Jesus is never distant to us but always in our congregations
and in our hearts.*
And so we thank You in Jesus' Name.
Amen

November 5

Then after this he said to the disciples,
"Let us go to Judea again."
John 11:7

His initial refusal to begin immediately would have
been misinterpreted.
He did not delay because He was afraid to go.
He did not delay because it was futile to make the attempt.
He may have delayed so that the death of His friend would
have been well-known by the time He arrived.
At some point we may determine to visit a family member
or friend before it is too late.
We may have done that already.
We treasure the kind of friend who would rush to our side
during our last hours.
But we need another kind of friend even more.
We need a friend who can rush to our aid after we die.
There has only ever been one friend like that.
He was the friend who left Galilee for Judea.
He was the great friend of Lazarus.
He delayed because He wanted His disciples to know that
the Resurrection was INTENTIONAL.

Heavenly Father, we thank You that the ministry of Your Son
was not inadvertent.
We thank You that He ministered by design.
We thank You for His attention to detail.
We thank You that there was never a misstep.
We thank You that He intends everything that happens to work
for our ultimate good.
We thank You for the assurance that He will intervene
at the end.
And He will raise us to everlasting life.
Amen

November 6

**The disciples said to him, "Rabbi, the Jews were just now
seeking to stone you, and are you going there again?"
John 11:8**

The answer of course was, "Yes!"
It is always noteworthy when someone takes it upon himself
to tutor the Lord from Glory.
Especially significant are those occasions when someone
deems it necessary to teach the Lord Jesus about death.
The irony is supreme.
As if Jesus had somehow overlooked the danger.
As if He had not noticed the hatred of His enemies.
Death was the prominent feature of His mission.
Just as death is the primary instrumentality of our redemption.
It was death which should have feared the Lord Christ.
He came to make death His prey.
He would stalk death like a hunter.
He would break the filthy neck of death on the Cross.
When Jesus entered Judea it was to slay death.
Death would die.
And Lazarus would rise.

*Heavenly Father, we praise You that our Redeemer did not
regard His own safety as a thing to be jealously guarded.
He came not to save Himself.
Thank You that He would go to Judea over the protests of
those who warned.
Thank you that He would go to ransom sinners like ourselves.
In Jesus' Name.
Amen*

November 7

Jesus answered, "Are there not twelve hours in the day?
If anyone walks in the day, he does not stumble, because he
sees the light of this world. But if anyone walks in the
night, he stumbles, because the light is not in him."
John 11:9-10

Jesus was not content merely to answer.
He must also teach.
But we are dull pupils.
And the lesson is not abundantly plain.
Apparently, Jesus speaks of the light of His Father's will.
He refers to the daylight of duty.
He means the light of plan, of foreordination, of purpose.
If death would be defeated danger must be confronted.
It would be better to die in the service of divine purpose than
to survive outside His Father's will.
It was not the presence of danger which influenced His timing
or His steps.
It was rather the Father's pleasure which determined His path.
That, and His love for sinners like ourselves.

Heavenly Father, we thank You for the spectacle of divine
resolve pulsating in human flesh.
We praise You for the indomitable will of our Lord
Jesus Christ.
We know that neither the counsel of friends nor the threats
of enemies could turn Him aside.
We know that He pushed on for Lazarus' sake.
We know that He pushed on for our sakes.
And we praise You that He won the victory.
Amen

November 8

After saying these things, he said to them, "Our friend Lazarus has fallen asleep, but I go to awaken him."
John 11:11

Consistently, Scripture refers to death as "sleep."
But the term applies to a believer's death alone.
Sleep is a temporary phenomenon.
Death for the believer is of shorter duration than sleep.
Though death is not the subject of the narrative, death is a part of the narrative.
The first warning in the Bible is a warning about death.
We may even say the first lesson in the Bible is a lesson about death.
God gave the world to our first parents as a platform for discovery.
There was but one thing to be left undiscovered.
That was the taste of the fruit on the tree.
That was the experience of sin in the taste.
That was the certainty of death with the sin.
Jesus was still teaching about death in the New Testament.
After two thousand years we still have much to learn.

Heavenly Father, we are ever dying.
How we thank You that Your Son came on purpose to waken.
We bid Him to ever work His purpose in us.
For Jesus' sake we ask it.
Amen

**The disciples said to him, "Lord, if he has
fallen asleep, he will recover."
John 11:12**

It should not surprise us that the disciples got it wrong.
They rarely caught on to what Jesus was doing the first time it
was explained to them.
Great as their privilege was, ours is greater.
We know the whole of the story in retrospect.
They were living the story out.
And our own first attempts at understanding and applying the
words of the Saviour often go far astray.
We will seldom err if we take the words of Scripture plainly.
"Seldom" does not mean "always."
"Plainly" does not always mean "literally."
Sometimes a too-literal interpretation inclines us in the
wrong direction.
The disciples were more clueless than usual in this instance.
It should have been obvious that if it were mere sleep Lazarus
would awaken on his own.
There would be no need to court the danger and visit Bethany
to do what anyone else could do.
What Lazarus needed was to be raised from the dead.
There was only one person who could do that.
Soon He would be on His way.

*Heavenly Father, we will always misunderstand Your words
without Your help.
Thank You for the extravagant measures You have taken to
give that help.
Thank You for the Holy Scripture as a gift of infallible truth.
Thank You for the Holy Spirit who is the infallible guide to
biblical meaning.
Thank You most of all for Your Holy Son who entered human
history to show us perfect godliness in three dimensions.
Thank You in Jesus' Name.
Amen*

November 10

**Then Jesus told them plainly, "Lazarus has died,
and for your sake I am glad that I was not
there, so that you may believe…"**
John 11:14-15

So then He told them plainly.
We may be grateful that the Lord Jesus condescends to our
mental sluggishness.
He did so in the First Century. He does so today.
This is the first of four registrations of Jesus' emotions in this
remarkable chapter.
The chapter is famous for the display of the Lord's tears, but
here He says, "I am glad."
The verse before us may be easily misunderstood so we must
approach it with care. He does not say He is glad Lazarus is
dead. He does not say He was happy that family and friends
were drowning in grief.
He does suggest that He was glad He was not there to prevent
the death.
Why?
Because the death of His friend afforded Jesus the opportunity
to provide an impetus to faith even greater than healing.
Christ's words force an inference not necessarily welcome.
In God's eyes an increase in faith is more to be desired than a
decrease in suffering.
This is not a truth happily received when we first encounter it.
One thing the Holy Spirit does over time is to bring us into
emotional sympathy with God's point of view.
The process is not always quick and easy.
Because we are not always readily cooperative.

Heavenly Father, we are sinners. We need to be changed.
Even when we come to the point of intellectual agreement we
don't always feel the force of convictions we confess.
By Your Spirit's power make us glad where Jesus is glad.
Make us to grieve at the things which grieve Him.
This is something we want. To be like Him.
This is what we ask for in Jesus' Name.
Amen

November 11

"But let us go to him."
John 11:15

Are these not precious words?
Do they not stir up hope at times when hope
seems impossible?
Is this not thrilling proof of the divine resolve?
"Master," they say, "they want to kill you down there."
BUT LET US GO TO HIM!
Who would say such a thing but Jesus?
A dead friend is by definition beyond reach.
There is no possibility of going.
All opportunity is past.
Not so with Jesus.
Death itself is permeable.
For Him death poses no barrier which cannot be annihilated.
Though Lazarus be entombed He will go to him.
And He will bring him back.

Dear gracious Father, we praise You for our
Saviour's resolve.
And we thank You that He not only resolves but
He also invites.
He bids His followers join Him.
They who share in the risk also share in the Resurrection.
We also resolve to follow.
Make it to be so now and forever.
We ask in Christ's own Name.
Amen

November 12

**So Thomas, called the Twin, said to his fellow disciples,
"Let us also go, that we may die with him."
John 11:16**

It is not easy to see humor in Holy Scripture.
We approach the Bible with a solemn reverence.
That reverence is fitting and proper.
In that frame of mind we are not receptive to humor.
And yet sometimes, heavily disguised, the humor is there.
There is something comic in Thomas' note of resignation.
In vain the disciples tried to talk their Master out of returning
to the danger zone.
It is as if Thomas is saying "Set your affairs in order my
brothers, this will be the end of us."
"We tried but He would not listen."
They commended their views as if offering a counsel
of prudence.
More likely it was a symptom of fright.
The absurd presumption persisted that they knew more about
human nature, death and what lay ahead than Jesus Himself.
Thomas is a character intriguing and complex.
We can see in him not a little of ourselves.
He is both a model and a warning.
He has enough love for Jesus to be willing to die with Him.
But he does not have the faith to believe that Jesus knows
what He is doing.

*Dear gracious Heavenly Father, Thomas complained but
he complied.*
Let us comply without complaining.
Let us follow the Lamb wherever He leads.
It will be our privilege and our joy.
In Jesus' Name we ask it.
Amen

November 13

Now when Jesus came, he found that Lazarus had already been in the tomb four days...So when Martha heard that Jesus was coming, she went and met him, but Mary remained seated in the house.
John 11:17, 20

The journey would have taken a minimum of three days.
Had Jesus left immediately He would have found His
friend entombed.
Luke famously contrasted the respective characteristics of the
two sisters.
Martha tended toward the practical while Mary concentrated
on Jesus' teaching.
Martha's actions in the passage are true to form.
The visitor is distinguished.
He should be met a distance out, so He could be escorted
in properly.
Good manners required this.
Mary's decision to remain in the house is more problematic.
We grant her the benefit of the doubt and assume her
reticence is benign.
It may be that her grief paralyzed her.
It may be that she didn't feel worthy to rush into the Lord's
presence unbidden.
What followed proved that Mary and Martha were not
dissimilar in all respects.
In one way the sisters' response would be identical.

Dear Father, we know that the Saviour ever approaches us.
Approaches us in our sorrow, approaches us in our
bewilderment, approaches us in our pain.
May we always run to meet Him.
May we welcome Him worshipfully and with love.
We are so grateful.
It is a wonder and a mercy that He approaches us at all.
Amen

November 14

Martha said to Jesus, "Lord, if you had been here, my brother would not have died."
John 11:21

The word "if" is not often a friend of faith.
There is something grammarians call the subjunctive mood.
That is the mood which follows the word "if."
The subjunctive takes us into a realm of unreality.
But God is real.
He rules over the Kingdom of the real.
God knows all contingencies.
He knows what could have happened.
He knows what would have happened, if.
The Bible is not a fairy tale.
Nor is it a product of anyone's imagination.
Jesus appears in actual history, in the space-time we humans share.
That is the place we meet Him.
That is the place He works.
He mends what is broken.
He heals what is ill.
He restores what is lost.
We should never say to God, "if you had only been here."
God's Providence has always been near.
God's Sovereignty is ever present.
It is true that Jesus was in Galilee when Lazarus died.
But His Name is Immanuel.
It means that God is here.

Dear Father, thank You for sending Your Son to be with us.
Thank You that His Name is Immanuel.
Thank You that He is always with us.
Thank you that He is always near.
Amen

November 15

Martha said to Jesus, "Lord if you had been here my brother would not have died." John 11:21

Martha means only to honor the Lord.
But her compliment is imperfect.
Her salute is subverted by an unspoken reproof gently hinted.
Jesus, she asserts, is mighty to heal.
So great was He that His physical presence would have deflected even the great thing called death.
So far, so good.
But He was not present.
He arrived, so she thought, too late.
We may be tempted to dwell much on what God could have done.
We may well mourn the lost advantage God missed or the present difficulty we endure because for whatever reason our prayers go unanswered.
Though the sentiment may be couched in the most respectful terms, this too is unbelief.
As if God had somehow been inattentive.
As if God somehow squandered an irrecoverable opportunity.
But He did not.
And He would not.
Because He cannot.
An unforgettable demonstration of God's faithfulness is about to commence.

Heavenly Father, we thank You that the Lord Jesus is never late and never remiss.
We know that "waiting" is the name of the school where faith is learned.
How quickly we long to graduate.
While we linger let us learn.
In Jesus' Name we ask it.
Amen

November 16

Martha said to Jesus, "Lord if you had been here my brother would not have died."
John 11:21

"If you had been here."
"Yes" the tempter is likely to whisper.
"But He was not here and because He was not here your brother is just as dead as he would have been had Jesus no power at all.
He is just as dead as he would have been if you had never met Jesus."
The temptation to indulge doubtful thoughts is not rare.
But the thoughts are diabolical.
Fight them as you would fight the devil.
Because they are of the devil.
The evil one wishes us to doubt the existence of a Being with the attributes of God.
If we believe in God anyway, the devil then tries to convince us that His divine attributes have nothing to do with us.
Power and sovereignty may be a good thing for God, but no advantage accrues to us humans.
Or those benefits may help others, but I cannot see the advantage.
God may be somewhere, and He may be doing something but that something is remote from my personal experience.
Jesus was born on this planet to explode that notion.
That is why He entered Bethany though Lazarus was four days dead.

Heavenly Father, we thank You for the life You have given us - suffering and all.
Help us resist the desire to compete with You as a rival Creator, imagining realities other than the one You have favored us with.
No matter what our disappointment, we know You will come to our "Bethany" and meet us in the hard places.
In You we trust and for You we wait.
Amen

November 17

(Martha said) "But even now I know that whatever
you ask from God, God will give you."
John 11:22

Martha wants Jesus to know that her devastation had not
destroyed her esteem for Him.
He still retains her confidence.
She is still certain that His connection to God is unbreakable.
She even believes God will do anything for Him.
But what follows proves that her confidence is more
theoretical than practical.
The "anything" did not include the possibility that she could
be appreciably helped in her present circumstances.
Comfort perhaps, or some form of consolation but Martha did
not expect Jesus to transform her crushing devastation into
unspeakable joy.
Evidently that had not crossed her mind.
The boundaries of her faith were not broad enough to
include resurrection.
We may be confident that Jesus raised more people from the
dead than those recorded in the Gospels.
Martha may have known of unrecorded cases.
She likely knew of Jairus' daughter at a minimum.
But her belief in the historical work of Jesus of Nazareth
in the past did not automatically inspire personal hope
for the present.
There was a gap in her faith.
And gaps are common to us all.

When our faith flags Lord, shore us up.
When we stagger, steady us.
Grow our faith from the historical to the personal.
Bring it home to us.
Make our confidence strong today in the place where we live.
For Christ's sake we ask it.
Amen

November 18

"but even now...whatever you ask..."
John 11:22

An accurate profession and an actual possession are two
very different things.
It is easier to talk about Christianity than to live the
Christian life.
It is easier to describe faith than to exercise faith.
What Martha said was perfect.
Even now, Jesus can do anything.
So great is His current power.
So great is His ongoing, unbroken intimacy with the Father.
But the confession of the lips does not always fully reflect the
disposition of the heart.
Faith builds a bridge between the two.
Martha knew that Jesus did not come for nothing.
Doubtless He would help in many ways.
His very presence was a comfort.
But He did not come for commiseration alone.
He was not there merely to pay His respects.
She may have expected Him to speak to the emotions
in her heart.
And so He did.
But He also came for something more.
He would speak to her brother in his grave.

Heavenly Father, we thank You that death is no impediment
to the Saviour.
The words of Jesus are priceless, but we thank You that Jesus
can offer more than words.
We thank You that He brings a ministry of power.
We thank You that He can alter events.
And we thank You that He came to this stricken family to
do just that.
May He come to our family and the families we pray for.
May He come in Word and power.
For we ask it in His own Name.
Amen

November 19

Jesus said to her, "Your brother will rise again."
John 11:23

The declaration was unadorned and without elaboration.
The Lord thought it unnecessary to provide details.
The promise was specific.
But the timing was imprecise.
All the promises of God should provoke joy.
But the more remote the prospect the less excited the response.
Israel spent 400 years in Egypt and 70 in Babylon.
There were 400 years between Malachi and Matthew.
Pious Jews were used to waiting.
There would be a general resurrection to be sure.
Was Jesus only repeating a dogma of Jewish Orthodoxy?
But He did not travel to Bethany merely to catechize.
His arrival suggested an imminent event.
The great question was always "When?"
On this occasion they had not long to wait.

Heavenly Father, may our faith grow by the study of
Your word.
May we always take the Lord Jesus at His word.
May we never be surprised when He acts.
We cherish the expectation that He will act FOR US.
In Jesus' Name.
Amen

November 20

Martha said to him "I know that he will rise again in the resurrection on the last day."
John 11:24

Martha was stricken by grief.
The wound was yet fresh.
She may have thought it strange that the usual formulas of consolation were not forthcoming.
Jesus' words carried potential for real comfort but only if the event He referenced was imminent and emerging.
Martha did not avail herself of that comfort.
Abraham waited a quarter century to receive a son.
Why would she expect to see a brother in a quarter hour?
But Jesus was not offering platitudes.
Still less was He rehearsing articles of doctrine.
The comfort He brought was meant to be immediate.
Jesus had come to Bethany to raise Lazarus from the dead.
It was a thing He meant to tend to with dispatch.
It had been a long journey.
But He would not sit down until Lazarus rose up.

Heavenly Father, we are greatly fortified by the possession of true doctrine.
But let doctrine always enflame and never dull our expectation.
May the truth prime us for the fulfillment of the promises.
We ask it in Jesus' Name.
Amen

November 21

Martha said to him, "I know that he will rise again in the resurrection on the last day."
John 11:24

For the believer reunion and restoration are certain but distant.
The joy may be real but the bulk of joy awaits the last day.
Meanwhile she must live in the present.
A mature faith brings heaven's joys to earth.
But even with faith waiting is seldom easy.
We resist a critique of Martha's faith.
We would not rebuke her grief.
Martha is orthodox.
She believes in eventual resurrection.
But she must live (she thinks) the rest of her biological life
bereaved of her brother's company.
That company must have brought much cheer in time past.
Even the presence of Jesus may not have felt like
compensation for what was lost.
But wait a moment.
Wait just a moment.
The compensation will be overwhelming.

Father, we thank You for the array of faith on display in
Holy Scripture.
We see already that the faith of Thomas is not the faith
of Martha.
We know the faith of Mary will be different from the
faith of Martha.
Lord we would be bold.
Give us a faith like Jesus.
Amen

Martha said to him, "I know that he will rise again in the resurrection on the last day."
John 11:24

We are human after all.
Because we are human our fallenness asserts itself at critical moments.
One symptom of that fallenness is an inability to feel the comfort which our convictions ought to provide.
Were we to abide in Jesus' visible presence we may imagine we would want nothing more.
The exchange suggests that Martha was more affected by her brother's absence than her Saviour's presence.
Think of it.
She believed in the promise of the Resurrection.
She beheld the presence of the Incarnation.
God in human flesh had come to reassure.
Still she was of a mind to mourn.
"If you had been here..."
We actually have the advantage over Martha.
We too believe the promises.
We too have Jesus' own comfort brought to us by the present and indwelling Spirit.
Not least, we have the advantage of knowing how this story will unfold.
And still we too may lament over what is no longer there.
May this account fortify us.
May it lift us to the place faith was meant to take us.

Heavenly Father, how we thank You that the Holy Spirit framed this stupendous miracle with the conversations which show the perspectives of those present.
May our faith be fortified by Martha's doubt.
May we be quicker to believe because she was slower.
We know she brought much excellence in her service to Jesus.
Let us profit from her experience.
Amen

**Jesus said to her, "I am the resurrection and the life.
Whoever believes in me, though he die, yet shall he live."
John 11:25**

How grateful we are for Martha's hesitation.
Her lack of comprehension called forth Jesus' great "I am."
Jesus here guarantees resurrection to all believers.
"He who believes in Me..."
That means the promise is good for all who receive what Jesus
says about Himself, about His relationship to God.
It means to believe what He says about what sin has done to us
and what only He can do for us.
There is no guarantee that we will avoid death physically.
On the contrary, the only way to experience resurrection is to
first experience death.
That's why He said, "though he die..."
There were exceptions in the past.
We remember Enoch and Elijah.
There will be exceptions in the future.
We think of believers who are alive at the Lord's
Second Coming.
But death will be but a fleeting thing for all the Redeemed.
Life will be the abiding thing.
The abiding and eternal reality.

*Heavenly Father, death is not a dreaded thing if it leads
to resurrection.
Death is to us a welcome thing because Jesus is
our resurrection.
So resurrection takes us to Him.
Father we thank You for the comfort this promise brings.
In Jesus' Name.
Amen*

"I am the resurrection and the life...Do you believe this?"
John 11:25-26

In Luke 10 Jesus credits the contemplative Mary for having
the better priorities.
The practical Martha was troubled over lesser concerns.
But servants enjoy advantages of their own.
In Cana, only the servants knew who changed the water
into wine.
Because Martha came out to meet Jesus she alone heard the
words spoken directly to her.
And what words they were!
Upon arrival Jesus begins immediately to tutor and disciple.
He chose to mold her character before He relieved her pain.
It was while she was in the lowest place that Jesus met her
with the deepest truth.
It was in her suffering that the Lord taught her the intimate
connection between resurrection and Himself.
Perhaps the fire of suffering melted her down to a greater
receptivity to the things of God.
Traditionally we hold Mary in the higher regard.
But it was the sister busy and beset who heard first the
declaration, "I am the Resurrection and the Life."

*Heavenly Father, we thank You for the context of the
great disclosure.*
*We know that Jesus offered these words not as a theological
abstraction but as the only possible remedy in a season
of desperation.*
*We know when we come to our last day nothing will
comfort us more than that we know Him who is the
Resurrection and the Life.*
For that we thank You forevermore.
Amen

"Do you believe this?"
John 11:26

He may have asked the question quietly with a sigh.
Or the words could have come like a peal of thunder to shake
her to the core.
The words may have been meant to comfort, or they may have
been meant to convict.
The amazing thing is that such a question came at such
a moment.
The Gospel and all it entails, the words, the works and the
historical events are not given to fill in all the gaps in
our knowledge.
Still less was the Gospel given to satisfy our curiosity.
We have what we have so that we might believe.
Our faith is meant to grow.
Living things grow.
If our faith is not growing, we might reasonably ask whether
it is alive.
It is striking that the Son of God would interrupt the wondrous
disclosure of His own identity to ask the question, "Do you
believe this?"
Not, "Are you religious?"
Not, "Do you believe in God?"
Rather the question is, "Do we believe everything Jesus
Christ says about Himself and the way it will radically
alter our future?"
Do we really believe this?

Dear Father, we do believe.
But sometimes we live as if we did not.
Sometimes our faith is weak.
Thank You for telling us of Mary and Martha and Lazarus
and Bethany.
That we might be strengthened.
Thank You in Jesus' Name.
Amen

**She said to him, "Yes, Lord; I believe that you are the
Christ, the Son of God, who is coming into the world."
John 11:27**

On the face of it, Martha's response is just as complete as
Peter's great confession at Caesarea Philippi:
"You are the Christ, the Son of the living God." (Mt. 16:16)
The confession brought strong commendation from the Lord.
Martha's subsequent attempt to overrule the Lord at the tomb
may leave us doubtful.
But Jesus does not reprove her. Neither shall we.
We may be confident that her habit of calling Jesus "Lord"
evidenced faith.
In common usage it meant no more than "Sir" but in this
context she was affording Jesus a more exalted honor than
the commonplace.
"Christ" was a reference with special meaning to the Jews.
The "Lord's anointed" meant someone designated for a
special task in Israel.
The Messianic expectation in Martha's generation was
excessively nationalistic.
The political and military aspects of the office eclipsed
the spiritual.
Martha's close contact with Jesus would have corrected
that view.
Her attribution of the title, "Son of God," evidenced the
highest praise of all.
She declared Him to be THE Son of God.
It is likely she already believed Him to be the Incarnate God.
It means that practical Martha was one of the profoundest
theologians of her generation.

*Father, we too believe that Jesus of Nazareth is Your only Son
and earth's only Saviour.*
May we proclaim that truth where we live, while we live.
May we send that message to the nations.
May it be the truth which dominates our lives.
Amen

**When she had said this, she went and called her sister
Mary, saying in private, "The teacher is here
and is calling for you."
John 11:28**

Martha is a precious figure in Holy Scripture.
The sisters and brother were among Jesus' best friends.
On his way to the Cross it was their fellowship which He
sought above others.
It is not hard to see why.
We note Martha's progress in grace.
Before, she had been frustrated when Mary lingered over
much in Jesus' presence, while Martha busied herself with
necessary duties.
There is irony here of course.
Here she invites her sister into the presence of the Lord.
Perhaps she should be better known for drawing her sister into
the Lord's presence instead of making an attempt to draw
her away.
In the space of two verses Martha assigns Jesus three titles.
In the verse before, he is the Christ, the Son of God.
Here He is "The Teacher."
And she, not Mary, had been the sole beneficiary of one of His
greatest pronouncements.
"I am the Resurrection and the Life," He said to her.
But another lesson was imminent.
That lesson would be accessible to all.
That lesson would be one of the greatest of all.

*Heavenly Father, we are glad to see the Lord's patience
with Martha.
We know how often patience is necessary with us.
We are glad to see Martha's progression in grace.
We too long to progress in grace.
Grant it Lord, we pray.
In Jesus' Name.
Amen*

Now when Mary came to where Jesus was and saw him, she fell at his feet, saying to him, "Lord if you had been here, my brother would not have died."
John 11:32

We are inclined to grant Martha an advantage over her sister when we see how she hastened to Jesus first.
And she was rewarded with some of the most dramatic words Jesus ever uttered.
But any advantage Martha enjoyed is offset by the posture with which Mary approaches.
It is the posture of worship.
She fell at His feet.
No sulking or recrimination here.
However crushed she may have been by His delay, still she worships.
Her words, which were identical to her sister's, leave something to be desired.
As if her endorsement of the Lord's power was subverted by her doubts about His punctuality.
But we believe her words were meant as a compliment.
Neither the practical bent of Martha nor the worshipful mind of Mary could anticipate the enormity of what was about to happen.

Dear Lord, we are hurt by some things and perplexed by many things.
But still we worship.
You are no less worthy for our pain or perplexity.
We trust.
And we know we cannot fathom the enormity of the wonders You will do, and the joy You will bring to our future.
Because of Jesus.
Amen

November 29

"...if you had been here..."
John 11:32

The sentiment is typically human.
But that a thing is understandable does not guarantee that
it is excusable.
Most of the time these "if only..." hypotheses should
be resisted.
Why?
First of all because Jesus COULD have been there but chose
not to be.
His absence was due neither to ignorance nor infirmity.
He was not there because He did not wish to be there.
He did not wish to be there because He had a better plan.
Can anyone doubt that it was a better plan?
To wish for anything other may be human, but it is
human folly.
When we worship we salute not merely a greater power.
We avow that we kneel in the presence of greater wisdom,
greater mercy and greater love.
His plan is what we would choose if we knew what
He knows.
His plan we would choose if we only loved with a
perfect love.

Father deliver us from the temptation of ever thinking we
could have done it better.
Let trust be a prominent component of our worship.
Let humility dominate as we approach Your holy throne.
Grant it for Jesus' sake we ask.
Amen

November 30

When Jesus saw her weeping ...he was deeply moved
in his spirit and greatly troubled.
John 11:33

What does this mean? We might well ask.
This is the second registration of the Saviour's emotional life
in a chapter where that part of His being is on full display.
In the first instance He was glad.
He had been glad for the opportunity to teach them a truth
so sorely needed.
But this response and the next two are deeply sorrowful.
The wording is unusually strong in the language in which
John was writing. The Lord was visibly moved.
In fact, He was shaken and overwrought.
Jesus of Nazareth, very God of very God was also
fully human.
He was not a composite being, part one, part the other.
He was fully human and fully divine.
We see from this verse and what follows that He was
INTENSELY human.
He loved fiercely, and He grieved deeply.
His beloved friend was dead.
The family were stricken and cast down.
It was almost too much for His human frame.
Is it ever permissible for a Christian to be troubled
and to groan? It cannot help but be.
The only perfect person ever to live on this planet has
shown us how.

Heavenly Father, we thank You that our Saviour did not stand
at a distance aloof.
We thank You that HE WADED IN.
We thank You that He plunged deep into the misery of human
woe in full participation.
We know that it was part of the ordeal of His suffering.
We believe it was a part of our redemption.
For that we bow down.
And we praise You in His Name.
Amen

December 1

And he said, "Where have you laid him?"
John 11:34

Jesus of Nazareth is taking command.
He has come to transform human sorrow.
He has come to ravage death by the authority of His own
sovereign power.
He will do what no other could do.
But in an act of divine condescension, He asks directions!
He enlists the bewildered onlookers in the miracle.
He assigns a role.
It is called human instrumentality.
Could the Incarnate God have found the grave on His own?
The question leads to an obvious answer.
He asks with a purpose in view.
He will use others in this serious business of resurrection.
He will employ the dying to raise the dead.
Indeed, dying is something He will soon embrace Himself.

Heavenly Father, we thank You that lowly callings may be
holy callings.
We thank You for the possibility of sure summons to
divine vocations.
We see the Lord employ the onlookers and enlist them in His
serious business.
We praise You Lord that Your Son Jesus Christ has given us
something to do!
And we thank You in His Name.
Amen

And he said, "Where have you laid him?"
They said to him, "Lord come and see."
John 11:34

The refrain, "Come and see" appears at critical junctures
in the Gospels.
In John 1, two of John the Baptist's disciples follow Jesus.
When He asked them what they wanted, they asked Him
where He was staying.
He bids them "come and see."
When the empty tomb is explored Matthew reports that the
angel invited the women to come see the place where He lay.
We may conclude that the Gospel accounts were meant to
be investigated.
Close scrutiny is invited so the undecided can make up their
own minds.
At the first Jesus invites prospective disciples to come and
see how He lived.
At the last those who loved Him are invited to examine the
place where He rose.
In Bethany the Lord is invited to see the place where a dead
man was laid.
Anyone may lead us to a grave.
Only Jesus can lead us out.

Lord, we have seen.
And the evidence is overwhelming.
We have seen more than enough to be convinced.
This Jesus is Your only begotten Son.
And so we praise You in His Name.
Amen

December 3

Jesus wept.
John 11:35

Short verse, big import.
The third and most famous reference to Jesus' emotional life
is in this verse. It is well known because it is the shortest verse
in the English Bible. Three words in the Greek original.
The words ought to be better known for other reasons.
It surprises some of us that Jesus would weep during this
particular time frame.
He knows that He is about to set everything right.
But His tears signal an unanticipated truth about God.
Why should the Lord weep when He knows very well He will
raise Lazarus in an instant?
His emotion corrects the notion that since God is eternal He is
unaffected by events taking place in a linear stream of time.
The fact that God abides in a kind of eternal "now" does not
render Him aloof.
The verse shows Jesus Christ to be an emotionally
engaged Saviour.
Though He knows He is about to turn their sorrow into joy,
He is not oblivious to their suffering, no matter how short
lived it may be.
He is very much in the moment. He suffers with them.
He is the Saviour who draws near to us.
He not only knows OF our suffering intellectually He actually
participates IN our suffering as a felt experience.
Jesus wept.
How grateful we are that it happened.
How grateful we are that we were told.

Gracious Father, of all the things seen on this planet surely
divine tears are among the most shocking.
We thank You for the visible demonstration of Jesus' care
for His people.
Teach us to draw near to scenes of suffering with a
like compassion.
Make compassion to be authentically felt on the inside
we pray. For we ask it in Jesus' Name.
Amen

December 4

So the Jews said, "See how he loved him!" But some of them said, "Could not he who opened the eyes of the blind man also have kept this man from dying?"
John 11:36-37

The proper answer is, "Of course He could have."
But He chose not to.
Not out of inattention or weakness.
Certainly not because of a lack of love did He permit His friend to die.
He was held back by the constraint of an omnipotent wisdom not understood by them or ourselves.
God will not prove His love for us by protecting those we love from suffering or death.
We do not say He will not protect them.
Obviously, we believe in divine providence.
We contend merely that He will not prove His love that way.
We do not say we should not ask Him to protect ourselves and our loved ones from suffering or death.
We believe in intercessory prayer.
We say He will not prove His love to us that way.
He will not prove His love for us that way for the simple reason that He has proven His love for us in a different way.
He proves His love for us by refusing to protect the One He loves from suffering and death.
Is that not sufficient?

Heavenly Father, Your love suffices.
And the proof of Your love is convincing.
We praise You for this overwhelming account of Christ's faithfulness to the family in Bethany.
And we thank You that there are thrilling parallels in our own experience.
In Jesus' Name we thank You.
Amen

December 5

**But some of them said, "Could not he who opened
the eyes of the blind man also have kept
this man from dying?"**
John 11:37

They offer their own variation of the ancient question.
It is a very human question, but not a very wise question.
It is an understandable question but not necessarily an
excusable question.
It is a question which cannot mask the suspicion that we may
know better than God after all.
The question suggests that everyone may have been better off
if only God had fashioned the world according to our
preferences rather than His own.
Death intruded because of human sin.
Human sin was made possible because of human freedom.
Human freedom made possible the doubting of
divine wisdom.
We are not likely to bring the cure by the same methodology
which brought the disease.

Heavenly Father, how patient You are with our
wearisome doubts.
But we profit nothing from second guessing You our Father.
So we ask Your forgiveness.
And we ask that You would keep us from dishonoring You in
this sinful way.
Amen

**But some of them said, "Could not he who opened
the eyes of the blind man also have kept
this man from dying?"
John 11:37**

Could Jesus have intervened and stopped Lazarus
from dying?
We earlier supplied the obvious answer to this question.
Jesus could have stopped Lazarus from dying.
He could have done anything.
He could have terminated human history at that moment
and cancelled death in the entire generation.
He could have assigned Lazarus a future identical to that
of Enoch and Elijah.
He could intervene in history.
He could overrule nature.
But speculations and theoreticals are seldom helpful.
Those questions are not much different from another
set of questions.
"Could He not implement a plan wrought of human sympathy
rather than divine sovereignty?"
"Could He not opt for human preferences instead of His
Father's will?"
The answer to those questions is, "No, of course not."
And we are left much better off with this divine "no" than
with any human "yes."

*Heavenly Father, we rejoice in the history and the eternity
You have mapped out for us.
Your gifts are better than our wishes.
May we rest in that.
Because of Jesus we trust You.
Amen*

December 7

Then Jesus, deeply moved again, came to the tomb.
It was a cave, and a stone lay against it.
John 11:38

He was moved ONCE MORE.
This is the fourth and final registration of the Lord's emotions
in this extraordinary chapter.
God's Person has been made visible.
God's emotions have been laid bare in the Man Christ Jesus.
The scene moves from the Man to the grave.
John writes as one inspired by the Holy Spirit.
John writes as one with acute memory.
He writes as an eyewitness.
He watched the Lord approach the grave.
Jesus was moved by the scene of His friend entombed behind
the stone no doubt.
But He may also have been moved by omniscient memory.
He could have well recalled the instant of every death from
Abel to that very moment.
He would have knowledge of every future death to the end
of history.
He would have been conscious of His own death waiting up
the road.
It was death itself that Jesus approached.
It was death itself He would destroy.

Heavenly Father, we thank You that our Champion felt deeply
within His heart.
We thank You that He moved swiftly with His feet.
We thank You that He did not shrink from confronting death
head on.
And we thank You that He would conquer.
Amen

December 8

Jesus said, "Take away the stone."
John 11:39

The words thrill.
Still, they are not as thrilling as the words soon to follow.
Here again the Lord invites fallen sinners into the sphere
of instrumentality.
What that means is that He is going to use them.
Though they have no idea what His shocking
words portend, He is going to use them.
He condescends to human partnership even in His
most stupendous works.
Even the work of raising the dead!
The onlookers were assigned a role.
They will participate if they acquiesce to
inexplicable commands.
All will be plain in time.
Theirs was to believe and obey.
He would use them.
He will use us.
Jesus would shortly do what only He could do.
But, in this case at least, He refuses to do everything.
He will not do what they could do.
Where he assigns a task He confers a glory.
Just how glorious they would soon discover.

Dear Lord, allow us to share in the work.
Give us Your assignments.
Command Your commands.
No matter how impossible or inexplicable the
commands may be.
In Christ's Name we ask it.
Amen

December 9

Jesus said, "Take away the stone." Martha, the sister of the dead man, said to him, "Lord, by this time there will be an odor, for he has been dead four days."
John 11:39

We wrote that Jesus' words were thrilling.
Now we see that Jesus' words were a thing opposed.
Jesus knew that death was an affront to the senses.
Did Martha suppose the Lord could not calculate how long her brother had lain behind the rock?
Did she think Him unfamiliar with the decomposition of the dead?
We cannot excuse the impulse to tutor the Son of God on any subject. It is especially outrageous to instruct the Lord on the implications of death.
Earlier Peter tried to turn the Lord from the Cross.
Later Pilate judged Jesus' death to be premature.
Yet Jesus is the only one who truly knows death.
No one in the New Testament who returns from the dead is quoted.
Neither before nor after death are they quoted.
None save One.
Only one is authorized to die, rise, and speak.
That One is about to teach a lesson on death to the whole planet.
He is about to render death a thing undone.

Lord Jesus, we would not teach You because we cannot teach You.
We want to be Your disciples.
We want You to be our teacher.
Tutor us especially Lord in this grim subject called death.
We would learn of our own death.
We would learn of Your death.
Make us diligent students.
That we might tell others.
Amen

Jesus said to her, "Did I not tell you that if you believed you would see the glory of God?"
John 11:40

It is a wonder and a mercy when the Lord Jesus condescends
to tell us anything once.
When He is forced to tell us twice, we should feel
doubly warned.
But the first rendition of these words to Martha
is unrecorded.
Everything the Bible tells us is true, but the Bible does not tell
us everything.
We could not live long enough to read the Bible if Scripture
told us everything.
It could be that when He told Martha her brother would rise
again He equated that with the glory of God.
But He did not tie the raising of Lazarus to Martha's faith.
It is more likely that the Lord is reminding her of a lesson that
John did not hear.
He told Nathanael that He would see angels.
He told His disciples that the death of Lazarus would lead to
the glory of God.
Faith rests on two foundations.
The first is the Word of God - especially the promises.
The second is the Work of God - especially the fulfillment
of promises.
Blessed is the one who hears, believes and sees.
Martha was so blessed.
And we are blessed to be told of her blessing.

Heavenly Father, we thank You for common things
like reminders.
And we thank You for uncommon things like glory.
We find both in Your Word.
And we rejoice in the discovery.
We thank You in Jesus' Name.
Amen

December 11

So they took away the stone.
John 11:41

It was a mercy that the objections gave way.
It was a low and contemptible irony that made them think He
would be surprised by what lay behind the rock.
He could have overwhelmed them with irresistible power.
But that was not His way.
His was the persuasion of gentle reasoning.
He pressed His case forward.
Once they understood He would not be turned aside they gave
themselves to the task.
They did what they could do.
They could not prevent death.
They could not reverse death.
But acting together in obedience they approached death.
They took away the stone.
It was a common enough beginning.
What followed was something they would think about every
day for the rest of their lives.

Father, make us to do the simple things we can do.
Allow us to see the impossible things only You can do.
That we may behold Your glory.
In Jesus' Name we ask it.
Amen

And Jesus lifted up his eyes and said,
"Father, I thank you that you have heard me."
John 11:41

Jesus lifted up His eyes.
Jesus may have been looking at the Father.
He was certainly looking to the Father.
Jesus as always is our Model.
We note that He prays.
We note how He prays.
He prays aloud.
He prays publicly.
In this case He prays briefly.
He thanks the Father for answers before answers come.
And of course, He asks for the impossible.
We may appeal to human agency for the possible.
Indeed, we may sometimes accomplish what is possible by
ourselves without any aid from others.
As for the impossible, our sole recourse is God.

Heavenly Father, even as we pray we thank You for prayer.
We know it is a gift which connects us with You.
We know it is a practice we share with the Lord Jesus.
Father may we always delight and be diligent in the
fellowship of prayer.
And may we see answers.
Teach us to pray prayers You delight to answer.
Give us answers which inspire strong confidence that You
have heard us.
We thank You that Jesus prayed.
And we thank You that for His faith He was heard.
Amen

December 13

And Jesus lifted up his eyes and said, "Father I thank you that you have heard me. I knew that you always hear me, but I said this on account of the people standing around, that they may believe that you sent me."
John 11:41-42

Here is an amazing thing. Jesus believed that His audible prayers spoken publicly would help bring the hearers to faith.
Not just the mighty miracles, but the prayers.
We might well think that hearing the voice from heaven at the baptism declaring that Jesus was the Son would have convinced everyone in Israel.
But here Jesus tells us the people needed something more.
They needed to hear Him cry up to heaven declaring that God was His Father.
And He declared that the God of Israel was a prayer answering God.
Doubtless Jesus would have found reason enough for prayer had no one been present.
He often repaired to a lonely place to pray undisturbed.
Doubtless prayer played a role in the mighty miracle which followed.
According to the Lord, the prayer was for those listening in.
Jesus was not exercising a random or rogue power independent of Israel's God.
He was an agent of the God of Abraham.
What He did was the latest installment of God's working in the history of His people.
Lazarus would be raised by the long-expected Messiah-King.
The Messiah was the man of prayer who acknowledged the source of His power. He was the man who gave thanks.

Heavenly Father, thank You that we may pray in Jesus' Name.
Now we ask that we could pray like Jesus.
We ask that we could pray with like results.
We ask if we could pray with like faith, being confident before the answer comes that it will come.
Work this faith in us by the ministry of Your Holy Spirit.
For we ask in the name of Your Holy Son Jesus.
Amen

December 14

...he cried out with a loud voice, "Lazarus, come out."
John 11:43

He cried with a loud voice when He gave up his life.
He cried with a loud voice when He gave back this life.
He could have cried louder.
A time will come when all in the grave will hear His voice.
We could assume that it was unnecessary for Jesus to raise
His voice at the grave.
Such was His power that He could will the reanimation of
Lazarus with the inaudible thoughts of His mind.
But His miracles were signs meant to teach.
They must know.
In Cana His sign was hidden from most.
It was one thing to replace the wine at a wedding.
Quite another to replace life at a grave.
They must learn who was responsible for the prodigy.
They must see how it came about.
Every detail of Christ's words and deeds brings sustenance
to our souls.
It would have been an experience unforgettable to hear the
Incarnate God cry aloud in human voice.
The command would have been no less irresistible had it been
spoken quietly.
But the drama of the volume made memory the
more indelible.

Heavenly Father, we thank You that our Lord went
to the trouble.
We thank You that He raised His voice.
We thank You that He raised the dead.
We thank You that we have heard His voice.
We thank You that we received His life.
For we too were once dead.
Amen

December 15

...he cried out with a loud voice, "Lazarus come out."
John 11:43

Who speaks to a dead man?
It is a fair question, for the dead cannot hear.
Death had no part in the original creation.
Death was a penalty imposed.
And death can be a penalty undone.
The one who imposed may also cancel.
It is Christ's own voice which carries the power of
cancellation and restoration.
It makes no less sense to speak to the dead than to
speak to the void.
It was the voice of God which spoke when there
was nothing.
It was the voice of God which spoke nothing into something.
God's own Son was the executive agent in Creation.
We should not be surprised that Jesus' voice can make
Lazarus hear and live.
It was the voice of Christ which created the stars.
It was the voice of Christ which brought forth the world.

Heavenly Father, we thank You that the speaking voice of
Christ was once heard on this planet.
How we praise You that the words were recorded.
We thank You that the voice of Christ will be heard on this
planet again.
Until then may we be His voice.
May we tell others what He said.
Because we know that once again the dead will
hear His voice.
Amen

December 16

...he cried out with a loud voice, "Lazarus come out."
John 11:43

For the third time in His recorded ministry Jesus raises
someone from the dead.
We may confidently assume that there were other
resurrections in addition to those recorded.
The dead are approached in varying degrees of decay.
Jairus' daughter was likely still warm.
The widow's son was being borne to his grave.
Lazarus had been dead four days as his sister was
quick to attest.
We are not told what form of consciousness those deceased
experienced before they were invited back.
Speculation is inevitable but, on this subject, we cannot know
what Scripture does not tell us.
It could be that they were conscious of waiting.
It could be that the sound of Jesus' voice brought the first jolt
of consciousness.
It is reasonable to think that their spirits knew some quiet
repose between death and resurrection.
Jesus called his friend by name.
We do not know the name of the little girl, but we know her
father's name.
We do not know the name of the widow or her son, but we
know they lived in Nain.
We know this man's name and the name of his town.
Christ may have designated Lazarus by name lest every grave
on earth be opened.
Such was the power of His command.
He approaches the grave. He lifts up His voice.
He will disarm death. He will make it to flee.

Heavenly Father, we thank You that Jesus knew
Lazarus' name.
We thank You that Jesus knows our name.
Father we thank You that Jesus approached Lazarus' grave.
And thank You that He will not leave us in the grave.
Amen

December 17

The man who had died came out...
John 11:44

The words are stark in their simplicity.
Still they are among the most dramatic of any recorded in
Holy Scripture.
For they record one of the most dramatic scenes ever beheld
in human history.
What happened was impossible by human calculation.
That was the whole point of the demonstration.
Jesus of Nazareth was a being both unique and divine.
His claims were authenticated by a manifestation of power
unknown to humankind.
He raised the dead with a word.
What He did was the fulfillment of His own prophecy.
He told His enemies at the Jerusalem Feast that the dead
would hear His voice.
He told the stricken Martha upon arrival that her brother
would rise again.
Events always unfolded just as He said.
That is because He was the Son of God.
We should have expected nothing less.

Heavenly Father, we thank You that such a thing
really happened.
We thank You that such a thing was faithfully recorded.
We thank You that such a thing will happen again.
We pray that we would bear faithful witness to the same.
In Jesus' Name.
Amen

December 18

The man who had died came out...
John 11:44

Every hour of every day in every country the dead are buried, burned or entombed.
But on one day in Judea of the First Century the dead came forth from the tomb.
He was alive because Jesus commanded life.
He rose because the dead hear His voice.
And the spiritually dead are deaf indeed.
Their inattention to Christ's commands certifies their death.
This Lazarus was alive.
For the words of Jesus bring life.
It was proof of the claims of the Man Christ Jesus.
Here then is ultimate triumph. Here then is ultimate healing.
Here is the ultimate display of authority.
Here indeed is the authentication of Messianic credentials.
Death is the last enemy. But death knows its Conqueror.
Here is the undoing of the curse brought down by Adam's sin.
To the dust we will return, yes, but there is someone who can bring our bodies back from the dust.
What Man is this who raises the dead?
He was a man earth-born but not of earthly origin.
He walked in Judea, and He stopped in Bethany where He worked this wonder.
He Himself soon died and was buried.
He was buried but He rose. He rose then He departed.
But He is coming again.

Heavenly Father, we acknowledge the historical reality.
We are grateful for the written record.
We have received the testimony of the witnesses.
Jesus Christ can raise the dead.
We believe in Jesus Christ.
We know that He will raise us as well.
And for that we offer everlasting praise.
Amen

December 19

Jesus said to them, "Unbind him, and let him go."
John 11:44

The detail is vital.
We are shown a pattern to be repeated.
We are given a principle to be mastered.
Yet again we see a glory of human instrumentality in the
sphere of divine activity.
Jesus condescends.
God is pleased to use us.
Boaz commanded that something be left for the gleaners.
This powerful Jesus reserves something in the miracle for the
powerless to do.
Who can command the dead to rise?
Not even the highest are able.
Jesus, and Jesus alone.
Who can cut graveclothes from the dead?
Even the lowest can manage that.
Sometimes only the lowest are willing.

Heavenly Father, we thank You for small assignments.
We believe all assignments from a great Master become
great assignments.
Lord, evermore command us.
We wish for nothing higher than to serve.
We can imagine no higher work than the raising of the dead.
For Christ's sake we ask it.
Amen

December 20

Many...therefore...believed...but some of them went to the Pharisees and told them what Jesus had done.
John 11:45-46

Of course, they believed. How could they not?
We do well to ask the question, because astonishingly, in the face of massive evidence, some still resisted.
Some ran to His enemies to sound the alarm.
Theirs was not a tremor of doubt.
Theirs was a vehemence of enmity as deep as hell itself.
The phenomenon called "undying faith" is something real and ought always to be celebrated.
But there is also an undying skepticism which itself is a form of faith.
We see the thing make its way from Bethany to Jerusalem.
It is a thing much to be wondered at, much to be lamented.
It is a thing anchored deep into a misreading of God's Word, a perversion of Israel's religion and a distortion of God's character.
It is the thing which killed God's Son.
Jesus had provided the highest form of proof for His claims.
He was met with the strongest imaginable hatred for His trouble.
When heaven came down, hell came up.
This Man who raised Lazarus must be stopped.
This Man who conquered death must die.

Heavenly Father, we thank You for that pardon the death of Jesus brings.
We thank You too for cleansing.
By that death and through that cleansing we ask that every stain on our character be removed.
Deliver us from every form of unbelief.
Let there be nothing in us which causes another to doubt.
We pray this in Jesus' Name.
Amen

December 21

...but some of them went to the Pharisees...
John 11:46

Some went to the Pharisees.
One wonders what they talked about.
They must have known they were in trouble.
The Pharisees were the spiritual elite of the land.
They had memorized the Law.
They missed nothing but the point.
Nothing escaped them but the truth.
Confident in their learning they conjured their own version of
what God must be like.
In fact, they reckoned Him to be someone very
like themselves.
They were sure He was someone far different from the
Nazarene carpenter who struck such terror in their breast.
The fact that Lazarus was alive again inspired no thought that
they could be mistaken.
They had become idol worshippers.
They clung to the idol-god fashioned in their own image.
In fact, they bowed down to themselves.
Either the idol must go, or Jesus must go.
For them the decision was not difficult.
They were creatures without qualms.

Father, make us resolute for Jesus.
For His enemies are resolute against Him.
Amen

**…but some of them went to the Pharisees and told
them what Jesus had done.
John 11:46**

And what things had Jesus done?
He traveled a great distance to show love for a friend.
He wept in empathy with those who grieved.
He spoke to a man who had been four days dead.
He brought the power of life to the scene of death.
He made death to tremble.
He forced death to relent.
He slew death in its lair.
The foul thing let go its prey.
We are left to wonder which part of His actions
caused offense.
Which act provoked a murderous response?
Jesus' authority over death proved His teaching
right and His opposers wrong.
But they showed no capacity for admitting error.
They would kill before they would confess.

*Lord, we know Jesus' enemies would kill before they
would confess.
Lord we would be Jesus' friends.
And so, we confess before we die.
Use our confession to make other friends for Jesus.
He brought life from our death.
And so, we praise Him.
Amen*

December 23

So the chief priests and the Pharisees gathered the council and said, "What are we to do? For this man performs many signs."
John 11:47

An enthusiasm for evil makes unlikely confederates.
The Priests and Pharisees were ever in opposition.
But the emergency inspired an alliance.
Jesus of Nazareth was a threat to both parties.
His preaching undermined the doctrinal authority of
the Pharisees.
His power challenged the political authority of the Priests.
Their options were few.
They could do nothing. Or they could repent.
They could admit that a Man of a character to heal the sick
and raise the dead must be an angel or something higher.
They could bow. Or they could battle.
They opted for war.
They declared war upon the Son of God.
The devil is nothing if not industrious.
His agents mimic their leader. They are never idle.
The children of light may procrastinate.
But the killers of light are impetuous. They are self-critical.
They rebuke their own inaction.
Their wickedness troubled them not at all.
But their hesitation to murder goodness shamed them.
It spurred them into action.
In a very short time this Council yielded results.
The Prince of Life would hang dead on a Cross.

Gracious Father, our life is full of choices.
Our enemies are eager to kill for their dark lord.
May we be willing to die for our great King.
May we always fight on Your side.
May we be faithful in the struggle.
And may our weapons be always forged in love.
In the name of Christ our Saviour we pray.
Amen

December 24

"If we let him go on like this, everyone
will believe in him..."
John 11:48

Behold the intersection of human perversity and
divine sovereignty.
This verse shines a light on the iniquity of conspirators
acted out in the history of Israel.
All men might believe in Israel's Messiah!
It was a calamity they must avoid at all cost.
Think of the depth to which they had sunk.
The best thing was their worst fear.
The divine side is hidden in the counsels of God.
God's part in the death of His Son is fathomed by the words of
Jesus and the theology of the Epistles.
God works His perfection through the willful rebels
who oppose.
He makes even the wrath of man to praise Him. (Psalm 76:10)
Here is mustered the brazenness of hell.
Here is the confession that the deeds of Jesus compelled
honest belief.
Here is the testimony that more time with like wonders would
sweep away all doubt.
Yet the determination to resist is breathtaking.
The enemies of God persist with unyielding purpose.
They are of a single mind.
Will the servants of the true King offer less?

Heavenly Father, we are shamed by the energy of the
devil's party. We are sluggish by comparison.
We know that He who is in us is greater than he who
is in the world.
May we prove it by our actions.
How we thank You for the Cross and the victory won thereon.
May we demonstrate all the power which flows from Christ's
cross and resurrection.
May the world see and be changed.
In Jesus' Name we ask it.
Amen

December 25

"...our place and our nation."
John 11:48

Their sin was multi-layered, but it lay mainly here.
Here is confusion of identity in denial of ownership.
The Psalmists knew.
"...we are his people and the sheep of his pasture."
Psalm 100:3
But the convictions of the Psalmists were alien to the mind-set
of the Priests.
We are what we are by the mercy of God.
We have what we have by sufferance.
We are tenants not landlords.
We occupy by Covenant not contract.
We enjoy what we have by the gracious good will of God.
And we have no claim on that good will apart from Christ.
It was not so much that the Priests and Pharisees did not
believe in God.
The problem was that they believed God existed to
serve themselves.

Heavenly Father, thank You for making us what we are and
giving us what we have.
Cause us to respect the Creator/creature divide.
Help us always to know the difference between ownership
and stewardship.
And make us faithful in that stewardship.
In the Name of Your own dear Son we ask it.
Amen

"...it is better for you that one man should die for the people, not that the whole nation should perish."
John 11:50

The devil only counterfeits; he cannot create.
He takes bits of what God made and he distorts.
The words are a near echo of John 3:16.
But they proceed from a vile mouth.
And they are spoken with evil intent.
The words frame a lie.
Caiaphas cares not a whit for the people or the nation.
He would gladly sacrifice the nation if only his own power and profit could be salvaged.
For us sinners' sake, the death of Jesus is necessary because we cannot atone for our sins.
From God's side the death of Jesus is necessary if He is to indulge His mercy without compromising His holiness.
Did the Priest know what he was saying?
Of course, he did not.
But God knew.
And that was enough.
Hate found a way to kill God's Son.
But love found a way to save the sinner by grace.
Better indeed!

Heavenly Father, thank You that You achieved the highest of ends by the lowest of means.
Thank you that this man's wrath toward the Lord Jesus was used to prove Your love for us in the Lord Jesus.
Cruel hands put our Saviour to death.
You showed Your mercy by that cruelty.
Thank You for this wondrous love that saved the souls of men.
Thank You that You overruled the conspiracies of the wicked to give so great a salvation.
Thank You in Jesus' Name, who died.
Amen

December 27

**He did not say this of his own accord, but being high
priest that year he prophesied that Jesus
would die for the nation...
John 11:51**

This is a remarkable verse pointing to a remarkable fact.
God could not honor the man, wretch that he was, but He
did honor the office.
Caiaphas was High Priest.
And Caiaphas prophesied.
Unwittingly yes, and he would have been horrified to know
the import of his prophecy.
But prophecy it was.
Jesus would indeed die for the nation.
Not for the reason that Caiaphas planned.
Not with the outcome that Caiaphas desired.
Not to deliver the nation from Rome.
Rome would destroy the nation in any case, the very thing
that Caiaphas feared.
Jesus died to save those who believe from the penalty of
their own sin.
Jesus died to offer sinners a way out.
But not all sinners wanted a way out.
Some sinners like Caiaphas preferred to fashion their
own remedies.
It was the way which seemed right to man but leading in
the end to destruction.
Caiaphas was of the Church of Lot's wife.
She preferred the fellowship of Sodom to the company
of angels.

Heavenly Father, thank You that You do rule and overrule.
Thank You for the means appointed for our salvation through
Jesus' own blood and sacrifice.
May we prize it, publish it, and depend upon it as our hope.
May it be true all our allotted days.
In Jesus' own Name we ask.
Amen

December 28

**...Jesus would die for the nation, and not for the nation
only, but also to gather together into one the children of
God who are scattered abroad.**
John 11:51-52

To the disciples the forecast of Jesus' death was deeply
puzzling and sternly resisted.
The purpose unfolded slowly to their understanding in the
fullness of years.
Writing under inspiration, John could now shine light on the
most consequential event in all of history: the death by
crucifixion of God's own Son.
He writes of the magnetic attraction of the Cross.
From the human side it was an act of judicial murder born of
the deepest hatred.
From God's side it was an intentional and atoning sacrifice
which proved infinite love.
For the patriotic Jew any sacrifice sufficient to cover sin was
the exclusive province of Israel alone.
Gentiles were not admitted into the Temple precincts.
But an Atonement by such a person could never be of local
significance only.
"The children of God scattered abroad" was not a reference
restricted to the Jews of the Diaspora only.
It was rather the way John described the elect of all ages
and places.
He meant those who would come to faith from every tongue
and tribe and nation.
Even at a distance of two thousand years the reference
was to ourselves.

*Heavenly Father, we were scattered abroad but You gathered
us together.*
You wooed us by the proof of love.
You drew us by the sacrifice of Your only begotten.
For that Lord we bow down.
For that we offer praise forever.
Amen

December 29

So from that day on they made plans to put him to death.
John 11:53

They set aside the former quarrel to serve the larger purpose.
The desire to see Jesus dead unified the wicked.
Their aversion for one another was overcome by their mutual hatred for Him.
If a man so powerful was to be nailed down on a cross they must sit down at a caucus.
And caucus they did until the time was ripe.
They had not long to wait.
The desire to see the wicked repent should draw all Christians together.
The Great Commission will not be advanced by efforts random and solitary.
Many must go down into the pit.
More must hold onto the rope.
We must sit together and caucus to be sure.
We already attained skill in that art by virtue of much practice.
But we must also advance.
We may also suffer and die.
The desperation of the times calls for the action of the church.
The other side still plots the devil's purpose.

Heavenly Father, let our actions always outrun our plans.
Don't allow us to be theoretical Christians.
Give us a resolve like Jesus.
For we ask it in His Name.
Amen

December 30

Jesus therefore no longer walked openly among the Jews, but went from there ...to a town called Ephraim...
John 11:54

Jesus did not turn aside to escape death.
Jesus turned aside to prepare for death.
His course was set.
The path was straight.
His resolve was fixed.
He would gather His disciples.
Their preparation was as necessary as His own.
If they were slow in apprehension it was not for lack
of warning.
Jesus would die according to the eternal counsels of
God not by the recent conspiracies of men.
It would be His way upon His day.
It was a thing divinely appointed.
It was an achievement long assured by the irresistible
determination of love.

*Heavenly Father, we thank You for the proof of the
Saviour's love.*
*We thank You that He loved His own and He loved
them unto death.*
*We thank You that by His death He atoned for
our sins.*
Amen

December 31

**Now the Passover of the Jews was at hand, and many went
up from the country to Jerusalem before the Passover to
purify themselves. They were looking for Jesus... the
Pharisees had given orders that if anyone knew where he
was, he should let them know, so that they
might arrest him.
John 11:55-57**

The irony becomes thick at this juncture.
It was the Passover celebration.
Israel's sons had been spared in Egypt.
The Feast helped them to remember.
God shielded their sons from the Egyptians with the blood
of a lamb.
So they must purify themselves!
The Priests and Pharisees set about the same by vowing that
God's Son would not be spared.
He would be given to the Gentiles.
The Messiah would be handed over.
Delivered for the purpose of death by slow torture.
Here we pass beyond the scope of human commentary.
Here we abide in the sphere of human tears.
Here we behold the Lamb.

*Heavenly Father, the scandal of Israel's treachery is
hard to imagine.
When we think of the wickedness that took your Son
to the Cross even prayer seems inadequate.
And yet we know that their guilt does not exceed our own.
It was for our sins He died.
So we could be saved by His grace.
And so we sing songs.
And so we praise.
Amen*

ORDER FORM

For additional copies of *The Path to Discipleship*

Make checks payable to: Rampart Publications

Send this order form to: Rampart Publications
PO Box 13455
Bakersfield, California 93389

I would like to order _____ copy/copies of The Path to Discipleship at a cost of $12.95 per book.

Please add 7.25% in sales tax for purchase within California.

Please add $3.95 for first book and $0.60 for each additional book to cover shipping and handling costs.

Book(s) to be shipped to:

Name: _____

Address: _____

City/State: _____

Zip code: _____

Telephone: _____

Email Address_____

For additional order options:
 Visit online: rampartpublications.com
 Call: (661) 747-0581

ORDER FORM

For additional copies of *The Path to Discipleship*

Make checks payable to: Rampart Publications

Send this order form to: Rampart Publications
PO Box 13455
Bakersfield, California 93389

I would like to order _____ copy/copies of The Path to Discipleship at a cost of $12.95 per book.

Please add 7.25% in sales tax for purchase within California.

Please add $3.95 for first book and $0.60 for each additional book to cover shipping and handling costs.

Book(s) to be shipped to:

Name: _____

Address: _____

City/State: _____

Zip code: _____

Telephone: _____

Email Address_____

For additional order options:
 Visit online: rampartpublications.com
 Call: (661) 747-0581

ORDER FORM

For additional copies of *The Path to Discipleship*

Make checks payable to: Rampart Publications

Send this order form to: Rampart Publications
                             PO Box 13455
                             Bakersfield, California 93389

I would like to order _____ copy/copies of The Path to Discipleship at a cost of $12.95 per book.

Please add 7.25% in sales tax for purchase within California.

Please add $3.95 for first book and $0.60 for each additional book to cover shipping and handling costs.

Book(s) to be shipped to:

Name: _____

Address: _____

City/State: _____

Zip code: _____

Telephone: _____

Email Address_____

For additional order options:
 Visit online: rampartpublications.com
 Call: (661) 747-0581